LIBERALISM

Old and New

TWAYNE'S STUDIES IN
INTELLECTUAL AND CULTURAL HISTORY

Michael Roth, General Editor
Scripps College and the Claremont Graduate School

LIBERALISM

Old and New

J. G. Merquior

Twayne Publishers • *Boston*
A DIVISION OF G. K. HALL & CO.

Liberalism Old and New

Copyright 1991 by J. G. Merquior.
All rights reserved.
Published by Twayne Publishers
A division of G. K. Hall & Co.
70 Lincoln Street
Boston, Massachusetts 02111

Copyediting supervised by Barbara Sutton.
Book design and production by Janet Z. Reynolds.
Typeset by Huron Valley Graphics, Inc., Ann Arbor, Michigan.

10 9 8 7 6 5 4 3 2 1 (hc)
10 9 8 7 6 5 4 3 2 1 (pb)

Library of Congress Cataloging-in-Publication Data

Merquior, José Guilherme.
    Liberalism, old and new / J.G. Merquior.
        p.   cm.—(Twayne's studies in intellectual and cultural
    history)
    Includes bibliographical references and index.
    ISBN 0-8057-8602-3 (alk. paper).—ISBN 0-8057-8627-9 (pbk.
    alk. paper)
    1. Liberalism—History.   I. Title.   II. Series.
JC571.M443   1991
320.5′1—dc20   90-21520

RAYMOND ARON

(1905–83)

in memoriam

This book is for Hilda, Julia, and Pedro.

Finis reipublicae libertas est.

—Spinoza, *Tractatus theologico-politicus*

Contents

Contents

Foreword

Twayne's Studies in Intellectual and Cultural History consists of brief original studies of major movements in European intellectual and cultural history, emphasizing historical approaches to continuity and change in religion, philosophy, political theory, aesthetics, literature, and science. The series reflects the recent resurgence of innovative contextual as well as theoretical work in these areas, and the more general interest in the historical study of ideas and cultures. It will advance some of the most exciting work in the human sciences as it stimulates further interest in cultural and intellectual history. The books are intended for the educated reader and the serious student; each combines the virtues of accessibility with original interpretations of important topics.

J. G. Merquior's *Liberalism Old and New* is the first volume to appear in the series. The book clearly and precisely examines the diversity of liberal doctrines and practices while emphasizing the crucial family resemblances within this diversity. It explores the development of the idea of liberalism from the classical period until our own day, with a focus on the early modern and modern periods. Merquior not only covers the standard figures in the liberal pantheon, but also moves beyond the Anglo-Saxon liberal tradition, demonstrating the interrelationships of liberalism in continental Europe and Latin America as well.

Merquior combines a thematic and national approach, showing how constellations of ideas and issues emerged as well as how specific national cultures produced distinctive contributions to the literature of liberalism. He discusses the various pressures that condition the growth of liberalism, and he attends to its various competitors in different periods and places. Brief but incisive, his book describes liberalism as a vital political idea with deep historical roots.

Liberalism Old and New provides a broad historical account of liberalism, even a defense of it, while engaging some of the major debates about liberalism in contemporary political philosophy.

MICHAEL ROTH
Scripps College and the
Claremont Graduate School

Preface

An overview of three centuries of the liberal idea can only be, in Arnold Toynbee's terms, "panoramic instead of microscopic." Just so, in this overview ideological summary takes precedence over philosophical analysis. I am aware that in many places the text is more indicative than inquisitive, but I hope some virtue has been made of necessity. For most of the best liberal theory today tends to be presented in the analytical mold, and there is a comparative scarcity of *historical* presentations of liberalism. Opting for the historical perspective has at least two advantages. First, it allows one to show that almost since its inception, liberalism has been plural and diverse. Old as well as new liberalisms are highly variegated, both in political positions and in conceptual underpinnings. This variety of discourses has enriched liberalism considerably in its political relevance, its moral scope, and its sociological acumen. The second advantage is that historical description uses the finest scholarship available, including many thoughtful recent reinterpretations of each major school of liberal doctrine. My debts to this scholarship are countless, and I should be glad if this book came to be read as largely an exercise in what the French call *haute vulgarisation*.

The historical diversity of liberalism is both inter- and intranational. Although liberal theory was and remains chiefly an Anglo-Saxon artifact, underpinned by a singularly continuous institutional practice—the "free institutions," of popular parlance—liberal thought also received signal contributions from elsewhere in the West. In keeping with the European range of this series I have tried to discuss not only the traditional French classic liberals like Montesquieu, Constant, and Tocqueville, but also a generous number of thinkers often neglected in standard accounts in English: Mazzini, Herzen, and Sarmiento; Troeltsch, Weber, and Kelsen; Croce and Ortega; Aron and Bobbio, along with several minor figures.

In employing the label "liberal" throughout the manuscript, I am aware that while most of the authors discussed considered themselves liberals, some of them did not. For the early classical liberals like Locke, Montesquieu, and Smith, the word was simply not available in its modern political sense. But some of the later liberal thinkers also avoided the label. For instance, Norberto Bobbio calls himself a "liberal socialist" rather than a liberal. Nevertheless, following what seems to me a well-established tradition, I have labeled both groups as liberals.

Since the completion of this book, a few further global discussions of liberal thought have come to my notice. They include three first-rate texts: Pierre Manent's comments on most authors composing his anthology *Les libéraux* (Paris: Hachette, 1986); Stephen Holmes's essay "The Permanent Structure of Antiliberal Thought," in Nancy Rosenblum (ed.), *Liberalism and the Moral Life* (Harvard University Press, 1989); and Andrew Vincent's reexamination of British liberalism in his "Classical Liberalism and Its Crisis of Identity," *History of Political Thought* (Spring 1990): 143–67.

As a Latin American taught in the heartland of the faith, I owe both myself and the reader a nonethnocentric view, but not a detached one either. For I write in unabashed commitment to the heritage and ideals behind the liberal label—almost a "dirty word" to many people today, both from the Right and the Left. This is a liberal book on liberalism written by someone who believes that liberalism, if properly understood, resists all vilification.

I am grateful to Michael Roth for his hospitable invitation to contribute this book to this timely series and for his helpful responses to my original draft. John Martin, at Twayne, was responsible for many a lucid improvement of the text, and Barbara Sutton supervised the copyediting most efficiently. None of them is, of course, in any way responsible for its shortcomings. Louise Finny typed the manuscript most graciously in Mexico City, where I wrote this book, in the summer of 1989.

1

Definitions and Starting Points

Liberalism

Nietzsche once said that only ahistorical beings admit of a proper definition. Thus liberalism, a manifold historical phenomenon, can scarcely be defined. Having itself shaped a good deal of our modern world, liberalism reflects the diversity of modern history, early as well as recent. The range of liberal ideas encompasses thinkers as different in background and motivation as Tocqueville and Mill, Dewey and Keynes, and nowadays, Hayek and Rawls, not to speak of their "elected ancestors," such as Locke, Montesquieu, and Adam Smith.[1] It is far easier—and wiser—to *describe* liberalism than to attempt a short definition. To suggest a theory of liberalisms, old and new, one ought to proceed by a comparative description of its historical manifestations.

In his influential 1929 essay "The Revolt of the Masses," the Spanish philosopher Ortega y Gasset declared liberalism "the supreme form of generosity: it is the right granted by the majority to minorities and hence the noblest cry that has ever resounded in the planet. . . . The determination to live together with one's enemies and what is more, with a weak enemy." Ortega's statement offers a convenient opening for our historical approach because it nicely combines the moral and political meanings of the word *liberal*. While obviously denoting liberal politics—the liberal rules of the game between majority and minority—Ortega's dictum also makes use of the first current meaning of the adjective *liberal* in any modern dictionary. Thus Webster's: liberal (1) originally suitable for a free man: now only in "liberal arts," "liberal education"; (2) giving freely, *generous*. Ortega's statement restores the word's moral meaning to its political sense—fittingly enough, since "liberal" as a political label was born in the Spanish Cortes of 1810, a parliament that was rebelling against absolutism.

In its golden age, the nineteenth century, the liberal movement operated at two levels, the level of thought and the level of society. It consisted of a body of doctrines and a group of principles that underlay the functioning of several institutions, some old (such as parliaments), and others new (such as the free press). By historians' consensus, liberalism (the thing if not the name) emerged in England in the political struggle that culminated in the 1688 Glorious Revolution against James II. The aims of the winners of the Glorious Revolution were religious toleration and constitutional government. Both became pillars of the liberal order, spreading in time throughout the West.

In the century between the Glorious Revolution and the great French Revolution of 1789–99, liberalism—or more aptly, *proto-liberalism*—was constantly associated with "the English system"— that is, a polity based on limited royal power and a fair degree of civil and religious freedom. In England, although access to power was controlled by an oligarchy, arbitrary rule had been checked, and there was more general freedom than anywhere else in Europe. Perceptive foreign visitors like Montesquieu, who came in 1730, realized that in England the alliance of law and liberty fostered a society more robust and prosperous than either the contemporary continental monarchies or the virtuous, martial, but poor republics of early antiquity. The thinkers of the so-called Scottish Enlightenment—David Hume, Adam Smith, and Adam Ferguson—saw the advantages of regular government and free opinion and their connection with economic growth and scientific progress stemming from the spontaneous activities of a class-ridden yet mobile civil society. The comparison with Britain convinced many a protoliberal that government should seek only a minimal action, providing peace and security.

Because liberalism was born in protest against the encroachments of state power, it sought to establish both a *limitation* of authority and a *division* of authority. A great modern antiliberal, the German jurist and political theorist Carl Schmitt, summed it up very well in his *Constitutional Theory* of 1928, where he wrote that the liberal constitution displays two main principles: one distributive, the other organizational. The distributive principle means that the sphere of individual freedom is *in principle unlimited,* whereas the ability of the state to intervene in this sphere is *in principle limited.* In other words, whatever is not forbidden by law is permitted, so that the burden of justification falls on state intervention, not on individual action. As to the organizational principle of the liberal constitution, Schmitt wrote that its purpose is to enforce the distributive one. It establishes a *division* of power(s), a demarcation of state authority into spheres of competence—classically associated with the legislative, executive, and judicial branches—in order to contain power through the interplay of "checks and balances." *Authority is divided so that power be kept limited.*

After the French Revolution and its interlude of Jacobin dictatorship, liberal thought (now called by that name) experienced new threats to freedom. Bourgeois liberalism had fought aristocratic privilege but was not prepared to accept a wide franchise and its democratic consequences. Therefore the liberal polity embraced what the greatest liberal theorist of the early nineteenth century, Benjamin Constant, dubbed *"le juste milieu"*: a political center, halfway between old absolutism and new democracy. Liberalism became the doctrine of limited monarchy and an equally limited people's rule, since voting and representation were kept restricted to a high-income citizenry.

This bourgeois polity, however, was only a transient historical form, soon to be replaced by universal male suffrage. The coming of democracy in the industrial West from the 1870s onward meant the definitive preservation of liberal achievements: religious freedom, human rights and the rule of the law, responsible representative government, and the legitimation of social mobility. Thus, late-Victorian society, the postbellum United States, and the French Third Republic initiated large, lasting experiments in liberal democracy—an epoch-making political mix. Switzerland, the Netherlands, and the Scandinavian countries took the same path, often earlier. Unified Italy turned to liberal politics, Spain managed to stabilize liberal rule, and the great Central European monarchies, Austria and Germany, veered from autocracy to semiliberal constitutions.

Not every democratic development emerged as a result of explicitly liberal forces. The English tories under Disraeli, the reactionary Bismarck, and the autocratic Napoléon III introduced or helped to introduce nearly universal male suffrage, often against the will of

liberal elites. The liberal democratic polity was by no means a creature of liberals alone. But this only proves that the logic of liberty
sometimes goes beyond the interests and prejudices of liberal parties, as if history vindicated liberalism even against liberals. In endorsing representative democracy and political pluralism, conservatives
and socialists alike, whatever their aims, patently yielded to liberal
principles.

In the twentieth century the general progress of democratic
liberalism has been less straightforward than it was in the nineteenth. The acute political turbulence entailed by the "European
civil war" of 1914–45 caused the breakdown of younger democracies such as Italy and Germany. Later on, the dilemmas of modernization in Latin America and elsewhere occasioned many an eclipse
of democracy from the mid-1960s to the mid-1980s. Nevertheless,
liberal democracy has remained the "normal" polity of industrial
societies, as shown in the postwar reconstruction of Germany, Italy,
and Japan, as well as in the end state of the politics of modernization in the "nics" (newly industrialized countries).

In 1989 the world witnessed the collapse of state socialism, the
chief rival of liberal democracy. This came after a painful process of
reform and soul-searching. In the West, by contrast, one often hears
of a cultural crisis, but almost nobody seems seriously to propose a
global change of institutions. For more than a century, democracy
has been the general idiom of legitimacy in the modern world. Now
it appears that the social and political pluralism of *liberal* democracies is something more specific: the only truly legitimate principle of
rule in modern societies.

The Italian liberal Luigi Einaudi used to describe liberal society
in terms of two aspects: the rule of law and the anarchy of minds.
Liberalism presupposes a wide *variety of values and beliefs,* unlike the
moral compact alleged by conservatives or prescribed by most radical utopias. Montesquieu, in *The Spirit of the Laws* (1748); suggested
that modern England was animated by the conflicting struggle of
"all the passions left free."[2] Classical liberalism, such as that of
Adam Smith, saw competition as leading to an almost Newtonian
world of social balance. Later liberals, such as Max Weber, chose to
stress the irreducibility of value conflict rather than the achievement
of balance. There are liberalisms of harmony and liberalisms of dis-
sonance. But in either case, liberalism takes a liberal view of human
strife.

As the liberal polity unfolded over time, the meaning of liberalism changed a great deal. Nowadays what *liberal* generally means in continental Europe and Latin America is something quite different from what it means in the United States. Since Roosevelt's New Deal, American liberalism has acquired, in Richard Hofstadter's celebrated phrase, "a social democratic tinge." Liberalism in the United States came close to liberal socialism—an egalitarian preoccupation that stops short of authoritarian statism, yet that preaches state action well beyond that minimal, night-watchman state once enshrined by old liberals. In all the history of liberal semantics, no episode was more important than this American shift of meaning.

On the other hand, the meaning of liberalism in its current revival, both in the United States and elsewhere, has only a tenuous connection with the mainstream U.S. meaning, and often even marks a departure from it. Over half a century or so, liberalism itself has become a highly diversified field of ideas and positions. Even before Keynes and Roosevelt—probably the theorist and the statesman who did more to alter the 19th-century legacy than anyone—liberalism already distinctly comprised more than one meaning.

Liberty and Freedom

This is a book on liberalism, not liberty. But no study of liberalism can omit a consideration of the various meanings of *liberty* and *freedom*. Moreover, precisely because liberty, like liberalism, has more than one meaning, sorting out the senses or kinds of freedom can throw some light on the varieties of liberalism.

Types of Freedom

What is freedom? In a work of social theory (as distinct from a work of general philosophy), the first thing to do is to discard the hoary dilemma of free will versus determinism. Since Montesquieu, it has been customary for discussions of social freedom to avoid engaging this thorny issue. By brushing aside the philosophical question of free will, one can focus on the more empirical, commonsensical subject of freedom and unfreedom among interacting members of a given community.

Modern analysts of freedom insist on the importance of this social dimension. A free action is an action from a desired or a neutral motive. An action lacking freedom amounts to an action performed not exactly "against one's will" but from an undesired motive. Some unfree actions are constrained by other people's will. *Social freedom* therefore may be defined as "the absence of constraint or restraint." Here, *constraint* and *restraint* refer to the effect, on any agent's mind, of other persons' actions, whenever such effect operates as an undesired motive of that agent's behavior.[3] The presence of an alternative, allowing room for choice, is a defining element of a free action.

Freedom is, therefore, freedom from *coercion:* it implies the nonimpediment by others of one's preferred course of action. Bearing this general meaning in mind, one can count at least four major embodiments of freedom throughout history.

The first embodiment of freedom is freedom from oppression as arbitrary interference. It consists in the free enjoyment of established rights and is associated with a sense of dignity. It is an old, indeed immemorial and universal kind of feeling and behavior. The land-bound peasant whose traditional rights, however meager, were respected by the feudal lord experienced such freedom as much as the lord himself when his privileges were acknowledged by the king. A nice illustration of it appears in Scripture (Acts 21: 27–39): when Paul of Tarsus, having caused a riot by addressing the crowd in Jerusalem, got scourged by order of a Roman commander, he said in protest, "Is it lawful to scourge a man that is a Roman, and uncondemned?" The apostle's words show that he felt lawfully *entitled* to a degree of respect, the violation of which meant oppression not only for him but indeed for the culture of imperial Rome.

It is precisely this same kind of freedom that any modern individual expects to enjoy as he or she performs social roles protected by law and custom. Let us call it *freedom as entitlement.* But although the enjoyment of freedom as entitlement involves a grasp of rights and procures a sense of dignity, it has little to do with the much more recent principle of *universal* human rights. The subject of the latter is man as such, whereas the bearer of entitlements was and is always a situated individual, embedded in specific (and historically varying) social positions.

The second kind of freedom, freedom to participate in the running of the affairs of the community at whatever level, became available to all free nationals in ancient cities like the Greek ones, and for this reason it was known from the beginning as *political freedom* (*polis* means "city").

Third is *freedom of conscience and belief.* Historically, its range became persistently significant first as a claim to the legitimacy of religious dissent (from papal Rome or other established churches) during the European Reformation. Before that, nearly all claims to religious independence had been treated as heresies and successfully suppressed. Though it was hardly the intention of the great reformers like Luther and Calvin, the Reformation inaugurated an age of religious pluralism. This in turn was secularized into the modern right of opinion, as mirrored in the free press and the right to intellectual and artistic liberty.

Fourth and finally is freedom as the embodiment of one's aspiration to live as one pleases. Modern people do not feel free simply because their rights are respected, or because their beliefs can be freely expressed, or because they freely take part in collective processes of decision making. People also feel free because they conduct their life by a personal choice of labor or leisure. *Freedom of self-fulfillment* conveys the gist of the matter. The point, stressed by John Plamenatz, is that people often set themselves goals and standards of excellence that have little to do with the common good or even the public assertion of belief—goals and standards of a *private* or individualistic character, yet that absorb a great deal of their exertions.[4]

Our classification of kinds of freedom follows roughly the historical order of their appearance. Freedom from oppression in the sense indicated above is an immemorial experience. Political freedom on the state level seems to have been an invention of classical Athens. Freedom of conscience first gained momentum during the Reformation and the ensuing wars of religion, which plagued Europe until the middle of the seventeenth century. Finally came the spread of individualistic liberty. Freedom as self-fulfillment and personal achievement, building on a basis of enlarged privacy, is very much a modern trend, underpinned by the growing division of labor in industrial society and more recently by the expansion of consumerism and leisure time.

At least two qualifications are in order here. First, a fair degree of freedom of opinion was part and parcel of ancient political liberty. Early in the fifth century B.C., Greek political life included the concept of *isegoria*, or freedom of speech not so much as freedom from censorship but as the right to speak freely at the citizens' assembly.[5] Furthermore, one should avoid the impression that the ancient world as a whole was lacking in individualist freedom, the fourth kind of liberty in our typology. But with these qualifications in mind, our chronological typology of freedom does seem to hold water.

Types of Liberty

Let us now briefly recall a few famous definitions of liberty in the liberal literature:

1. "Liberty is the right to do whatever the law permits" (Montesquieu, *The Spirit of the Laws*, bk. 12, ch. 2).
2. "Liberty means obedience to the law we prescribe to ourselves" (Rousseau, *Social Contract* (bk. 2, ch. 8).
3. Modern liberty is "the peaceful enjoyment of individual or private independence" (Benjamin Constant, "Ancient and Modern Liberty").

Political philosophers (for instance, Norberto Bobbio) often distinguish a classical *liberal* concept of liberty from a classical *democratic* concept of liberty. In the liberal concept, freedom means just absence of coercion. In the democratic concept it means *autonomy,* that is, the power of self-direction.[6]

In his celebrated 1958 Oxford lecture, "Two Concepts of Liberty," Isaiah Berlin, pitted *negative* against *positive* freedom. He defined negative liberty as freedom from coercion. Negative freedoms are always freedoms *against* someone's possible interference. Examples are the freedom to enjoy entitlements (against possible encroachments); the freedom to express beliefs (against censorship); and the freedom to privately satisfy tastes and the free pursuit of private goals (against imposed standards). Positive freedom, on the other hand, is essentially a desire to be self-governed, a yearning for autonomy. Unlike negative freedom, it is not freedom *from* but freedom *to:* the aspiration to self-mastery, to deciding for oneself instead of being decided for. While negative freedom means independence from interference, positive freedom is concerned with the appropriation of control.

The Canadian philosopher Charles Taylor corrected Berlin by warning that both kinds of liberty, positive and negative, are often caricatured in the heat of ideological debates.[7] Critics of positive freedom, for example, tend to stress that partisans of positive freedom end up justifying the tyrannical rule of "enlightened" elites by asserting "true" or "higher" human ends (like the formation of the "new man" under communism). Inspired by lofty ideals of humankind, these utopians generally turn out to be grim virtuosi of *moral substitutionism:* in the name of our higher self, they simply decide our lives for ourselves. But stark defenders of negative freedom are just as blind to certain compulsive psychological dimensions of freedom of choice. As Taylor noted, at first sight, positive liberty is an "exercise concept" and negative liberty an "opportunity concept." For negative freedom, all that is required is the absence of significant obstacles; no actual performance is needed.

Moreover, in the pursuit of my freely chosen goals (negative liberty) I can face internal fetters (for instance, my desire to travel may clash with my sloth). Thus the very use of negative liberty can often involve lots of self-mastery, and therefore the psychology of positive freedom.

Liberal thinkers of a more historical-minded complexion also realized that the distinction between negative and positive liberty is not so sharp. Bobbio, for one, finds that freedom as independence and freedom as autonomy share a common ground, since both imply self-determination. History itself has begotten a progressive integration of both kinds of liberty—so much so, that in our social liberal age, one can conceive of the two as complementary perspectives. Whatever the individual can decide by himself or herself must be left to his or her will (which vindicates negative or "liberal" liberty); and wherever there is need for a collective decision, the individual must participate in it (which vindicates positive or "democratic" liberty). After all, concludes Bobbio, each of the two doctrines answers a different question. Negative liberty addresses the question, "What does it mean to be free for the individual taken alone?" Positive liberty concerns itself with another question: "What does it mean for the individual to be free *as member of a whole?*"[8] In liberal democracy, both questions are conspicuously germane, and the significance of their answers is far from academic.

Three Schools of Thought

Another way to stress the differences between kinds of freedom and liberty—one closer to the familiar ground of the history of ideas—is to discern three main schools of thought on liberty. Each is identified with a major European country—England, France, and Germany.[9]

England

The English school of liberty theory, running from Hobbes and Locke to Bentham and Mill, sees freedom as the absence of coercion, or (in Hobbes's celebrated view) the absence of external obstacles. When he described such freedom as a social liberty, Hobbes deliberately clashed with the humanist tradition—the worship of civic values and therefore of self-rule and *political* liberty (our second historical freedom, or "Rousseaunian" liberty). This notion can be traced back to *polis* democracy and has never died altogether. In the Middle Ages, a town was said to be free when it could make its own law ("*civitas libera quae possit sibi legem facere*"). But the ideal of political rule was rekindled—and much enhanced—by Renaissance humanists, first in Florence[10] and then in the rest of Europe.

Hobbes, writing with the English civil war before his eyes, desperately wished to dissociate the modern concept of freedom from this tradition. He criticized both Machiavelli and the poet Milton for their republican views and redefined liberty away from civic enthusiasm. Instead of extolling civic virtue, Hobbes lauded *civil,* or nonpolitical, freedom. His claim was that once government is in place, freedom is no longer a matter of self-rule but something to be enjoyed "in the silence of the laws."

Hobbes's phrase is crucial, for it equates liberty with everything the law permits by the mere fact that it does not forbid it. Political liberty, the foil to his own definition, had always been conceived of as freedom *through* law (and lawmaking) instead of as something *outside* the law. Hobbes's reformulation is the source of the English idea of negative liberty, though its classical formulation within liberal thought was made by a Frenchman, Montesquieu.

France

The "French" school of liberty, as a theoretical model, prefers Rousseau to Montesquieu. Jean-Jacques Rousseau, a son of free Geneva, Calvinist born like Milton, returned to Machiavelli and the republican principle. To him, the highest freedom was self-rule, and politics should be the mirror of autonomous selfhood. Rousseau was as keen an individualist as anyone; in fact, as the main forerunner of romanticism, he was the chief originator of individualism in literature and religion. But when it came to social freedom, he put the citizen much higher than the bourgeois—and political liberty well before civil freedom. The eloquence of his *Social Contract* redirected the concept of liberty from the civil back to the civic. Though Rousseau never envisaged anything like revolution, much of the Jacobins' revolutionary terrorism of 1793–94 was carried out in his name.

Many have argued that Rousseau was a kind of ideological schizoid, a begetter of individualism in culture on the one hand and a forerunner of totalitarianism on the other. But this notion is utterly ill founded. Rousseau never meant for democracy (or republic, the word he favored) to curtail freedom.[11] The true aim of his exaltation of democratic rather than liberal liberty was not to damage individualism but to destroy *particularism*. Particularism reflected the spell of an old force in French politics: *patrimonialism*.

The French monarchy, long beset by the problem of controlling a divided polity, had evolved a patrimonial concept of power. Sovereignty meant private property at large—and the king was the sole owner. Centralization was a greater problem for French kings than it was for English kings. In England the feudal aristocracy self-centralized and the crown built itself from the strong position afforded by the Norman conquest, but in France fragmentation was the rule. Hence, there were several regional Estates in France, in contrast to the old English *national* parliament. In its bid for centralization, the French Crown bought the aristocracy off with notoriously massive office-selling, and the upshot was a whole edifice of particularist interests and unequal strongholds.[12]

Early royalist political thought in France, such as Jean Bodin's 1576 *The Six Books of a Commonweal*, tried to use the concept of sovereignty, to fight feudal anarchy. But enemies of royal power, like the Huguenots in the sixteenth century, dreamed of strengthening the Estates as public institutions able to check the Crown. Rousseau's strategic contribution to the history of political discourse consisted in using Bodin's brainchild—undivided, indivisible sovereignty—to eliminate the power of rulers as a particularist source of oppression, rather than to strengthen it. In the apt words of Ellen Meiksins Wood, "Where Bodin subordinated the particularity of the people to the (alleged) universality of the (royal) ruler, Rousseau subordinated the particularity of the ruler to the universality of the people."[13]

Rousseau articulated a powerful rhetoric on behalf of political or democratic liberty against the odium of privilege—something early liberals like Montesquieu were not above upholding. But Rousseau was so taken by the need to depatrimonialize power that he lost sight of the other key issue: the question of the *range* of power. For as

Constant remarked, "the legitimacy of authority depends on its object as much as on its source."[14] Constant saw that by focusing almost exclusively on the source of authority (popular sovereignty), Rousseau's social contract could be used as a weapon against freedom as independence, endangering privacy and the life of individuality. Political freedom was good, if only because it ensured individual independence. John Locke, a generation after Hobbes, had realized this. But if freedom was to be full freedom, it had to flourish beyond the civic sphere as well, in the silence of authority, so to speak. Montesquieu taught that authority had to be divided lest it be tyrannical; Constant warned that sovereignty had to be limited lest it be despotic. Rousseau had replaced autocracy with democracy. The next task was to prevent democratic despotism.

Germany

Very early in the nineteenth century, an outstanding German humanist and diplomat, Baron Wilhelm von Humboldt (elder brother of the great naturalist Alexander von Humboldt and founder of the Berlin university), called for limiting rather than simply controlling central authority. In *On the Limits of State Action*, Humboldt expressed a deep-felt liberal theme: the humanist concern for personality buiding and self-improvement. Educating freedom, and freeing in order to educate—this was the idea of *Bildung*, Humboldt's Goethean contribution to moral philosophy.[15]

The *Bildung* ideal is terribly important in the history of liberalism. Besides having a strong influence on epoch-making liberal thinkers like Constant and John Stuart Mill, it is the logical structure behind a long-prevalent German concept of freedom.[16] The concept is akin to political liberty in that it also stresses autonomy, yet it revolves not around political participation but around the unfolding of human potential.

Immanuel Kant, the Königsberg sage in whose austere rooms hung a portrait of Rousseau, asserted that man, not as an animal but as a person, ought "to be prized as an end in himself."[17] This was another key dimension of German concepts of freedom: *autotely*, or self-realization. Kant placed autotely at the center of morality. Though he never confused politics with morals, Kant advocated republicanism as a liberal polity in which personal independence would at least fuel a legal order closer to morality than the selfish warring monarchies of his time.

When G. W. F. Hegel (1770–1831), the greatest of the post-Kantian philosophers, wrote his *Philosophy of Right* in 1821, he transferred Kant's autotely from ethics to politics and from the person to the state. He then idealized the state as a worldly embodiment of the Spirit, a progress of reason through history. In Hegel's state there is freedom, but it is rational liberty—not simply freedom from coercion, but freedom as an unfolding power of self-realization, the very stuff of *Bildung* in a lofty political version. For as in Kant's morality and as in Humboldt's *Bildung*, so in Hegel's politics: in all three cases there runs a common drive, autotely. Such was the soul of the modern German concept of freedom. It was positive liberty, to be sure, since it was most conspicuously an instance of "freedom to"; but it was positive liberty with a cultural vengeance.

The English theory, put briefly, said that liberty means independence. The French (Rousseaunian) concept was that liberty is self-rule. The German school replied that liberty is self-realization. The political environment of the English theory was the classical liberal polity; the political environment of the French theory was the democratic principle; and that of the German theory was the "organic" state, a mix of traditional and modernized elements.

The Individual and the State

To come closer to concrete history, we need to sketch a further typology than this one. For it is possible to distinguish two main liberal patterns within the Western political evolution; specifically, two basic patterns in the relationship between state and individual.

Here there is an English paradigm and a French one. The distinction between two liberalisms with a national hue, one English and the other French, was made forcefully in Guido de Ruggiero's *History of European Liberalism,* which was the standard work on the subject during the interwar period. De Ruggiero noticed that while the English species of liberalism was all for limiting state power, the French variety sought to strengthen state authority in order to ensure equality before the law. The French version also sought the demolition of a "feudal" order well entrenched in social privilege and the power of the Church.

This difference has social roots. Although English social structure kept a strong class basis, the estates hierarchy characteristic of traditional society had early been eroded by the emergence of free farmers and the equally early conversion of the nobility to agrarian capitalism.[18] This, together with the early achievement of a unitary state, set a pattern in which the state rested on independent individuals, whose relationship with the state was more *associative* than subordinate. The English upper classes were masters of the state.

French society, by contrast, maintained a closed hierarchical structure for a long time. When the Revolution deprived this structure of its political legitimacy, the logic of the situation made it necessary *to use the state to free the individual,* guaranteeing his rights. The new state, allegedly embodying the general will, stood high and mighty as the sole legitimate authority, largely impervious to the mediation of associative institutions belonging to civil society. As a consequence, while in England the state-individual relationship was basically relaxed, in France it often became tense and dramatic, pitting the citizen against state power in heroic, defiant solitude, like a character in classical tragedy. Meanwhile, the state, made into a jealous seat of the general will by the fictions of omnipotent representation (assembléisme) and of plebiscitary rule (Bonapartism), oscillated between democracy and despotism.[19] Hence the concern of French liberals like Tocqueville to acclimatize in France an American-like associative fabric that would be able to put a brake on state power. We shall meet these two patterns again, especially the French one, as we trace the fortunes of liberalism in the two last centuries, both in Europe and elsewhere.

2

The Roots of Liberalism

This chapter and the next three will be the most historical chapters in this historical-perspective book. I shall devote two sections here to pointing out some roots of liberalism from the Reformation to the Enlightenment and the early nineteenth century; chapters 3, 4, and 5 provide a bird's-eye survey of liberal theory from wigged whigs to latter-day neoliberals. Over the course of three centuries, liberalism was truly enriched both in themes and in topics, but the enrichment of liberal doctrine was seldom a linear process. Advances in one direction were often offset by setbacks. Any impression of triumphalism should be avoided since liberalism has had to learn important things from the challenge of rival ideologies.

Early Modern Sources

Classical liberalism, or liberalism in its original historical form, may be broadly described as a body of theorization advocating a constitutional state (that is, central national authority with well-defined and limited powers and a fair degree of control by the ruled) and a large amount of civil freedom (or freedom in the individualistic, Hobbesian sense discussed in Chapter 1). Classical liberal doctrine consists of three elements: the theory of human rights; constitutionalism; and "classical economics" (roughly, the branch of knowledge inaugurated by Adam Smith, systematized by David Ricardo, and illustrated, among others, by Mill). I shall deal with rights and constitutionalism in this section and with classical economics in the next.

Rights and Modernity

The formative struggle of liberalism was the vindication of *rights*—religious, political, and economic—and the attempt to control political power. Modern culture is normally associated with plenty of *individual* rights; historically, one can say that liberty has to do with the rise of modern civilization, first in the West, and then in other areas of the world. The formula, therefore, seems to be liberty equals modernity equals individualism. We can safely look for the roots of liberalism in the historical experience of modernity. But where to begin? Granted that the scale and growth of individualism is a hallmark of modernity, where is the point of breakthrough, the epochal watershed?

An eloquent answer to this question was given by the so-called reactionary school of social theory—the French publicists like Maistre and Bonald, who were writing in hostile reaction to the Great Revolution. Their view was that the evils of the Revolution harked back—through the Enlightenment—*to the Protestant Reformation* of the 16th century. The great original culprit was Luther, who had set the demon of individualism loose. From then on, they argued, criticism and anarchy started to undermine the social order and its foundations, the principles of authority and hierarchy. These reactionaries agreed with our equation of modernity and liberty, but they evaluated it in starkly derogatory terms.

But others, even loyal Protestants, saw the Reformation not as the begetter of modernity but, at most, as an important ancestor. A typical and most influential example was Hegel. To Hegel, Christianity, with its metaphysics of the soul, was the historical cradle of the principle of individuality. Greek freedom had been a glorious achievement, but it did not develop human individuality. The Reformation brought about a strong assertion of individual conscience, Hegel said, but even in the Christian West freedom as individuality did not attain an active form until the Revolution and Napoleon. Then it was that a "civil society" composed of worldly independent individuals received its proper legitimation, most visibly in the Code Napoléon, the civil law of postrevolutionary Europe. Before that time individuality, the driving force in the culture of modernity, had lived a long chrysalis stage. Therefore the modern watershed was not so much 1500 as 1800—a considerable displacement.

The Protestant theme of the inviolability of conscience was a powerful seminal contribution to the liberal creed. But in the history of liberal institutions, was the link between conscience and freedom this straight and direct? The Protestant sects that upheld freedom of conscience before Catholic intransigence often themselves lapsed into intolerance and repression. The burning of the physician Miguel Servetus in Calvinist Geneva (1553) became a cause célèbre of the Protestant rage against heresy; very soon persecution was practiced, as Erasmus had sadly foreseen, on both camps, Reformation as well as Counter-Reformation. Understandably, for a time advanced political thought respected religious freedom, but feared fanaticism as much as power—a time extending from Richard Hooker (1554–1600), the main defender of the Elizabethan settlement, to Hobbes and Spinoza in the mid-1600s.

Shortly before World War I the prominent liberal Protestant theologian Ernst Troeltsch (1865–1923) made a strong case for severing modern religious culture from the Reformation. Challenging the pieties of the German middle classes, which worshipped Luther's fight against Rome as a foretaste of modern liberty, Troeltsch saw the Reformation as fundamentally unmodern. Far from announcing modern pluralism, Troeltsch said, its leaders had held fierce theocratic beliefs worthy of the Middle Ages. Troeltsch was deliberately contradicting his teacher at Göttingen, Albrecht Ritschl (1822–89). For Ritschl, Luther had freed Christianity from mystical withdrawal by redirecting religious energies into service in the world and into the strict observance of everyone's duties toward family, occupation, and the state. But according to Ritschl, the individual led a religious life chiefly through his or her membership in the established church. Not so, countered Troeltsch: true faith originates in personal experiences. In England, as against Lutheran Germany, Calvinist dissent managed to create a climate of bold reform. But on the whole, Protestant individualism came to the fore only in the free-floating mystical movements of the *eighteenth* century, like pietism. In Troeltsch's revision, modern Protestanism therefore owed very little to the authoritarian scripturalism of the Reformation.[1]

Some strands in the Reformation did prefigure modern liberal pluralism and its respect for the heterodox individual. A few sects like the Socinians, an Italo-Polish current of the early seventeenth century, and thinkers like Milton, the poet-prophet of English Puritanism, preached toleration well in advance of their age. In Milton's "Areopagitica" (1644), subtitled "a speech for the liberty of unlicensed printing," the case for freedom of conscience unfolded into an argument for freedom of opinion.

Religious toleration also became a keystone of Locke's proto-liberal system. His *Letter concerning Toleration* (1689), full of sympathy for Dutch Arminian dissenters, stated that persecution is contrary to charity and is therefore un-Christian. Locke stressed that the Christian care of souls requires "inward persuasion" and hence free assent instead of coercion.

In the "natural theology" of William Paley (*The Principles of Moral and Political Philosophy*, 1785), the argument for toleration turned utilitarian, claiming that "truth itself results from discussion and from controversy." In the meantime the leading continental *philosophe*, the deist Voltaire, pointed out in his own *Treatise on Toleration* (1763) that while toleration never stirred social upheaval, intolerance had caused many a bloodbath. Thus toleration, so earnestly advocated by the Puritan-bred John Locke, became the object of secular justifications. The fight for religious rights fueled the idea of general individual rights, one of the very springs of liberalism.

Rights: Natural Law and Consent

The foremost force in the conceptual legitimation of the modern idea of rights was the modernization of natural law theory. The notion of a law of nature had been a very old one. It could be found in the Stoic philosophy, in the works of Cicero (notably *De republica* and *De officiis*), in Roman imperial jurisprudence (notably Gaius and Ulpian), and in the fathers of the Church. The basic tenet of natural law theory is that there is a higher law, "a right reason [*recta ratio*] according to nature," as Cicero put it (in *De republica*, bk. 3, ch. 22). This unchanging reason applied to command and prohibition is "right" inasmuch as it enables people to tell good from evil by consulting no more than their mind and heart, their inner moral sense. Cicero himself had suggested that there was a kinship between such law of nature and the law of nations—in effect, a common law of mankind.

There are significant differences between the natural law theory of the ancients (classical jusnaturalism) and later developments, medieval and early modern. Before the Principate (which began with Augustus in the first century B.C.), the Romans had regarded liberty as an acquired civic right rather than as an innate attribute of humans.[2] But a few centuries later, a conceptual shift occurred in the *Digest*, the body of case law that integrated Justinian's sixth-century *Corpus Juris Civilis*. It included a definition of *liberty* as "one's natural faculty of doing what one pleases." This definition was a prefiguration of negative freedom, phrased in unmistakable jusnaturalist language.

The concept of rights underwent even deeper changes during the transition from antiquity to the Middle Ages. Our notion of right denotes a proper claim, often on things (as the right of ownership), and it has a strong subjective side. The Roman concept of *ius*, by contrast, was quite objectivist.[3] Ulpian, in the third century A.D., and the *Institutes* said that "justice is the continuous and lasting determination to assign to everyone their *ius*" (the famous principle *suum cuique tribuere*). This simply meant that a judge should always look for the just outcome to a dispute. The medieval commentators of the *Institutes*, like Azo of Bologna (ca. 1200), construed Ulpian's dictum as meaning that people ought to acknowledge and respect one another's *claims*. Induced by the entanglements of feudal relationships, medieval lawyers ended up by blending two concepts that had originally been separate in Roman law: *ius* and *dominium*, or property. Initially, *dominium* referred solely to possessions and not to interpersonal relations. But in the thirteenth century the great glossator Accursius conceived of dominium as any *ius in re. Any* right that could be defended *erga omnes*—that is, against any other people—and that could be alienated by its owner came to be seen as a *property* right.

In the late Middle Ages, this creative fusion of *ius* and *dominium* was deepened. In turn, nominalist thinkers like Gerson in Paris blended the concept of *ius* with the natural faculty of *libertas*. According to Richard Tuck, a leading expert on the history of natural rights theory, the end result of the resistance to Franciscan evangelism was the conclusion that individuals have a right of *dominium* over their lives and goods. This right derives not from civil law or social intercourse, *but from people's very nature* as human beings.[4]

In the early modern age, natural law concepts affected primarily *public* law.[5] But the robust new concept of natural rights as wideranging subjective claims soon invaded the theory of the polity, and the "social contract" model emerged as the political version of natural rights theory. The social contract model, which was the centerpiece of early modern political thought from Hobbes to Rousseau, served the natural rights idea with a vengeance. Its individualist premises, as distinct from its political conclusions, turned out to be crucial ingredients in the rise of liberal thought.

Contractarianism did not spring automatically from the medieval concept of subjective rights and its jusnaturalist framework. Instead, a new development took place. The Jesuit Francisco Suárez (1548–1617), chief publicist of the Counter-Reformation, shared the recognition that Luther and Machiavelli had dismissed natural law. Luther's dark view of human sinfulness was scarcely compatible with the jusnaturalist assumption that people, however fallen, could grasp God's will and so reflect divine justice in ordering society. Nor did the Machiavellian reason of state have room for criteria of preternatural justice.[6] Consequently, Suárez and others believed that the Catholic counterattack against both Protestantism and secularism demanded a full return to the natural law perspective.

Suárez was not oblivious to the late medieval developments in legal theory. He opened his treatise *De Legibus ac Deo Legislatore* ("On the Laws and God the Lawgiver," 1612), by observing that *ius* does not mean simply "that which is right" but also denotes "a certain moral capacity everyone possesses". He illustrated this capacity by mentioning the owner's hold on his possessions. Besides realizing how functional such rights were in commerce, Suárez saw that Catholics, too, needed these rights in order to resist Protestant power in the reformed countries.

Suárez was at pains to see that subjective rights were subordinated to a holistic frame, a moral-social whole defined by a traditional view of natural law. This synthesis of Thomism and the nominalism of Ockham provided the Iberian world with a lasting political mold.

Suárez's contemporary, the Dutchman Hugo Grotius (1583–1645), saw otherwise. In his great work of 1625, *De iure belli ac pacis* ("On the Law of War and Peace"), he defined the state, or political society, as "a community of rights and sovereignty" (II. IX. VIII. 2). The state was a group separated from the rest of mankind by particular rights. Grotius set out to rescue universal moral standards from Renaissance skepticism. He posited a *minimalist* ethics, composed of only two principles: the legitimacy of self-preservation and the unlawfulness of wanton injury of others. This originated a new look for natural law theory. Just as Machiavelli had severed political analysis from ethics, Grotius redefined natural law apart from theology.

Grotius, as an aide and adviser to the great statesman Jan van Oldenbarnevelt, had spent many years trying to prevent a clash between orthodox Calvinists and the Arminian minority in the Netherlands. In 1612 Oldenbarnevelt made Grotius, barely thirty, pensionary (chief executive) of Rotterdam. Unfortunately, seven years later Oldenbarnevelt failed miserably to contain the ambitious Prince of Nassau, a hero of the Calvinists, and was executed. Grotius (after betraying his master) got a life sentence and escaped in a huge basket that his devoted wife had sent to prison full of books. He ended his existence in a shipwreck as ambassador of Christina of Sweden to France, but was honored all over Europe as the founder of international law. In Grotius's bold recasting of jusnaturalism, natural law no longer rested on the nature of things but on the nature of man. Above all, he used jusnaturalism to build an individualist account of society—the very opposite of Suárez's holist views.

This uncompromisingly individualist approach was precisely the gist of contractarianism. Legitimate authority came to be seen as based on voluntary covenants made by the subjects of a state. As Hobbes wrote in *De Cive* (ch. 14, 2), obligations derive from promises—that is, from clear choices of the individual will. Grotius still believed (as Hobbes did not) in natural sociability, but like Grotius, Hobbes broke with the old view of society and polity. Rejecting the idea of natural order, Hobbes started from the individual and saw society as a collection of them.[7] This rationalist and individualist way of modernizing natural law[8] made jusnaturalism, in the now-venerable words of Otto Gierke, "the intellectual force which finally dissolved the medieval view of the nature of human groups."[9]

Now protoliberal thought was a mix of Lockean contractarianism and Montesquieu's constitutionalism. John Locke (1632–1704), the first largely influential liberal thinker, theorized a social contract that established lawful government in individualist terms, as Hobbes had, although Hobbes's *Leviathan* (1651) proposed absolute monarchy where Locke defended limited government. For all their shared individualism, however, there is a world of conceptual difference between Hobbes and Locke, one an absolutist, the other a protoliberal—and the heart of the matter is Locke's fruitful reelaboration of the notion of consent.

The need for consent as a ground for legitimacy had surfaced in political theory well before Locke, first in Marsilius of Padua's *Defensor Pacis* (1324) and then in the conciliarist or antipapist movement within the Church in the fifteenth century. Marsilius had held that in state and Church alike, the people—or their majority—have the right to elect, "correct," and if need be depose rulers, whether secular or ecclesiastical. Ockham (ca. 1300–49) is generally credited with the first derivation of governmental legitimacy from consent based on natural law. Later, several major theorists such as Hooker, Suárez, and the German Johann Althusius (d. 1638), one of the fathers of federalism, also valued consent as the source of political obligation.

The rethinking of natural law by Grotius and Hobbes had been accompanied by a strong emphasis on will. This old Augustinian concept[10] had been much emphasized by Ockham's nominalist stress on the idea of subjective rights. Nominalists, including Ockham, had extolled human free will along with God's. Suárez had sought to attenuate the role of the will in the myth of natural law, but Ockhamists found natural law binding because it was said to be God's will.

The idea of consent, as the source of legitimate authority, implies will that is politically expressed. But consent can vary around two axes. First, consent can be given either on an individual or on a corporate basis. Second, consent to a government can be granted either once and for all or periodically and conditionally, in which case it can be reclaimed (or not) according to the citizens' opinion about the quality of governmental performance.

For most previous consent thinkers, consent was a corporate act of the community that had been given in the past.[11] The orginality of Hobbes and Locke was that they stressed consent *by the individual*. The innovation of Locke (in his *Second Treatise on Government*, published in 1689) was to make consent (even if tacit) periodical and conditional. Locke's work, to quote one of his ablest modern interpreters,[12] inaugurated "the politics of trust." Locke saw rulers as trustees of citizenship and memorably envisaged a right to resistance and even revolution. Thus, consent became the basis of *control* of government.

Locke's contractarianism marked the apotheosis of natural rights in the modern individualist sense. Hobbes before him and Rousseau after him had devised social contracts in which the individuals utterly alienate their power to king or assembly. In Locke, by contrast, personal rights come from nature, as God's gift, and are far from dissolving into the social compact. While Hobbes's pactarians give up all their rights except one—their lives—Locke's individuals give up just one right—the right of doing justice by oneself—and keep all the others.[13] By enshrining property as a natural right, prior to civil and political association, Locke enhanced a trend five centuries old: the postclassical fusion of *ius* and *dominium*, of right and ownership. By enthroning the right of resistance he enlarged the individualist principle of will and consent. And consent, rather than tradition, is the gist of legitimacy in liberal politics.

Constitutionalism

So much for the rights element, the first and most important of the three components of classical liberalism. On the second component, constitutionalism, one can be considerably briefer. A constitution, written or not, consists of those rules that govern government.[14] It is tantamount to the rule of law, which stands for the exclusion of both the exercise of arbitrary power and the arbitrary exercise of legal power.

Varying theories for the Western roots of constitutionalist doctrine and for its legitimacy have been presented. In the nineteenth century, the great Oxford historian William Stubbs (1829–1901) piously entertained the notion that the Gothic parliament had been a political assembly. Refuting Stubbs, Cambridge's Frederick William Maitland (1850–1906) demolished the legend and established that the English medieval parliament had instead essentially been a court of law. A. V. Dicey's classic study, *The Law of the Constitution* (1885), showed the rule of law to be the essence of constitutionalism.

Stubbs, in his monumental *Constitutional History of Medieval England* (1873–78), also lent credence to another, cruder legend: the notion that English freedom stemmed from a stock of Teutonic, hence Anglo-Saxon, liberty. "Freedom was in the blood," wrote Stubbs, and the blood came from the German forests with the Saxon invaders, well before the Normans and the Magna Charta.

Maitland's pupil at Cambridge, J. H. Figgis, responded with a more serious theory. He traced constitutionalism, the law of liberty, to the contractual bonds of feudalism. What else, Figgis argued, could have given medieval society, with its rudimentary economy, the privilege (especially in England) of a centralized state circumscribed by fundamental guarantees for its subjects? Modern scholarship has disagreed with Figgis's view. After all, Japan had feudal structures too, but it did not develop anything like Western constitutionalism. The American constitutional historian Charles McIlwain reacted against the feudal theory by stressing the role of Roman law in medieval political thought.[15]

More recently, Brian Tierney has singled out an alternative explanation. In Tierney's view, the roots of constitutionalism in the West were largely ecclesiastic. Figgis had underscored the Gerson-to-Grotius line, from conciliarism in the fifteenth century to modern jusnaturalism in the seventeenth.[16] Tierney, however, showed that conciliar doctrines like consent had been around long before the age of Gerson, in the glosses on canon law since 1200. At that time, a lively debate began to oppose partisans of papal theocracy to defenders of ecclesiastical power and even independent secular authority. In Plato, Aristotle, and Cicero the problem of the origin of obligation was overshadowed by the question of the best regime. But at least since John of Paris (1255–1306), an early Thomist, the jusnaturalist problem of *legitimacy* had been haunting political philosophy. Early modern political thought from Hobbes and Locke to Rousseau was devoted to it. These thinkers addressed the issue of legitimacy (and its answer, the doctrine of consent), in an individualist cast of mind, whereas their medieval predecessors were under the spell of hierarchy and of the whole.

Conclusion

Our search for the roots of rights concepts and constitutionalism has found a rather ironical picture. We started our inquiry sure in the knowledge that modern liberty, the historical phenomenon that is at once the ground and the result of the liberal movement, is tied up with the growth of individualism. As individualism did not flourish on a large scale before the modern age, we naturally turned to modernity as the watershed of liberty in its full contemporary meaning. Given its pivotal role in fostering freedom of conscience, it was only logical for us to look at the Reformation. But the time of Luther and Calvin turned out to be at most a prologue to the culture of individualism, since the Reformers' theocratism was fundamentally authoritarian, whether in Lutheran conformism or in the social dynamism of the Puritan sects. We then followed Hegel and Troeltsch and located modern freedom in the new religiosity of 18th-century mysticism and in the civil society of postrevolutionary Europe (and, it goes without saying, the United States).

Yet the deeper we probed into the roots of rights and constitutionalism, the more we found that decisive conceptual departures had been achieved in that long and still shadowy laboratory of Western culture: the Middle Ages. Azo of Bologna, Accursius,

Ockham, and Gerson proved to be almost as crucial as the early modern jusnaturalists and contractarians—Grotius, Hobbes, Pufendorf, Locke, and Rousseau. Nevertheless, modern political thought, like modern political culture, was not just a matter of combining the ideas of rights and consent that were both already present in medieval jurists and philosophers. Such a combination, invaluable as it was in itself, had an extra dimension, one distinctly postmedieval: an individualistic, nonholist, and nonhierarchical view of society. Ultimately, this is what separates the world of Locke from the world of Aquinas, Ockham, and Gerson—and brings the social contract of early modern thinkers close to our own liberal democratic universe.

The Enlightenment Heritage

Liberalism is often said to derive largely from the Enlightenment. This is to a great extent true, but in order to realize it, we must recall the nature of that intellectual age. One of its foremost interpreters, Paul Hazard, argued that the Enlightenment was basically an attempt to replace religion, order, and classicism with reason, progress, and science.[17] Its background was the new expansive sense of mastery over nature and society that seized Western Europe around the middle of the eighteenth century, in the wake of an impressive growth of population, trade, and prosperity that followed an era of economic depression. As such, the Enlightenment meant above all a "recovery of nerve," in Peter Gay's accurate formulation.[18] As it unfolded in the work of Voltaire and Diderot, Hume and Adam Smith, Lessing and Kant, it amassed a complex set of ideas comprehending human rights, constitutional rule, and *liberism,* or economic freedom. Enlightenment thought came to overlap with most of the ingredients of the classical liberal creed, without being always liberal in strictly political terms.

"*Nous cherchons dans ce siècle à tout perfectionner*": Voltaire's comment apropos the humanitarian penal reforms advocated by Cesare Beccaria—one of the peaks of reform thought in their century—catches the gist of the age. More often than not, the *philosophes* were practical-minded authors. With the exception of Kant, they did not attain the intellectual stature of Descartes or Leibniz, of Grotius or Hobbes, but then, their aim was quite different. Improvement through reform—such was the name of their game. The perfectibility of man, and hence of the world, was their first belief. Even

Rousseau, no believer in progress, was relatively hopeful about man, provided the right social contract was adopted or the right education procured (as he stipulated in *Émile*, his 1762 pedagogic treatise that appeared in the same year as his republican catechism). As the *philosophes* sought to put perfectibility into practice, they approached the essence of Kant's famous identification of the Enlightenment with the emancipation of mankind from tyranny and superstition.[19]

Political Thought

Locke reinforced his theology of natural rights with a clear concern for the rule of law. No other strategy would suit his supervision of corporate consent into the great liberal theme of (revocable) consent as (periodical) control. To this extent Locke, the rights paladin, also inclined toward constitutionalism. But a full-blown explication of constitutionalism came only with Montesquieu, because *The Spirit of the Laws* offered what Locke's *Second Treatise* did not: an extensive consideration how to distribute authority and how to regulate its exercise, if liberty was to be enlarged or simply preserved. In short, Montesquieu gave protoliberalism that institutional depth that the contractarian tradition lacked. For this, and also for his powerful adumbration of a sociological account of law and politics, Montesquieu, the second great forefather of classical liberalism after Locke, is rightly deemed one of the initiators of the Enlightenment.

The historical bloc formed by the Renaissance and the age of the baroque, the full blossom of "court civilization" in the "Europe of the capitals"[20] had witnessed a major shift in the conception of law. The widespread reception of Roman jurisprudence contributed to the emergence of a new relation between rulership and legal norms. Whereas law had previously been seen chiefly as a mere framework of governmental action, it now came to be seen in a new light, as an *instrument* of power.[21] The most characteristic political ideology of the Enlightenment, enlightened despotism, made extensive use of the new perspective—the "Machiavellian" view, so to speak—of norms as tools of power. But the classical formulations of the theory of enlightened despotism represented modifications of absolutist doctrine precisely in that they subjected royal power and the new instrumental approach to law to the climate of opinion generated by the ideology of freedom and improvement.[22]

Thus the locus classicus of the concept of enlightened despotism, Frederick the Great's *Essay on the Form of Government and the Duties of Sovereigns* (1771) (which was written in French for Voltaire), offered an implicit contractarian basis in its stress on monarchic duties. It depicted the king as the first servant of the state, morally if not legally accountable to his subjects—whom the Prussian sovereign went as far as to call "citizens." The main proponents of progressive absolutism in Western Europe, the French economists known as Physiocrats (though they did not endorse the social contract concept) distinguished "legal despotism" from mere despotism by speaking of a functional monarchy as an autocracy identified with the protection of freedom and property, intelligently refraining from meddling with the free play of the market. In the discourse of enlightened despotism, what Frederick stressed was "enlightened," not "despotism." Thanks to the impact of the Enlightenment, absolutism underwent a curious metamorphosis into a paradox: responsible autocracy—at the level of legitimacy if not at that of the actual exercise of power.[23]

The political theories of the *philosophes* fall into three main positions. Voltaire (and for a time Diderot) were close to enlightened monarchy, as were the Physiocrats and their friend Turgot. A protoliberal, Anglophile parliamentary model of sorts was held, very influentially, by Montesquieu, with his constitutionalist thesis of the need for a separation of powers. Finally, a republican position, strongly democratic in spirit, found its preacher in Rousseau.[24] Holbach's utopia, "ethocracy" (1776), combined the moralist and anticommercialist pathos of Rousseau with a defense of representative bodies (like parliaments) sharing sovereignty in order to prevent royal despotism—not so far from Montesquieu. Most important, lessons from Locke (natural rights), Montesquieu (division of powers), and Rousseau (the democratic element) coalesced into the new republican system erected at the time in independent America—and then helped shape the constitutional views of the French Revolution.

Still, generally speaking, the Enlightenment was not in essence a political movement. It was practical-minded, but its reformist zeal was geared to penal codes, systems of education, and economic institutions rather than to political change. This was also true outside France. Gibbon's main achievement was in "philosophical history," Beccaria's in penal reform, Lessing's in drama criticism, aesthetics, and the philosophy of history, and Kant's in the theory of knowledge and ethics. Hume left a few thoughtful political essays besides his *History of England* and his crucial work in philosophy, but he wrote as a utilitarian tory, not as a political modernizer. As we shall see, there was even a *conservative* Enlightenment. In the end, if we wish to identify the major contributions of the Enlightenment to the liberal worldview, we have to turn to another area—the theory of history. Here, despite some pathbreaking insights by Voltaire, the main work by far was done by the Scottish Enlightenment.

Historical and Economic Thought

The Enlightenment called its way of looking at events, or the succession of the ages, in search for deeper meanings and broad patterns "philosophical history." Its primary content was the history of civilization, but this in turn had a more specific focus, the "history of civil society," to paraphrase the title of Adam Ferguson's 1767 book. Mindful of Montesquieu's interest in the underlying causes of social forms, Scottish philosophical historians such as Ferguson, Adam Smith, and John Millar mounted among themselves a stages (or stadial) theory of mankind's development. Some stadial schemes stressed modes of livelihood, like Millar's (and his master Smith's) four historical systems of subsistence, from hunting and pastoralism to agriculture and then to "commercial society." Ferguson's own sequence concentrated rather on the state of manners and distinguished three stages: savage, barbarous, and polished. The Scottish social theorists insisted on a progression from rudeness to refinement. It was with Ferguson and with Rousseau's famous *Discourse on the Origin of Inequality* (1754) that the phrase, "civil society" started a new semantic career. Where the word *civil* in *civil society* had previously corresponded to *civitas* and had traditionally meant "political," in Rousseau and Ferguson *civil* was related to *civilitas,* meaning "civility" or "civilization." As such, it referred to the state of morals and manners without any necessary connection with politics. (Hegel and Marx subsequently established "civil society" in this nonpolitical sense.)

The road from rudeness to refinement described in the Scots' stadial schemes was also a road from poverty to prosperity. A purple page at the close of Book 1 of *The Wealth of Nations* by Adam Smith (1723–90) states that even the "industrious and frugal peasant" in a commercial society was far better off than "an African king, the absolute master of the lives and liberties of ten thousand naked savages." The secret of the superiority of even the lower strata of "civilized society," said Smith, was due to the much higher productivity of its division of labor. Several authors at the time shared this realization that economic strength meant new, better standards of living for even the toiling masses. Locke, for one, observed that though they controlled huge expanses of land, American Indian chieftains were fed, clad, and lodged worse than a day laborer in England simply because the latter belonged to an economy where the yield of the land through industry and property was so much more advanced.

One can see that the Enlightenment was discovering or inventing economics. But the great foundational text of classical economics, *The Wealth of Nations* (1776), was not altogether original in its analysis and prescription of market mechanisms. That had been pioneered by convinced liberists like the Physiocrats. To their leader, François Quesnay (1694–1774), physician of Madame de Pompadour, Smith dedicated his magnum opus. Smith's own contribution lay in his careful discussion of the division of labor as the underlying factor of modern prosperity.

The creation of classical economics was accompanied by a considerable shift in values. At the time when Smith, a professor of moral philosophy at Glasgow, turned to economics, there had been an ongoing debate among the *philosophes* concerning the good or evil of luxury. Voltaire and Hume justified luxury on utilitarian grounds (since it provided employment), but Diderot and Rousseau found it worse than useless—they saw it as harmful. An old historical wisdom blamed luxury for the enervation and hence the decline of great empires, Rome being the most conspicuous. Against this moralistic humanism, other writers asserted a new outlook that legitimized affluence. The defense of opulence often substituted the high-minded industriousness of diligent merchants and artisans for the frugal ethics of civic virtue upheld by moralists like Rousseau, pitting a principled work ethic against the civic ideal. But the partisans of affluence sometimes claimed that social well-being was not so much the result of any virtue, private or civic, as the unintended consequence of many selfish acts. The very pursuit of self-interest, they argued, led to general prosperity and ultimately to social harmony.

This line of argument, well known since Bernard Mandeville's 1714 *Fable of Bees* and its wry slogan, "private vices, public benefits," was taken up by Hume and Smith. Correcting Rousseau, Smith pointed out that although the rich sought to gratify their endless desires out of pure vanity, their stomachs were no bigger than those of the poor, and they could not, by their consumption, starve the rest, as Rousseau suggested in his *Discourse on Inequality.* To the contrary: the taste for luxury, however silly in itself, energized the economy and in so doing created widespread if unequal affluence. Moreover, expanding economies, as both Montesquieu and Gibbon acknowledged, were not likely to collapse as the ancient empires had; the arts of commerce succeeded where the genius of war had failed.[25]

Little by little, profiting from the increasing discredit of the idea of martial glory, *interests* came to the fore as a new ethical paradigm, as "tamers of the passions." Albert O. Hirschman's perceptive study, *The Passions and the Interests—Political Arguments for Capitalism before Its Triumph,* features Smith prominently. But in a sense Smith is the villain of the story, for he did not share Montesquieu's view (also embraced by the leading pre-Smithian economist in Scotland, the mercantilist Sir James Steuart) that the rise of a commercial society would bring more political order by controlling wilder, riotous passions of the "feudal" kind. To the contrary, Smith thought noneconomic drives were harnessed into feeding each man's "wish to better his condition." Vanity and the craving for recognition goad most of mankind to pursue riches through hard work (the "toil and bustle of this world," in Smith's words). For Smith, therefore, "interest" itself becomes as hot a passion as the old longing for glory, and by the same token economic motivation ceases to be an automatic prop of social stability, as in the other ideological cases discussed by Hirschman.[26]

One should be wary of suggesting too darkly Faustian or demonic an image of Smith's view of emergent capitalism. For all his keen awareness of some serious "disadvantages of the commercial spirit," such as the numbing effects of humble work in the increasing division of labor (his remarks foreshadow Marx's critique of alienation), Smith held fast to the Enlightenment idea that trade was a high road of improvement. As he wrote in *The Wealth of Nations,*

> Commerce and manufactures gradually introduced order and good government, and with them, the liberty and security of individuals, among the inhabitants of the country, who had before lived almost in a continual state of war with their neighbors, and of servile dependency upon their superiors. (bk. 3, ch. 4)

If Smith was far from presenting a rosy picture of nascent capitalism in his psychology of economics, his sociology of economics fully vindicated the superiority of "the commercial spirit."

Here we have to emphasize at least two aspects: freedom and justice. As for freedom, Smith leaves no doubt that he thought the fourth stage in the march of civilization, commercial society, meant an increase in independence since it drastically reduced the degree of personal dependency characteristic of most social relations in agrarian society. Like Hume, Smith set little store by the humanist nostalgia for a world of elite citizenship, a realm of civic virtue sustained by slave labor or at the very least by patron-client bonds. Smith never forgot that the conquering ardor of the Roman legions had been no choice, but was an outlet for the constant indebtedness of agrarian societies resting on slave toil and bound to seize the land and labor of their neighbors. Ancient society, for all the exquisiteness of its flower—city democracy—had been a barren plant, capable neither of sustained growth nor of lasting liberty.

In the classical worldview of the civic ideology, *praxis*, the action of free men, was placed high above *poiesis*, production or manual work. Why? Because while the end of poiesis lies in the product, hence beyond the activity that produces it, praxis or action is an end in itself. Smith was the first major social theorist to turn this valuation upside down: in *The Wealth of Nations*, the praxis of politicians, jurists, and soldiers is roundly demoted, whereas production gets the upper hand. Trade and manufacture, not politicking and war waging, furnish the model of worthy behavior. And this change of values entailed the dismissal of the elitist bias inbuilt in civic nostalgia.

The civic ideologists, to whom we shall return in the next section, were above all worshippers of virtue. Smith, however, chose justice over virtue. In so doing he was following the key concern of another tradition of discourse that rivaled that of civic humanism: the natural law tradition of jurisprudence, which was crucial, as we have seen, in the formation of the concept of rights. Central to Smith's analytical enterprise was the elucidation of economic growth. As clearly stated in the full title of his great book, *An Inquiry into the Nature and Causes of the Wealth of Nations*, he was founding the theory of development. But one of the main points he makes is that since commercial society leads from poverty to prosperity, with need neither for conquest nor for the haunting prospect of decline, the same higher stage of civilization, although certainly unequal in social structure and largely unvirtuous in its morals, was far less unjust than its agrarian predecessor had been. For all its members could at least enjoy equal access to the means of subsistence, due to the general diffusion of affluence. Put together, the archfamous "invisible hand" passages in Smith's *Theory of Moral Sentiments* (1759) and in *The Wealth of Nations* amount to a perception that the self-interested individual can unintentionally both maximize the wealth of society and help to distribute it more widely.[27]

Smith's achievement was to cope with the problem of natural law—justice—in terms of a new kind of political economy—the theory of growth—and to show that, at least in historical perspective, the burden of distributive justice—that is to say, the balance between rights and needs—could be taken care of by what he called "the system of natural liberty" and its spontaneous evolution toward wealth and welfare. A true enlightener, Adam Smith gave the theme of progress its socioeconomic depth. An originator of liberal thought, Smith welded the idea of progress into the case for liberism. Small wonder that he was a consistent critic of privilege and patronage. As interlocking pillars of premodern society, privilege and patronage were left largely unscathed by the spokesmen of civic virtue. But they became natural targets of liberalism as the voice of modernity.

Progress and Liberism

The themes of progress and liberism, so prominent in Smith, were substantial additions to the two earlier formative elements of the liberal creed, rights, and constitutionalism. Politically, liberalism could restrict itself to the latter two. But liberalism, besides being a political doctrine, was also a worldview, identified with the belief in progress. The Enlightenment gave liberalism the theme of progress, chiefly theorized by classical economics. Between Hume and Smith, the Scottish Enlightenment added to Locke's theory of rights and to Montesquieu's critique of despotism a powerful framework: a new account of western history. Its meaning was progress through trade thriving on freedom—on civil, individual *modern* freedom.

Progress was certainly an Enlightenment belief, but was it also a liberal one? The ideological cluster of rights/constitutionalism/progress/liberism suggests it was. Yet some critics have argued that the ideology of progress was in fact anything but libertarian. Many years ago, in a thought-provoking study, *The Liberal Mind*, Kenneth

Minogue distinguished "two liberalisms." One is a libertarian rejection of crippling traditions, but the other is hard to tell from authoritarian utopianism or the despotism of progressivist blueprints. It tends to be an intolerant search for efficacy, order, and harmony.[28] The "liberal mind" is often prone to the ugly sin chastized by Michael Oakeshott as rationalistic *constructivism*, or wholesale social engineering of an abstract, a priori salvationist kind.[29]

The widespread reformism of the Enlightenment came close to an enterprising liberalism, but not, I think, to its neoconservative caricature. For a historical approach shows that the actual experience of enlightened reforms had a distinct libertarian flavor. Voltaire's fight against torture and censorship, Beccaria's humanization of penal practices, the avoidance of state support for religious persecution or discrimination, the elimination of caste and gild privileges, the liberalization of trade, the abolition of serfdom in Josephinian Austria were not felt as despotic measures, except by the obvious vested interests damaged in the process, but as truly liberating advances. The restless, self-sacrificing emperor Joseph II in Vienna was surely an autocrat, but his earnestly attempted (and largely failed) revolution from above (though by no means liberal in its methods) held a genuine prospect of emancipation for peasants and Protestants, Jews and the common man. As a rule, even when the Enlightenment was illiberal, it ended up clearing the ground for freer institutions and a (on the whole) less unequal society. If the bold reformism of the enlightened despots was not libertarian in intent, most of its results helped increase freedom and equality.

Politically speaking, what caused a revulsion from the Enlightenment was neither progress nor reform but revolution, in the form of Jacobin violence. The true historical—and hysterical—embodiment of authoritarian salvationism was not enlightened reformism but Jacobin voluntarism: the willful tyranny of virtue under Robespierre and Saint-Just.[30] Ideologically, the Jacobin fanatics were more akin to the discourse of virtue of civic humanism than to the largely unvirtuous hedonism of legitimizers of commercial mores like Hume and Smith. By contrast, the quintessential preacher of progress, Condorcet (1743–94), was philosophically a Humean. He had little concern for virtue, and in his politics tried to stress two elements—knowledge and consent—that were perfectly alien to Jacobin voluntarism. Condorcet may be deemed the very opposite of Robespierre. The antithesis of their republicanisms symbolizes the gulf between Jacobinism and mainstream Enlightenment.

The more one senses the distance between Enlightenment and Jacobinism, the more one appreciates the common ground between the Enlightenment and liberalism. Understandably, in Restoration and Orléans France (1815–48) some of the foremost liberals like Constant were full of the Enlightenment heritage. The same happy combination of Enlightenment and liberalism can be found in the greatest art of the age, from Goya to Beethoven.

Romanticism

Goya, Beethoven, and Stendhal were not romantics, but all were major forces in shaping romanticism. In France, the romantic school was born in league with *légitimiste* or Restoration politics. The great critic Sainte-Beuve wrote that romanticism is royalism in politics. Yet from a European viewpoint Victor Hugo was more accurate when he declared that romanticism was liberalism in literature. For Hugo himself conducted the transformation of French romanticism from royalism to advanced liberalism.

What made liberalism and romanticism mix? A recent study by Nancy Rosenblum quickly answers that it was the experience and appreciation of modern individualism. The two movements coincided in that they both cherished privacy. The romantic imagination could flourish only within a deep respect for private fantasies; hence romanticism *was* liberalism in literature, in its disregard for classical decorum and in its subversion of classical rules. Likewise, liberalism held the private realm as something invaluable in itself, not just as a means to anything else.[31]

Small wonder, then, that a central liberal moralist like John Stuart Mill traced his concern for spontaneous individuality to romantic roots. Individualism could put on either a calculating mask (Bentham) or an expressivist countenance (its romantic face), but liberalism had room for both of them. (Indeed, each of these images, the rationalist-utilitarian and the romantic-expressivist, corresponds to a "national" school of liberal thought. While utilitarian liberalism belongs to the English concept of liberty as social independence, the liberalism of expression recalls the German concept of freedom as psychological and cultural autotely.)

The romantic or protoromantic origins of modern individualism have been cogently tapped by Colin Campbell's 1987 book, *The Romantic Ethic and the Spirit of Modern Consumerism.*[32] Literary history, Campbell begins, had long shown that by the mid-eighteenth century the English middle classes were reinterpreting Protestantism in a sentimental rather than a Calvinist direction. Against the austere asceticism of the Puritan mind, this new piety saw pleasure as a natural companion of virtue and indulged in feelings of sympathy, benevolence, and melancholy. Sentimentalism set in, soon to be reinforced by the evangelical movement. John Wesley (1703–91), the founder of Methodism, was an Arminian—that is, an opponent of the Calvinist doctrine of predestination, in which sin was inextricable from fate. Wesley stressed passion and prophecy, making the drama of personal conversion into a prototype of romantic experience. Typically, he became an admirer of Rousseau, the preacher of inner religiosity.

The theory of the romantic ethic therefore starts from the recognition that Protestantism has been humanized (and modernized) by mysticism—a process that shaped modern culture as much as the rationalization of the world brought about by ascetic capitalism. The work ethic built the modern economy and technology, but the romantic ethic makes them tick by dint of a perpetual, protean demand, dictated by modern hedonism.

The romantic face of individualism was not limited to sweet hedonisms and dreamy fantasies. It also came in a darker mood, connected with a rather grim view of economics. Evangelicalism, founded by Wesley in an optimistic, Arminian spirit, reached the end of the eighteenth century in a more somber vein. Soon afterward, the evangelical creed, though keeping its accent on faith rather than ritual, clashed with the theism of the divine William Paley, which was so instrumental in secularizing Locke's stand for toleration. Paley's *Natural Theology* (1802) was the peak of religious optimism at the time. Against its sunny vistas, Evangelicalism proclaimed an Age of Atonement, a vision of depravity redeemed by apocalyptic vicissitudes. In this ghastly predicament, bankruptcy was interpreted as a sign of punishment, and the evangelical believers were liberists to a man since they saw the market as a potential weapon against sinfulness. As their able student, Boyd Hilton, observes, evangelical catastrophism was rifer among Low Church Protestant rentiers than among the early industrialists, who often were more secular minded and tended to espouse Ricardian economics instead of the tragic sense of life exuded by the drama of sin and salvation.[33] Insofar as aging Evangelicalism was a religious romanticism, its odd theological justification of liberism provided liberalism with one more powerful link with the romantic culture. Only in the second half of the nineteenth century, with the rise of a meliorist mentality, did the Age of Atonement begin to recede. But before it did, it had romanticized the mind of a substantial part of the Victorian middle classes. And because such a romanticization was a strongly individualistic drive, it significantly contributed to the rise of a liberal culture.

3

Classical Liberalism, 1780–1860

"Sir, the first whig was the devil."

—*Dr. Johnson to James Boswell, 28 April 1778*

By tracing the roots of key elements in the liberal creed, such as the concept of individual rights, the rule of law, and constitutionalism, we arrived at a fairly comprehensive picture of *protoliberalism*—an ideological cluster of values and institutions that historically cleared the ground for the full-blooded liberal polity that became the advanced form of government in the nineteenth-century West. On the level of political thought proper, these elements were to be incorporated, with different degrees of emphasis, into the writings of the main classical liberal thinkers—from Locke and Montesquieu to the American federalists, and from Constant to Tocqueville and John Stuart Mill.

The classical liberals, taken together, made two decisive contributions to the development of liberal thought. First, they welded liberal traits into a coherent advocacy of the secular liberal polity that was then taking shape in representative governments of the age. Second, they introduced and developed two further themes in liberal thought: democracy and libertarianism. Together, these essential themes constituted a defense of the individual not only against oppressive rule but also against the encroachments of social constraint.

Locke: Rights, Consent, and Trust

Hobbes's *De Cive* is divided into three parts, each of which is named after a key concept in the ideological background against which liberalism developed: *libertas, potestas,* and *religio*. Hobbes's aim was to define the relations between state power (*potestas*) on the one hand, and liberty (freedom as independence) and religion (ideological power) on the other. Hobbes discerned two ideological causes of the English civil war. The academic intellectuals taught the magnates of the realm ancient models of civic liberty. At a lower social level, the Puritan "saints" disseminated the right to dogmatize in the name of a holy inspiration. The civic intellectuals rekindled once again the Aristotelian idea that the city is natural—that is to say, that men are naturally social animals. But in the circumstances of 1640 England, the result was sheer disorder. The Puritans, too, made their faith into a motive of subversion and regicide. As Bishop Samuel Butler said in his *Hudibras,* their "stubborn crew of errant Saints" was wont to "prove their Doctrine Orthodox/By Apostolick Blows and Knocks."

Seeing all this, Hobbes inferred that the principle of political order could derive from neither nature nor Grace.[1] It had to be an art, the technique of law as well as of a social contract enabling the state to humble at once fractious grandees and religious zealots and prevent society from collapsing into chaos. In the frontispiece of *Leviathan,* the giant sovereign, "king of all children of pride," bears a sword and a crozier: he wields spiritual as well as temporal power, since he has to deter both a warrior aristocracy and the charismatic sects. In order to protect *libertas, potestas* had to keep self-righteous *religio* at bay.[2]

Hobbes's protoliberal successors kept his theoretical principle—contractarianism—but dropped his political recipe, absolutism. In Locke's prime, with the risk of civil war at a safe remove, they felt danger from another problem. What now bothered the friends of liberty was that the king, acting as an autocrat, might use the state not as an arbiter but as a *monocracy*—a concentration of political and ideological power. The Catholic leanings of the Stuart succession, in the person of James II, meant just that. *Libertas* no longer found itself protected by *potestas;* on the contrary, *potestas* threatened to use *religio* to crush *libertas.*

The struggle against Stuart autocracy came to a head with the Exclusion crisis, around 1680. (At stake was Parliament's possible exclusion from the throne of the Duke of York, who five years later became James II.) The rift between "tories" and "whigs" began at this moment. Tories were the king's partisans; whigs were those who resisted the policies of the crown. In 1680 a treatise written much earlier by a contemporary of Hobbes, Sir Robert Filmer, came into print. Its title was crystal clear: *Patriarcha: A Defense of the Natural Power of Kings against the Unnatural Liberty of the People*. Filmer claimed that society was but a family writ large. Therefore, all authority was of a parental nature, which in those days of unquestioned male dominance meant *paternal* nature. To Locke, however, a scholar deeply involved with whig opposition through his lifelong association with the first Earl of Shaftesbury, this analogy between political and paternal authority was completely false.

Locke devoted the first of his *Two Treatises of Government* to a downright refutation of the patriarchal thesis. To Locke, the people's liberty was quite "natural"—in fact, it was God's gift to man. Royal power was more necessary than natural, and it existed preeminently for the protection of the citizens' natural freedoms. Chapter 15 of the *Second Treatise* emphatically separates "civil power" from two other kinds of domination: paternal power and despotic power. An old typology, endorsed by Grotius (in *De iure belli ac pacis*, bk. 2, ch. 5) had said that power over people can derive from three sources: generation, consent, or crime. Parental power springs from generation. Despotic power, equated with domination over slaves, allegedly comes from conquest in just wars; hence slavery is a retribution of unjust aggression. Which does "civil" (that is, political) power resemble, the parental or the despotic type? Locke's answer was adamant: neither, for political power stems entirely from consent. Now, as Norberto Bobbio has shrewdly noticed, while the speciality of Filmer's patriarchalism was the fallacious conflation of political and parental power, the blurring of the distinction between political power and despotic domination was Hobbes's doing. Hobbes's *De Cive* made no distinction between the sovereign and the slaveowner since in both types of power rested at bottom or a promise, whether it was a promise between individuals pledging obedience for the sake of peace, or of vanquished persons promising to serve if their life be spared.[3]

The *Two Treatises* deployed both a theory of consent and a theory of trust. The theory of consent accounted for the legitimacy of government (and compared absolutism to a state of war on society). The theory of trust showed how rulers and subjects ought to understand their reciprocal relationship. Neither theory was ever relinquished by the subsequent liberal traditions, for all their diversity. They also inaugurated a new truly seminal type of *telos*, or goal, in political theory. For while the ancient and the medieval thinkers had written with a Platonic view to design the good society, and while Hobbes was concerned with the conquest of order, Locke's political philosophy was the first highly influential one that aimed at establishing the conditions of *liberty*.

From Locke to Madison: Civic Humanism and Modern Republicanism

The basis of the Lockean theories of trust and consent was his theology of natural rights. But rights theory in natural law language was not the only kind of discourse the whigs practiced; as challengers of absolutism and champions of toleration, they were the first liberals in modern history. Another, vastly appreciated species of antiabsolutist idiom was the ideology of civic humanism or classical republicanism. It, too, left a big mark on classical liberalism.

Anglo-Saxon political thought between the Glorious Revolution and the issuing of the American Constitution was once viewed as a straight march from Locke to Bentham—that is, from natural rights liberalism to utilitarian democracy. This traditional view was formulated by the English Harold Laski and the American Louis Hartz.[4] Hartz interpreted the American founding fathers as fervently Lockean. Liberals and Marxists alike thereafter told a typical whig tale in which liberty was propelled by the winds of history; they asserted the progressive nature of the commercial society and parliamentary institutions, both helped by modern rights concepts.

But recently John Pocock of Johns Hopkins has proposed a masterful revision of this view. Pocock's main book, *The Machiavellian Moment* (1975), has created a whole school in the history of early modern political thought.[5] Pocock realized that Locke was too radical a consent theorist to be the official thinker of the Glorious Revolution. He also questioned the Lockean picture of Independence republicanism. Pocock discovered an anguished gentry that had deep misgivings about the rise of capitalism. Their genteel citizenship clung to civic humanism as a refuge from commerce and corruption.

This republican gentry, well read in Cicero, Plutarch, and Polybius, fluently spoke a civic vocabulary of liberty and citizenship. Beginning with the "country party" led by Bolingbroke (1678–1757), the tory leader under Queen Anne (who later masterminded the opposition to Walpole and befriended the towering names of Augustan literature, Swift and Pope), these republicans' mouths were full of ideals of virtuous self-rule. They poured abuse on governmental jobbery and ministerial corruption. Their gospels as modern texts were Machiavelli's *Discourses on Livy* (posth., 1531) and Harrington's *Oceana* (1656), the republican voice in English Puritanism.

Central to Pocock's analysis is the idea that the Machiavellian moment inaugurated a "new paradigm" in the conceptualization of politics. The Machiavellian paradigm gave pride of place to *time.* Before Machiavelli, the western vision of politics had turned on timeless values. Even in Florence the rival views of Guicciardini the elitist and Giannotti the populist still looked for an unchanging, balanced constitution, a wall of order against the sea of history. Machiavelli was the first boldly to turn *to* history, not away from it. Conscious of the unpredictable interplay of chance and courage, *fortuna* and *virtù,* he favored political innovation. Nothing less could save Florence from the twofold threat of foreign conquests and Medici despotism. The old values of universal monarchy, as dreamed of by Dante, had to go. The republic had to turn heroic or perish.

Pocock saw this rather tense civic ethic as permeating the whole Atlantic tradition of discourse. Far from being individualist and capitalist, he claimed, early American ideology was humanist-republican in the wake of an English appropriation of Machiavellian themes. During the Puritan interregnum, James Harrington had started fearing for the future of independent freeholders, the gentry whose status had been enhanced by the end of feudalism. Harrington wished to go on (against Cromwell) with gentry militiae (a pet idea in Machiavelli), and he suspected commercial property of bringing about dependency. During the Stuart Restoration, many neo-Harringtonians imagined that there had once been an "ancient constitution," a Gothic past of liberty peopled by landholding warriors. (Harrington himself had never believed in the myth of the ancient constitution.) But otherwise they agreed with the Puritan gentry republicans: the neo-Harringtonians opposed a standing army, decried ministerial corruption, and later resisted the two main "commercial" institutions that had been created at the turn of the century, the Bank of England and the national debt. The republican "country party," old whig by 1680, turned tory when Bolingbroke, defeated in Anne's succession by the Hanoverian whigs, went into the wilderness as the antagonist of Robert Walpole.

Pocock argued that this country party ideology survived right up to late-eighteenth-century republicans and radicals. He noted that Thomas Paine began his *Rights of Man* (1791) by denouncing credit, that bête noire of civic humanists. And Pocock construed the antifederalism and anti-big government of Jefferson and Madison as a remake of country party doctrine. In opposition to Georgian commercialism, his young America was born "in a dread of modernity."

Criticism of Pocock's thesis was not wanting. Countered seventeenth-century Oxford expert Keith Thomas, before the Glorious Revolution the pivotal issues in political argument had been sovereignty, obligation, and the right to resistance—a Hobbesian and Lockean lexicon, hardly a humanist-republican one.[6] Isaac Kramnick, a leading critic of Pocock in the 1980s, claimed that classical republicanism, with its stress on agrarian elites and its nostalgic mood, had little to offer to the urban lower middle class whose property was small and mobile (that is, commercial) and whose bugbear was political and social privilege—the gentry's monopoly. Unsurprisingly, these lower strata supported egalitarian radicals like Wilkes and Paine. Kramnick insisted that for all their attack on corruption, radicals like Paine owed more to Locke than to the civic ideology.[7]

In his more recent work, Professor Pocock shifted his focus. Instead of tracing the survival of classical republicanism, he now proceeded to apply his remarkable analytical powers to modern whiggism.[8] Old whigs, we may recall, had invented the myth of the ancient constitution. Restoration tories replied that there had been no such thing, implying that royal power could grow, as it had on the continent, unembarrassed by ancestral liberties. Now, in a clever move, modern whigs of the Walpole age quietly embraced this old tory dismissal of the ancient constitution—and threw by the board the civic ethic. Modern whig scribblers like Joseph Addison, one of Adam Smith's favorite readings, pitted politeness against "primitive" virtue; Daniel Defoe (of *Robinson Crusoe* fame) exchanged the civic militia for the cultivation of manners; and the Scottish enlighteners rounded it up by building their stadial account of human evolution.

In 1988, in a superb lecture at the London School of Economics and Political Science, Pocock portrayed a British "conservative Enlightenment."[9] With Hume, Gibbon, and Smith as its central figures, this conservative Enlightenment tried to defend the Hanoverian dispensation from the onslaughts of counterelites, both religious and radical-republican. But its ideology was of a definitely liberal-modernizing sort. In a sense, it had Hobbesian underpinnings, for it insisted on political order and social peace under the full protection of sovereign power. Meanwhile, by contrast, the American colonies, hurt by British assertion of imperial power, reverted to a Lockean discourse. Jefferson used a natural rights language *and* the thesis of the ancient constitution to claim that by settling in America, the English colonists had entered the state of nature and therefore were free to erect a social contract; British authority prevailed over their federative but not their legislative (i.e., taxing) capacities. Pocock explicitly acknowledged that Lockean populism, sidestepped in England in 1688, was adopted by the American insurgents in the 1760s and 1770s.

As David Epstein has shown in *The Political Theory of "The Federalist"* (1984), the authors of the Federalist papers (James Madison, Alexander Hamilton, and John Jay) were very much in the tradition of Lockean populism. Epstein took pains to show that they had been proposing a "strictly republican" or "wholly popular" form of government; that the American republic, in size and system, could only be very different from ancient democracy (hence *The Federalist*'s snipes at Rousseau's antiquarianism); that the republican argument of *The Federalist* is based on a realistic psychology that encompasses people's political and not just their economic impulses; and that while ancient democracy in small republics overlooked the problem of justice in favor of the good of the whole, "civilized societies" couldn't avoid a great deal of diversity and consequently had to face the problem of ensuring the good of each part—namely, justice.[10]

By equating popular government with a large federal republic, the *Federalist* papers attempted to cope with the task of balancing interests and factions, freedom and justice. As Madison wrote, by "extending the sphere," "you take in a greater variety of parties and interests," thereby making less probable a majority encroachment on the rights of others. But Hamilton and Madison were aware that this federal solution *meant saying farewell to classical republicanism.* They realized that a large and heterogeneous republic would lessen the need for civic virtue by weakening "factions" within a vast national whole. Moreover, Hamilton counted on a specific passion—the love of power and fame—to attract the rich to virtuous public life, even if in a commercial society virtue could be at most only "a graceful appendage of wealth." Whereas Jefferson was dreaming of agrarian virtue within autarky in Rousseaunian Arcadia, Hamilton was deepening the psychological grasp of liberalism and Madison was devising a republican machinery that suited the manifold morals of a commercial society. Jefferson remained in thrall to local direct democracy, but the Federalist republicans became keen on representative government. They wished to employ political liberty to protect and enhance civil freedom at large. In other words, they were intent on using the "French" concept of liberty as a way to foster the experience of "English" liberty.

Politically speaking, classical liberalism had enough room for elements of the civic ideology as well as for liberalist-progressivist tenets of Enlightenment origin, let alone for natural rights beliefs stemming from Locke and Paine. In the American case (the only major instance of republican implementation of the age), a further conceptual strand proved no less important: the constitutionalist concern. This concern went beyond the old Polybian idea of social balance reflected in the constitution (with the aristocracy represented in the Senate and the people in the commitia) and followed Montesquieu's advice to separate and balance the *powers* or branches of sovereign authority. The constitutional theme runs from Montesquieu to Madison. But in Montesquieu (as in Locke) the specter haunting liberty was still the latent despotism of monarchic power. In *The Federalist* concern for a new danger emerged: unchecked majority power. The same concern reappeared in Constant's criticism of Rousseau: it is not enough to transfer power—it must be also clearly *limited*.

Limiting power was of course the rationale of Locke's play of trust and consent. And of late, we seem to be witnessing the revenge of Locke on the interpretations that displaced him from the canon of early American republicanism. Thus, as Thomas Pangle claims, the American refurbishment of the republican ideal meant an unprecedented commitment to private and economic freedom, in a daring departure from both the Protestant and the classical traditions. But this departure was nourished in Locke's subtle equation of the biblical God with the rational law of nature. The pursuit of happiness and the protection of property were Lockean motifs at the center of the moral vision of modern republicanism.[11]

Whigs and Radicals: The Birth
of the Liberal Democratic Idea

Liberal republicanism in the Founders' America enlarged on the Lockean idea of a commonwealth in that unlike Locke it stipulated elective offices across the board. It also beckoned with a substantial democratic potential within liberal institutions. Last but not least, it envisaged a liberist economy. The American federation was rightly perceived as the freest form yet taken by a whig polity and as such it both fascinated and repelled Simón Bolívar (1783–1830), the unity-seeking, conservative leading liberator in the south of the Hemisphere.

This is a nice stage in our story to overview the birth, growth, and transformation of whiggism as the historical ancestor of liberalism. We have seen that whiggery was born out of the assertion of rights against royal power and had at least two aims: religious freedom and constitutional rule. After their successful struggle against the Stuarts, whigs in this sense governed Britain from Walpole to the elder Pitt, or in dynastic terms, under the first two Georges (1714–60). They fostered commercialism and the expansion and consolidation of the first British Empire. Driven into opposition in the long reign of George III, they managed to return briefly to office in 1806, led by the advanced liberal Charles James Fox (1749–1806), the great parliamentarian opponent of the younger Pitt.

By then, there was already a recognizable stock of whig positions. First was moral latitudinarianism, a reluctance to accept that there is one best way of life or a common good definable by any ethical monism. Second was individualism, with the attendant rejection of "organic" views of society. Third was responsible—that is, accountable—government. Fourth was an Enlightenment plea for progress and liberism (or a preference for liberism justified by the belief in progress). The first whig position, moral latitudinarianism, was alien to the code of values of the Harringtonian "civic" republicans. Nor were the second and fourth of these positions held by civic republicans; they were only halfway individualists, and they were basically innocent of progressivism, being rather inclined to contemplate history as an ominous promise of moral decadence and political decay. But in the English context of the Glorious Revolution, so peculiar in Europe as a whole, the third whig position—namely, responsible government—quickly became a shared principle and was the flag of Bolingbroke's tories after 1714 just as it had been a whig program against the Stuart crown.

During the 1830s, the whigs were again in power, led by two lords, Grey and Melbourne. They passed the first Reform Bill (1832), broadening the franchise in favor of the upper middle classes. It was at that time that whigs began to be called "liberals." Despite the modest scale of the electoral reform, the shift from whig to liberal was linked to a shift *in the direction of democracy,* since the old whig battles for religious freedom and constitutional rule had been largely won. But a few other connotations are contained in the substitution of the liberal label for the whig one. At the level of the political elite, the liberal leadership gradually slipped from the hands of aristocrats such as Russell and Palmerston and was taken over by an archbourgeois, William Gladstone (1809–98), who actually came from the "heretic" liberist toryism of Peel. At the ideological level, the change from the Palmerston to the Gladstone type signified a replacement of Enlightenment insouciance (tinged with unbelief) with the high seriousness of Victorian virtue. Liberalism became to a large extent a kind of lay evangelicalism, fraught with reforming campaigns undertaken as moral causes.

The olympian secularism of whigs as distinct from liberals as well as their taste for elitist compromises survived a little longer across the Atlantic. In antebellum America, there was a whig party before the free soil issue blew it up. Its main leader, Henry Clay, headed the opposition to Andrew Jackson's Democrat party, a Jeffersonian movement representing states' rights and frontier populism. Yet just as at midcentury in England the patrician whigs of the Reform Club marched into the big stream of Gladstone's bourgeois liberalism, in the 1850s, the American whigs with their battle cry (Daniel Webster's "Liberty and Union") marched into the Republican party of Lincoln. Both evolutions from whiggism into liberalism were conducted within a democratic horizon.

Initially, the democratic proposition was the doing neither of whigs nor of liberals. Apart from the American formula of republican federalism, the idea of representative democracy had at least three sources. One was the Lockean left, as embodied in the natural rights theory of Tom Paine (1737–1809), the militant of two revolutions, the American and the French. Brought up as a Norfolk Quaker, Paine believed, like Locke, that men form societies to secure their natural rights, not to surrender them. Another source was the plebiscitary democracy recommended by Condorcet, the

Girondin *philosophe* who died a victim of the Jacobin Terror. Third, democracy was also promoted by the utilitarian school founded in London by Jeremy Bentham (1748–1832). Paine and Bentham are often dubbed "radical" thinkers, and indeed the utilitarians came to be known as "philosophical radicals." When the British liberal party was formed after the Reform Bill and the repeal of the corn laws (1846), it had three main components: whigs like Russell (the Reform prime minister), liberist ex-tories like Gladstone, and Benthamite radicals. So the empirical historical record justifies seeing the utilitarians as members of the big liberal family.

Bentham's first ideological hit was his critique of the great jurist William Blackstone (1723–80). Blackstone's Oxford lectures had given a lucid and humane exposition of common law. But his jusnaturalist (Grotian) assumptions and his conservative constitutionalism incensed the young Bentham (*A Fragment on Government*, 1776), steeped as he was in the enlightened reformism of Helvétius and Beccaria. Bentham rejected Locke's emphasis on *natural* rights, which he mocked as "nonsense upon stilts." From Locke, noted he, the law must receive its principles, from Helvétius its content. Such content was a rule of utility, always corresponding to reason and soon to be equated with "the greatest happiness of the greatest number."

Bentham's gifts to liberalism include a zest for intelligent administrative and judiciary reform and, most important, a larger view of the ends of the state, which for him should promote welfare and equality as well as enforce freedom and security. Bentham's case for democracy was characteristically tough-minded. He had no difficulty in admitting that majorities may be dead wrong. In the long run, however, the general consent is the surest sign of general utility because the majority, having a natural interest in their greatest happiness, have also an interest in discovering and correcting mistakes. Moreover, as democratic rule thwarts "sinister interests," mistakes are more likely to be detected.[12]

What of liberal individualism in all this? Bentham never stopped arguing that the burden of proof ought to fall on those wishing to restrict the private pursuit of happiness. He thought it absurd to reason about other people's happiness without reference to their own feelings. In this, he was quietly moving utilitarianism far away from the outlook of Helvétius, for Helvétius, in his treatises *On the Mind* (1758) and *On Man* (posth., 1772) had shown the most uncompromising, uniformist egalitarianism. Bentham shared the antiaristocratic frame of mind of Helvétius without overlooking individual diversity. Unlike the romantics, who would be constant critics of utilitarianism, Bentham held fast to a cosmopolitan sense of the brotherhood of man and was so universalist a thinker that he coined the word *international*. Because he never forgot that individualism is the soul of liberty, Bentham, the great Westminster eccentric, insisted all his life on reform and codification—yet ultimately refrained from the utopian constructivism in which the early socialists indulged. As Shirley Letwin perceived, his was a rather "modest sort of utopianism," free from the illusion that politics or political blueprints can direct the whole life of society or alter the entire fabric of human nature.[13] If, as is so often noticed, ethically speaking, utilitarianism often sounded shallow, sociologically it meant liberation: liberation from high-minded definers of the "common good," ascetically impinged on the anonymous individual by self-appointed elites, with the inevitable consequence of cant and repression. Deep down, therefore, the connection between utilitarianism and democracy seems far from contingent.

In the name of progress, the utilitarians sponsored several healthy reforms in late Georgian and early Victorian Britain—for instance, in schools, factories, and sanitation. Edwin Chadwick, who lived with Bentham at the time of the master's death, sat on countless committees for legislating along these lines. Modern English jurisprudence started with the Benthamite John Austin (1790–1859). Other disciples, like James Mill and the classicist George Grote (a Reform Bill MP), were among the main founders of the University of London. The Benthamites were the greatest reformers in young industrial England, the main providers of rational institutional change in a change-hungry modernizing society.[14]

By demanding genuine comprehensive democracy (including the secret ballot) and promoting wide-ranging reform, the utilitarians surpassed whatever remained of whig elitism in the original arrangements of American republicanism. Another liberal tenet—liberism—was quickly implemented. James Mill, who authored the first English textbook of economics, worked as an intellectual liaison officer between Bentham and David Ricardo, whose *Principles of Political Economy* (1817) gave classical political economy its classic formulation. Still, liberism did not mean dogmatic laissez-faireism. Far from being an article of faith in the classics of economics, rigid laissez-faire was preached much later by noneconomists like Herbert Spencer.

British state policy after 1830 was increasingly interventionist, and a great deal of responsibility for it may be attributed to the influence of Benthamism up to the 1870s. The question is whether the utilitarians were antiliberists or simply nondogmatic liberists. As has been aptly said, Bentham and his followers favored better government, not more government.[15] Bentham's reforming zeal consistently sought to remove laws restricting freedom, and this made him an early friend of liberism. So were Benthamite reformers like Chadwick. Moreover, early Victorian collectivism, however real, was far more social than economic. The best historians' considered conclusion still is that the century as a whole was indeed an "age of laissez-faire"[16]—and as in practice, so in theory. Their flexibility on this point by no means makes the utilitarians, or the classical economists, less liberists.

The First French Liberals: Constant to Guizot

Let's now turn to the fortunes of liberalism outside Anglo-Saxonland. In early-nineteenth-century Germany, there existed at least two major strands of liberal thought: the cosmopolitan republicanism of Kant's postrevolutionary pamphlets, notably his *Perpetual Peace* (1795), and the *Bildung* liberalism (briefly discussed in chapter 1) of the great humanist Wilhelm von Humboldt (though Humboldt's youthful essay on the limits of the state was published much later). But in Germany until the revolution of 1848, the dominant political philosophy was Hegelian, and Hegel was no liberal. Rather, his *Philosophy of Right* (1821) represented a grand endeavor to insert modern "civil society," with its vigorous bourgeois individualism, into the framework of a holist state accommodating the traditional hierarchies of the ancien régime. Like Suárez two centuries earlier, Hegel attempted to straddle two ages. His synthesis fully accepted the work of the Revolution in legitimizing bourgeois society. Yet he shunned the political consequences of 1789, and he emphatically rejected the social contract idea—the very nub of liberalism and democracy, from Locke to Rousseau. His deification of the state was by no means socially reactionary (and in fact put him at loggerheads with the Prussian conservatives), but neither was it compatible with the liberal concept of political freedom.[17]

The strongest alternative to Hegelianism—German nationalism, starting, in the war effort against Napoleon, in the passionate speeches of Johann Fichte (1762–1814)—was even less hospitable to liberal concerns. In 1793, Fichte wrote in praise of the French Revolution and extreme contractarianism. But a few years later he redefined freedom as the development of one's "higher" self, extolled the "ethical" state, abused modernity as the "age of absolute sinfulness," and put state reason at the service of an unabashedly authoritarian nationalism, operating through compulsory education into nationhood. In the process he also found time to concoct a classic antiliberist tract, *The Closed Commercial State* (1800). Thus, Fichtean eloquence pledged German nationalism to a long animus against liberalism.

While liberalism led a wretched life in Germany, in post-Napoleonic France liberal doctrine flourished even more than it did across the Channel. From Constant to Guizot and Tocqueville, the most prestigious liberal thinkers of the age were French, as they were right up to the political prime of John Mill, around 1860. Even before the Restoration, France had already counted original liberal contributions, quite apart the aristocratic protoliberalism of Montesquieu and its pervasive international influence. (He was mandatory reading for Madison, Constant, Hegel, Bolívar, and Tocqueville, to name just a few.) Take for instance the very interesting case of Abbé Sieyès (1748–1836). Sieyès was the man responsible, at the beginning of the Revolution, for building a new concept of legitimacy. He defined legitimate authority in the new France in terms of national sovereignty. This was nothing remotely like an "ancient constitution"—precedent and prescription (the very things that Edmund Burke was to reproach the Revolution for dropping) meant no more than a long usurpatory oppression in France. Representation was redesigned against hierarchy: vote and eligibility were predicated on property, no longer on status. A sworn enemy of privilege, Sieyès blended Rousseau's misty general will with something quite un-Rousseaunian: representation. All power to the Third Estate! So the big problem in Rousseau—undivided sovereign power, even when transferred from king to people—remained intact. But Sieyès was a fan of modern freedom. Brilliantly, he played Adam Smith off against Rousseau. If direct democracy is an anachronism, he claimed, it is because in a civilized society the division of labor applies to politics as well. People get represented so that they may do something else. Politics is not a duty—it is a trade, a function entrusted by the many to the ruling few.[18]

The other great godfather of French liberalism is a godmother: Germaine, Mme de Staël (1766–1817), the dazzling daughter of the Swiss banker Necker, the last, cleverest, and most popular of Louis XVI's ministers. Her mother almost married Gibbon in Lausanne; she married a Swedish diplomat and then became the mistress first of Benjamin Constant (liberalism) and then of August Schlegel (romanticism). Exiled by Napoleon, Mme de Staël converted her filial piety into an influential assessment of the Revolution. Her *Considerations on the French Revolution* (posth., 1818) told a simple tale. There had been a good revolution in 1789, which brought civil equality and constitutional rule, thereby aligning France with England. (Staël thereby joined the illustrious company of liberal French Anglophiles, which includes Voltaire, Montesquieu and Guizot.) Then there came a bad, nasty revolution, 1793, which brought Terror and violent egalitarianism. Her tale was quite new in that it broke both with the traditionalists' wholesale condemnation of the Revolution and with the left's defense of Jacobinism.[19]

As a liberal, Germaine was a whig, not a democrat. Her political Anglophilia was an avoidance of republicanism. And under the spell of the German romantics (which she introduced to Europe in a remarkable book, *On Germany*, in 1800), she valued religion. For liberty needs morality and morality feeds on faith, though of course that faith was Protestant principle and not papist bigotry. Let Condorcet's children, the *idéologes*, scorn religion—no wonder they are republicans. Seasoned liberals know better. Tocqueville would remember this link between freedom and Christianity.

Benjamin Constant, as indicated (Chapter 1), popularized the idea of modern liberty as an individualist phenomenon. A Protestant Swiss like his friend Germaine, he also stressed the religious springs of freedom. But his liberalism was less patrician, more virtually democratic than hers. All in all, his rich, thoughtful political theorizing made two decisive points. First, the vindication of modern liberty; and second, the institutional limitation of authority. This was his Montesquieu-like solution, adumbrated by Sieyès in his late, Directoire stage, to the Rousseaunian problem of undivided sovereignty. Let us insist once more on this. Rousseau, warned Constant, is right about the *source* of authority, which is the social contract as a symbol of popular sovereignty. But he forgot about limiting the *extent* of the same authority, and this left undetermined the crucial matter of the relations between the rulers and the ruled.[20]

Writing after the dictatorial surges in the French Revolution, Constant perceived, in particular, that Rousseau's republican ideal of collective appropriation of absolute sovereignty, and even the very rule of law, so praised since Montesquieu, could in turn be appropriated by tyrannic minorities ruling in the name of all for the sake of justice; and to this extent he was prepared to break not only with republicanism but also with previous liberal thought.

Between Constant, its great constitutionalist after Sieyès, and the rise of Tocqueville, French liberalism prospered among the so-called "doctrinaires." Their leader was Royer-Collard (1763–1845), who, like Constant, saw sovereignty as a potential danger. An engrossing orator, Royer-Collard was constitutional but no devotee of parliamentary power: for him the Chamber, unlike Sieyès' assembly, had no authority over ministers. As a Restoration liberal, Royer judged the Revolution with less benevolence than Constant and de Staël. He cherished the conquest of civil equality but thought that the disappearance of the ancien régime had "dissolved" society, clearing the ground for administrative centralization. The grip of power on atomist society frightened him—the same ghost that would haunt Tocqueville.

From the "doctrinaire" circle came the chief minister of Louis Philippe (1830–48), François Guizot (1787–1874).[21] A Protestant and an academic historian from the provincial bourgeoisie, Guizot explained western history in terms of the rise of his own class. The 1789 event had done no more than declare its advent, as had 1688 in England. Modern civilization reflected the strength of two distinct impulses, one national, the other liberal. Nation building made for unity, whereas the struggle for human emancipation caused liberty to grow.

Guizot justified French absolutism on historical grounds because it greatly helped the national impulse. Yet he regretted that absolutism had stifled the liberal impulse by curtailing the Reformation in France. In 1789, the adoption of the principle of national representation promised to liberalize the country, but the Jacobins and Napoleon spoiled it all. Consequently, 1789 had established a society but not a polity. It fell to the 1830 revolution the task of completing the Great Revolution by implanting constitutional monarchy and responsible government. But as Louis Philippe's minister, Guizot was haunted by the prospect of further revolutionary upheavals and therefore stubbornly refused to broaden the franchise. With twice the population of Britain, France had many fewer electors than Britain did after the Reform Bill.

The Calvinist in Guizot led him to relinquish the old liberal glorification of popular sovereignty, with its underpinning of optimistic assumptions about human nature. He replaced popular sovereignty with a meritocratic "sovereignty of reason." Politics should be left to be "capacities" of bourgeois elites, while a national program of basic education would gradually lift the rest of the nation to moral and intellectual standards worthy of full citizenship.

Oddly enough, while in theory his parliamentarianism was more advanced than the Restoration doctrinaires', Guizot's political practice was fairly reactionary, leading straight to the revolution of 1848. French liberalism was born, in the salon of Mme de Staël, as a moderate break with the reactionary exorcism of 1789. Guizot gave it too conservative a face—so conservative that it looked, in practice if not in spirit, much like reactionarism under a new guise. Not for nothing did he try to conjure up a moneyed aristocracy as a new, rightful ruling class. Under his oligarchic, authoritarian diet, liberalism was shorn of its democratic germs. As a young historian under the Restoration, Guizot had greeted the leveling effects of the bourgeois ascent. But as a statesman he starkly opposed liberty to the dynamic of equality. In the end, he left French liberalism well behind Constant.

Liberalism Analyzes Democracy: Tocqueville

The other tall figure amidst French liberal thought alongside Constant, Alexis de Tocqueville (1805–59), hated Guizot and made equality and democracy the ruling concerns of his work. Tocqueville described himself as "a liberal of a new kind." And indeed he differed significantly from his French predecessors. He was, if anything, as keen and passionate as any of them when it came to the life of liberty, stressing that "a nation that asks nothing of its government but the preservation of order is already enslaved in its heart." Again, he kept a heartfelt concern for the moral basis of liberal institutions and especially for its religious grounding. If the Protestant Constant made of religion a lifelong preoccupation, Tocqueville was probably even more devout; his intimate papers show that his Jansenist background shaped his vision of man and morals. Nor was he less of an Anglophile, in his love for parliamentary authority, than any of the constitutional liberals before him.

In other important aspects, however, Tocqueville took a rather different path from his predecessors. He didn't balk, for instance, at praising the feudal past. Aristocracy, in the eyes of this Norman squire, was nothing bad in itself. And his contempt for the middle classes was a persistent aristocratic trait in this strange liberal-democrat. Tocqueville's wistful appreciation of feudal freedom made him paint the ancien régime as not only the condition but the very cause of the French Revolution. A despotic centralist tradition nourished by absolutism, having emasculated the aristocracy, reasserted itself with the Jacobins and Napoleon, only to engulf French freedom once more in the Second Empire. Such was the thesis of his study of 1856, *The Ancien Régime and the Revolution*. Needless to say, in this reading 1789, like 1848, was but an episode; in the long run, France suffered from a chronic propensity to authoritarian rule. The reason for this was, in Tocqueville's opinion, the atomization of society brought about by administrative centralism (which he took care to distinguish from the functional centralization of government, necessary to national unity). As one can see, Tocqueville endorsed the lament, dear to the doctrinaires, of a *"société en poussière,"* except that he located its cause not in the shock of the Revolution but in a protracted growth of administrative tyranny under absolutism. Moreover while Royer-Collard was concerned with the state, Tocqueville focused on the state of society and became the sociologist of classical liberalism.

A second, crucial discrepancy between Tocqueville and previous liberals had to do with the issue of individualism. It is worth recalling that the word *individualism* made one of its first appearances in the English language in Henry Reeve's translation of Tocqueville's *Democracy in America* (originally published in two parts in 1835 and 1840).[22] In French the term appeared much earlier, in the reactionary writings of Joseph de Maistre. From 1825 it was often heard among the disciples of Saint-Simon, founders of technocratic socialism.

Tocqueville distinguished between egoism and individualism. Egoism, he said, is a moral category, the vice of selfishness. Individualism is a sociological concept, denoting a lack, not of virtue per se but of public or civic virtue. It is a peaceful disposition that separates one from one's fellow citizens, exchanging society for the small company of family and friends. While egoism plagues all times, individualism is a characteristic of *democratic* society. In his trip to America, Tocqueville admired the civic stamina of town meetings in New England. But he saw it as a corrective rather than a reflection of democracy. The puzzle can be easily solved if one bears in mind the meaning of the word *democracy* in Tocqueville. Sometimes he used the term in its normal political sense of a representative system resting on broad suffrage. But more often than not he employed it is a synonym for egalitarian society, by which he meant not a society of equals but one where hierarchy was no longer the rule or the accepted principle of social structure.

In this democratic context Tocqueville saw individualism as a social pathology, a widespread self-centeredness, arising from an egalitarian society ridden by materialism, competition, and resentment. In his *Ancien Régime* he found individualism already in privileged society before the Revolution. For a whole chapter (bk. 2, ch. 8) he expatiated on how the French had become at once more alike and more aloof, fragmenting the nation into jealous small interest groups that cleared the ground for the "true individualism" of modern democratic society.

No such dislike of individualism was discernible in either Constant or Guizot. For them, individualism was a good thing, the heart of "modern freedom" in Constant's sense. Tocqueville by no means overlooked the value of personal independence, but his misgivings about the growth of individualism in democratic—that is, modern—society show that he kept his distance from the bourgeois high regard for negative freedom and its model of *homo oeconomicus*. A fine recent interpretation by Jean-Claude Lamberti[23] spots the originality of the Tocquevillian approach to the problem of individualism. Unlike reactionaries such as de Maistre and Bonald, who blamed the Revolution for unleashing individualism, Tocqueville pointed out a social source for it—the leveling of "conditions," or in his jargon, the democratic trend.

By the same token, Tocqueville felt a strong distrust for the middle classes (which had been sacred to Guizot), for they were the natural bearers of enhanced individualism. This opposed a tradition of thought extolling the civilizing effects of the rise of the bourgeoisie. Montesquieu, Tocqueville's own chief reference, thought of the commercial spirit as a begetter of order, peace, and moderation (the "taming of the passions" theme analyzed by Hirschman).[24] Constant in his youth in Edinburgh had fallen under the spell of Scottish stadialism and celebrated the contrast between the "spirit of conquest" and the "spirit of commerce."[25] To Tocqueville, however, democracy, not trade, sweetens manners—but at the price of individualist isolationism. He did not accept the Enlightenment belief in the civilizing force of commerce, but neither did he follow the conservative idealization (so prominent in Burke) of Church and chivalry in the Middle Ages as factors of refinement, bygone pillars of a genteel word defaced by the rise of vulgar commercialism.

Tocqueville made the antibourgeois mood into a potent cultural motif. All his life he cold-shouldered the liberist exaltation of *homo oeconomicus* professed by economists like Say and Bastiat. As Lamberti suggests, his taste for independence resembled much more the romantic heroism sung by his distant cousin, Chateaubriand, a *légitimiste* royalist turned liberal after 1830, than the bourgeois ethos of Guizot. Tocqueville's liberalism, like that of the Swiss economist Simonde de Sismondi (1773–1842), was of a political, not an economic nature.

At 36, Tocqueville, made glorious by the publication of *Democracy in America,* entered the Academy as "the new Montesquieu." As Raymond Aron saw, Tocqueville took over from *The Spirit of the Laws* a critical perspective on the interpretation of equality. In Montesquieu's monarchies, freedom was bound up with the distinctions between estates of the realm and the feudal feeling of honor. Montesquieu's despotisms, on the other hand, were systems dominated by equality within general enserfment. Tocqueville defined democracy by the drive toward equality, and he showed that equality does not make (necessarily) for liberty. Democracy breeds individualism and individualism means materialist aspirations and lack of civic virtues. To Lamberti, Tocqueville wrote what was to be the last flight of civic humanism.

What pre-Tocquevillian French liberalism feared most was despotism, the tyranny of the state. In this Constant differed very little from Locke, Montesquieu, and Jefferson. But Tocqueville discovered a new threat to liberty: the conformism of opinion. The "democratic instinct," using centralism as a lever, seemed about to level minds as well as ranks and conditions. The second part of *Democracy in America* spoke of "a new kind of despotism": the "tyranny of the majority." A sweet serfdom could endure, under the well-meaning tutelage of a paternalist state—but it would spell unfreedom nonetheless.

By stressing so much the dangers of equality, Tocqueville may seem rather close to his detested Guizot, the antidemocratic authoritarian liberal. As John Plamenatz observed, it was rather fallacious to claim that the feudal past had been more unequal but also freer than French society after the absolutist centralization. For if the feudal past was certainly less equal than modern society, it was by no means freer, unless one limits the assessment of freedom to the upper echelons of the social structure.[26] How far had Tocqueville gone, in his aristocratic nostalgia, from the loyalty to the Enlightenment vision displayed by the previous French liberals! In 1805, Constant wrote a whole essay on the perfectibility of mankind. Perfectibility, he stated, was nothing but the tendency toward equality.[27] These were precisely values Tocqueville didn't share or about which he was highly ambivalent.

On the other hand, Tocqueville was more sanguine than Guizot about the institutional power of liberty. He gladly envisaged antidotes against the centralist drift. Hence his hopeful prescription of local self-rule and voluntary association—the two things, together with the tonic effects of religion, that he praised as American warrants of freedom within social democracy. The "new liberal," in sum, was a pessimist but not a fatalist. He even trusted that the right polity could breed liberty. In America, he thought, free mores had made the political institutions free; in France, free institutions just might create liberal mores. This, too, was very Montesquieulike, for Montesquieu had famously asked how laws can help forming a nation's character (*Spirit of the Laws*, bk. 19, ch. 27). Social causality is a two-way street.

Tocqueville paid little attention to the emerging industrialism of his time. He did travel to Pittsburgh, but he ignored its steel plants (other French visitors at the time, like Michel Chevalier, were far more curious); he was appalled at Manchester's factory life, but he didn't think beyond moral revulsion. Even his more perceptive remarks on industrialization turned out to be beside his main point, the march toward more equality and the need to choose between liberty or benign despotism as forms of democratic society. Tocqueville saw that industrialism tends to strengthen the illiberal effects of administrative centralization by weakening the position of the worker. The more the division of labor advances, the more dependent it makes the servants of machinery. (We are not far from Marx's alienation thesis.) In the long run, however, the workers, by the sheer force of their numbers, will become increasingly assertive and restless and will press the state to quicken the pace of leveling. A tutelary Leviathan will be established, striking an agreement between a largely formal principle of popular sovereignty and the further progress of bureaucratic centralism. As one can see, the prophetic value of this scenario can only reinforce the democratic theory in Tocqueville's sense. Other variables, by contrast, were overlooked by him.[28]

From 1840 onward, Tocqueville's work moved away from democracy to focus increasingly on revolution.[29] One might say that his sophisticated sociological musings ended up sharing Guizot's obsession with revolutionary threats. This is rather ironic, since French liberalism had begun by discarding the reactionary demonization of the Revolution. One senses here the peculiarity of French classical liberalism: a constant reference to the Revolution, its origins, its endless sequel. Unlike English liberals between Locke and Mill, the French were not justifying a polity but were groping for one, in the checkered course of French politics from Waterloo to Sedan. The French conservatives were generally reactionaries who wanted to extirpate the work of the Revolution root and branch. The liberals, on the other hand, wished to finish the Revolution without finishing *with* it—that is, without jeopardizing its social gains. On this at least Constant, Guizot, and Tocqueville did agree; but it still left plenty of disagreement as to the methods of normalizing political liberty in the world of civil equality created by the Revolution (or, in Tocqueville's terms, ratified by it). Tocqueville was capable of listing some "liberal instincts" in the democratic evolution of modern society. But basically he left them in the shadow and mostly gave the impression that as a sincere friend of liberty he was just resigned to democracy as equality.

A final point is in order before we take our leave of the French classical liberals. Guizot's little affection for laissez-faire and Tocqueville's lukewarm attitude toward commercial society seem to support those who claim that early liberalism was *not* an ideology of the commercial and industrial bourgeoisie but the creature of a declining aristocracy or of learned strata more intent on reason and free debating than on interest, market, and progress. Lamberti's description of Tocqueville as a belated civic humanist tallies with such a revisionist interpretation, to which an Italian scholar, Ettore Cuomo, has devoted a whole book.[30] Neither of them quotes Pocock, but both their works seem to suggest Pocockian themes persisting well beyond their original Harrington-to-Jefferson span.

The Libertarian Saint: John Stuart Mill

The crowning texts of classical liberalism, those by John Stuart Mill (1806–73), evince a conspicuous influence of Tocqueville. Mill was a Francophile who cherished two aspects of French thought that he sadly missed in England—theory and progressive politics of a radical kind. Early in his life he had flirted with Saint-Simonian ideas or, better said, with the Saint-Simonian ethos. In his *Autobiography*, the genre's classic of the century, Mill wrote movingly of his mental crisis of 1826, when he underwent a nervous breakdown as he came to doubt the value of his desiccating, archintellectualist drill of an upbringing, earnestly conducted by his father James, a fervent Benthamite.

Mill's quest for feeling instead of pure analysis led him to discover Coleridge, Carlyle, and Saint-Simon. Coleridge, the founder of English romanticism, was as such the very opposite of Bentham. Carlyle, the future Sage of Chelsea, inveighed against Mammonism, the "cash nexus" (capitalism), and the "Mechanical Age" (industrialism). His fiery prose (in *Sartor Resartus, 1833,* and *Past and Present,* 1843) did not spare the utilitarianism of Bentham and James Mill; it satirized the "felicific calculus," the Benthamite's gauging of pleasure and pain, as an awful "grinding-mill." The pun was not lost on the young Mill, who was in full if belated oedipal rebellion. Saint-Simonianism offered him a very different kind of progressivism, with a mystique of altruism and sacrifice instead of the cool satisfaction aimed at by utilitarian ethics.[31]

Mill, having sown his romantic oats, marched into middle age as the author of two rationalist masterpieces, the *System of Logic* (1843) and the *Principles of Political Economy* (1848), which, in spite of their agnosticism, became textbooks in still-clerical Oxbridge. And he stood loyal to liberal individualism in his firm rejection of the authoritarian technocracy recommended by the greatest Saint-Simonian, Auguste Comte (1798–1857). By the early 1850s, however, he became engaged in practical issues, which he approached in a spirit of militant left liberalism. Mill's change of heart was due to his enthusiastic reaction to the 1848 revolutions—an upheaval that scared Comte to death but that Mill hoped would republicanize all Europe. He was also very much under the influence of his wife, Harriet Taylor, a devoted libertarian. To her memory is dedicated Mill's most famous essay, *On Liberty* (1859).

On Liberty owes to Tocqueville its abiding concern with the tyranny of opinion. Fearing the prospect of "Chinese" uniformity, Mill warned of the need for preserving "the antagonism of opinions." In his more political treatise, *Considerations on Representative Government* (1861), he advocated proportional representation as an electoral system with a view to ensuring respect for ideological diversity. Mill also shared with Tocqueville a regard for civic morals and a faith in the educational value of democratic participation. But here the main agreement between the two leading late-classical liberals stops. Their worldviews were far from identical. Mill endorsed both the Tocquevillian alarm before social rather than political despotisms and the Tocquevillian antidote, namely, participatory democracy; but he had none of the Frenchman's aristocratic nostalgia or religious penchant. The son of a self-made civil servant and himself a bureaucrat at the same department (the India Office), Mill had a very different background and outlook; and as an economist, he also stressed liberism, a liberal theme largely overlooked by the French political (as distinct from economic) theorists. Significantly Mill's defense in his *Principles* of laissez-faire as a general practice went unaltered through the seven editions of the work during his lifetime. Whatever socialist sympathies he may have felt in his mature years they never implied any shift towards dirigisme.

Representative Government is a curious departure from James Mill's brief for democracy, the *Essay on Government* of 1820. Mill junior kept universal suffrage, but neither equal voice nor the secret ballot. In order to give more weight to the educated—an elitist purpose—he resorted to a system of plural voting so that the better qualified could cast more more than one vote and get votes from more than one constituency. This attempt to balance participation and competence, democratic access and enlightened rule,[32] actually derived from a liberal goal that was at a far remove from James's. For James Mill prescribed democracy in order to minimize oppression, whereas John Mill prescribed it in order to maximize responsibility.[33] For the same reason, John Mill discarded secret ballots.

Still, the distance between John Mill's qualified democracy and his father's plea for universal suffrage tells us much about the evolution of the liberal temper. As John Burrow has pointed out, in Mill's cautious arrangements for representative self-rule protected against majoritarian tyranny little is left of the optimistic utilitarian gamble on the ultimate rationality of mankind.[34] Officially he might talk as a loyal heir to the progressivism of the Enlightenment and his utilitarian masters, but at heart, Mill, like Tocqueville, was a pessimist liberal. Reviewing the second volume of *Democracy in America* in the *Edinburgh Review* (1840), Mill objected that Tocqueville had overstated the impact of equality and underrated the dynamism of commerce. After all, quipped Mill, French Canada was as egalitarian a society as the United States, yet it lacked that mobile entrepreneurship, that impatient thirst for progress, that was also so conspicuous in inegalitarian Britain. On the face of it, this seems a hearty return to the Enlightenment paean to progress. But Mill no longer saw commercial society as an age of improvement. In his essay "Civilization" (1836), he stated that its effect was an increase in everyone's dependence on society and a general "relaxation of individual energy." Needless to say, such an entropic view of history was in stark opposition to early utilitarianism. Historical angst was not Bentham's forte.

Mill's underlying pessimism did not prevent him from asserting progressive claims. He proposed agrarian reform as a solution to the Irish question and producers' cooperatives as a way to democratize property. He wrote a passionate feminist tract, *The Subjection of Women* (1869). Since the day in his adolescence when he was arrested for distributing birth-control propaganda, his reforming zeal never abated; and in the 1860s he was the progressive MP at Westminster. So the resulting picture differs considerably from the Tocquevillian syndrome, since for all his elitism Mill's political complexion was far more advanced than Tocqueville's. That is why so many still think of him, as it would never be possible to think of Tocqueville, as an intellectual bridge between classical liberalism and liberal socialism.

On Liberty was read as a manifesto for individualism. It forbade state interference in regard to "self-regarding" conduct, and it exalted the freedom of "pursuing our own good in our own way." He saw freedom as essential to self-development, a theme he borrowed from Humboldt. Unimpeded individuality and a comprehensive sphere of privacy are necessary for the cultivation of personality. In addition, he showed that freedom is vastly instrumental in fostering progress. His aim as a utilitarian liberal, that is to say, as someone not arguing from any "natural right" position, was to give freedom a central place in utility, demonstrating its key role in happiness as well as in character building.[35] After Mill dropped the passive concept of the mind held by Bentham and his father, his own idea of happiness became inseparable from activity, and from the activity of choice in particular.[36]

This German trait of autotelic liberalism was combined with a concern for autonomy (political liberty) and with a taste for both experience and experiment. Liberty was inter alia an openness to experience in that it meant a disposition to be critical, to be free from prejudice and dogma. Conservatism was to Mill above all a bad epistemology, based on intuition instead of induction, on received wisdom and unexamined belief instead of an inquiring cast of mind. Mill prescribed at once moral experimentation and strength of character, thereby catering to two sides of the Victorian soul, the ascetic and the aestheticist, or in the terms of Heinrich Heine and Matthew Arnold, the Hebraic and the Hellenic.

Chiming with the liberism of the *Principles* and the inductivism of the *Logic, On Liberty* quickly became a libertarian bible. Mill had woven various liberal strands of thought together. Political liberty, negative freedom, self-development; freedom as entitlement, freedom of opinion, freedom as self-rule, freedom as privacy and independence. The old Protestant plea for conscience, in a secularized form, was there; and so was the Enlightenment approach to liberty as the instrument of progress. Indeed, *On Liberty* was admirably complemented by the work on *Representative Government*, since the former was a protest against the tyranny of opinion and the latter a recipe against the tyranny of the majority.

Scholars, however, hotly dispute the authenticity of Mill's message. Gertrude Himmelfarb in the United States and Maurice Cowling in England have portrayed Mill as a blinkered radical, mesmerized by the insufferable bluestocking Harriet Taylor into repudiating his own youthful repudiation of utilitarian shallowness.[37] F.A. Hayek and more recently John Gray chided Mill for unrealistically severing individuality from the social contexts and cultural traditions. Others, sticking to a closer reading of the great 1859 essay, reject this accusation. Mill may have entertained starry-eyed elitist ideals, but in *On Liberty* he balanced his fears of a tyranny of majoritarian opinion with an explicit insistence on the need for *general* self-development and for avoiding inculcation of every kind.[38]

In the 1860s, Mill once more dissociated himself from Comte's position on account of the latter's "liberticide" tendencies. Thus Comte's scientism—a nineteenth-century dream of enlightened despotism—served as foil to Mill's own intentions. The positivist church would have meant paternalism, and paternalism was precisely what Mill was keen to reject, in the name of individual liberty. Macaulay's criticism—that he exaggerated in his picture of conformism in an age of strong characters and so many eccentrics—is much more to the point.

The Oxford scholar Larry Siedentop has drawn an instructive distinction between the French and English branches of classical liberalism epitomized by Tocqueville and Mill. The English were chiefly philosophers of mind, like the two Mills; and the very openness to peaceful evolution of British society kept their liberalism poorer in historical and sociological content. By contrast the French school was made up of historians and jurists, and its liberals were wont to treat political institutions as a function of social conditions. Also, they paid special attention to historical change and generally adopted a comparatist perspective.[39]

Siedentop's antithesis opposes a psychological to a historico-sociological liberalism, holding water despite Mill's keen interest in French history (Michelet) or political sociology (Tocqueville). But if we turn to the internal history of English liberalism, there is no gainsaying that Mill's liberal program, for all its undeniable reticence before democracy, largely surpassed in social spirit and moral scale the whig formula, for which he felt but the utmost contempt. In this as in many other things Mill remained faithful to the progressive thrust of the Benthamite circle. Much respected by Gladstone, whose biographer, John Morley, was Mill's disciple, John Stuart Mill symbolized the final valediction of liberalism to its long patrician past.

Toward Social Liberalism: Mazzini and Herzen

It is fitting to round up our overview of classical liberalism by glancing at other parts of Europe. By midcentury, two figures, both émigrés in London, stood out as great and influential paladins of liberty. One was the Italian Giuseppe Mazzini (1805–72), an almost exact contemporary of Mill. The other was the Russian Alexander Herzen (1812–70).

Mazzini contributed two things to the liberal catechism: nationalism and youth. In his student years he joined the Carbonari sect, which was fighting a secret war to unify Italy and liberate it from Austria. But in 1831 he founded Young Italy, a quickly spreading organization campaigning for a unitary republican state in the whole peninsula. By the end of the decade, he had to exile himself and in London wrote the essays later collected as *The Duties of Man*

(1860). His moral tone was clear, and the book was addressed to the workers, despite Mazzini's stress on generation rather than class struggle.

Because in his eyes liberalism meant no more than a vulgar materialist liberism, Mazzini considered himself an opponent of the liberal school. His socioeconomic outlook derived from Sismondi and the communitarian socialists in industry, led by Robert Owen (1771–1857). And his democratism was tinged with social Christianity à la Charles Kingsley (1819–75) and Lamennais (1782–1854). In his *History of European Liberalism,* de Ruggiero reproached him for espousing a mystical antiindividualism wholly unfit for the backward Italy of the time.[40] But social Christian that he was, Mazzini was adamant in his rejection of socialism, which he thought illiberal as well as amoral because materialistic.

The revolution of 1848–49—"the People's Spring"—made Mazzini a triumvir in a short-lived Roman republic. But unification was eventually to be controlled by the liberal-conservative Count Camillo Cavour (1810–61) on behalf of the Piedmontese kingdom, brushing aside the generous republicanism of Mazzini and Garibaldi (1807–82). In Mazzini's highly idealistic liberalism, the national cause of the Risorgimento was perfectly compatible with a universalistic humanitarianism and a European federation. His prestige was immense, and in the Victorian heyday he was a true conscience of liberal republicanism. Gandhi saw in him, together with Tolstoy, one of his Western inspirations.

After the failure of the 1848 revolution came Herzen's *Letter of a Russian to Mazzini* (1849). Leaving Russia for exile two years before, Herzen, who had been under the spell of Hegelianism in his country, had decreed as a radical-left Hegelian that the bourgeoisie had "no great past and no future." It was a traditionless class, incapable of substituting political economy for aristocratic honor. When socialism was miserably defeated in 1848, he saw bourgeois Europe as a new decadent Rome, the socialists as the persecuted early Christians, and the Slavs as the new barbarians. Despairing of his erstwhile historicism, he wrote in *From the Other Shore* that history has no goal—and so much the better for individual freedom, which could say good riddance to every utopia demanding huge sacrifices for the sake of the future.

Having lost all hope of a proper revolution in Europe, Herzen did not turn apolitical or reformist. He just turned slavophile (before his exile he had been a leading westerner). Writing to Michelet,

Mazzini, Proudhon, and the German socialist Georg Herwegh (until he found out that Herwegh and the beautiful Mrs. Herzen were too fond of each other), Herzen circulated his conception, and inception, of a Russian socialism.[41] Like previous slavophiles, Herzen welcomed the fact that the Russian "barbarians" had not been infected by Roman law and property rights. Russia, he promised, would never be either Protestant or bourgeois. At the same time, he departed from slavophile orthodoxy by finding the village commune too dull, dumb, and conservative an institution; and he even dared to celebrate the wild modernization of Peter the Great, the crowned Jacobin.

By the 1860s, Herzen showed a remarkable intelligence of western social evolution. In a polemical series of articles addressed to the novelist Turgenev, *Ends and Beginnings,* he considered the age of the bourgeoisie, as had Mill and Tocqueville, to be the realm of mediocrity. But he stressed that the rise of the middle classes had stabilized capitalism and promoted the social and material advancement of the masses; and he went so far as to predict the workers' embourgeoisement in an era of widespread prosperity. He preached bloodless reforms to the czar. Yet in the Russian political spectrum of the time, he was definitely on the far left. When the first revolutionary organization, Land and Freedom, was founded in 1861, it borrowed its title from Herzen's widely read journal, *The Bell.*

Herzen left a political testament in the *Letters to an Old Comrade* (1869). Addressed to Bakunin, they were actually written in self-criticism, mainly of his own despondent attitudes after 1848. Reinstating a fair amount of historicism, Herzen now looked at state and property as something historically functional, as kinds of stepping-stones for human development. He scolded the revolutionary vanguards for their "petrograndist" attempt to impose their will on the masses. He roundly condemned communism for its "galley slave" idea of equality, and he gave his blessing—to Bakunin's fury—to the moderation of the First International. Herzen, being neither a constitutionalist nor conversant with economics, was never a liberal in the full western sense, but this did not prevent him from powerfully contributing to the libertarian vision in the liberal creed.

Our four late-classical liberals, for all their differences, did share some common ground. The conservative liberal Tocqueville taught the elitist Mill the civic value of self-rule and the dangers of majority power. Mazzini liked Mill enough to invite him (in vain) to his émigré home at Blackheath. And Herzen thought Mazzini worthy of receiving one of his major assessments of the post-1848 situation. 1848 itself found all four on the republican side, albeit with different hopes and attitudes. This was a long way from the timid constitutional royalism and the oligarchic census of Royer-Collard and Guizot—though not so far from the politics of the early utilitarians.

The Discourses of Classical Liberalism

Well after the acme of late-classical liberalism—the flourish of Tocqueville, Mill, Mazzini, and Herzen in the middle decades of the nineteenth century—William Butler Yeats asked in a poem called "The Sage,"

> What is Whiggery?
> A levelling, rancorous, rational sort of mind
> That never looked out of the eye of a saint
> Or out of a drunkard's eye.[42]

Yeats, of course, was no liberal, whig or otherwise; and maybe that was why he criticized as "whiggery" something that was actually more like Benthamism, in its opponents' view. As for mid-Victorian classical liberalism, it certainly had at least two saints—Mazzini and Mill. And I would like to propose our lyrical hedonist, Herzen, as a good candidate for the place of liberalism's "drunkard." One thing, however, none of them ever was—a whig. Which again only shows how long had been the road trodden by liberalism, even at that stage.

In a more serious vein, we might as well conclude by stressing the conceptual diversity of classical liberalism. Early classical liberalism already knew at least three kinds of theoretical discourse: natural rights theory, civic republicanism, and stadial history, as in the political economy and social theory of the Scottish Enlightenment. The evolution of liberal doctrine evinced a progressive detachment from the civic ideology, until in early American republicanism, Lockean jusnaturalism plus stadial views (the theme of the commercial, or civilized, society) got the upper hand. Then by 1800, the Benthamites placed themselves at a further distance from the civic discourse and liberalism again spoke with the voice of utility, not with the voice of rights or civic virtue.

The early French liberals, resuming the stadial perspective, created yet a new mode, the political theory of commercial society, most typically in Constant. Nearly all French classical liberals wrote in a historical idiom, resting their claims on a comparatist, Montes-quieuan grasp of the underlying causes of macropolitical change. Tocqueville's analyses were simply the subtlest form of this historico-sociological mode of political discourse. Mill knew and admired this alliance of liberalism and theoretical history, but in his own work he reverted to the utilitarian approach.

By 1870 the discourses of liberalism added up to five, although in more than one case they were combined: natural rights, civic republi-canism, political economy, utilitarian, and comparatist history. The first had medieval roots and a seventeenth-century jusnaturalist take-off. The civic mode originated in Renaissance humanism. And the three remaining discourses stemmed from the Enlightenment, with Montesquieu, Hume, and Smith as their main theoretical sources. In broad outline, such was the conceptual profile of classical liberalism.

But pointing out the enrichment of the discourse of political theory from protoliberalism to late-classical liberalism is not enough. Underlying the early classical liberals' way of addressing the nature of the polity and the meaning of liberty in the nineteenth century was a big divide from the days of Locke, Montesquieu, and Smith. This divide was caused by the impact of the Atlantic revolutions of the late eighteenth century on political theory. The American and French revolutions introduced a new principle of legitimacy, based on na-tional sovereignty instead of dynastic rights, into liberal theory.

And here it was Rousseau, far more than any of the earlier liber-als or protoliberals, who made the decisive contribution. By giving the contractarian discourse of rights a democratic twist, Rousseau was the main ancestor of the notion that the nation, and not the king, was the ultimate seat of political authority. Now the question was how to square the old liberal concern with limiting power with the new, postrevolutionary principle of legitimacy. Such was the task that exercised the minds of Constant and Guizot, Tocqueville and Mill, and that made them "classical liberals" in a modern sense.

4

Conservative Liberalisms

Liberal Conservatism and Conservative Liberalism

The legacy of classical liberalism was a balance of democratism and libertarianism. The earlier conquests of protoliberalism, such as respect for rights and constitutional rule, were preserved. But from Madison and Bentham to Constant, Tocqueville, and Mill, clear advances were made in the social scope and moral range of the liberal creed. While the robust historical optimism of the Enlightenment was seriously qualified between the era of the federalists and utilitarians and the era of the great Victorian liberals, liberism was generally upheld and classical liberals were basically true to the democratic promise and the libertarian potential of the liberal idea. Classical liberalism conducted its institutional inventiveness, conceptual imagination, and analytic bite in a secular frame of mind. Even when its theorists, like Constant and Tocqueville, attached great importance to religion, their mode of theorizing was no longer dictated by theological concerns. In this at least, the lay spirit of the Enlightenment imposed itself most consistently.

Classical liberalism did not hog the whole stage of liberal thought. By the mid-nineteenth century several liberal currents emerged that differed considerably from the positions and modes of discourse of classical liberals, represented by Tocqueville and Mill. The new currents were also quite unlike the later developments known as "new liberalisms" and characterized by their "social" content. Such currents, some of which were contemporary with the last stage of classical liberalism, can be gathered under a single reasonable label: *conservative liberalism.*

When the Duke of Newcastle asked him to drop the old label *whig,* Lord Russell, the Reform prime minister, retorted that *whig* has the advantage of saying in one syllable what *conservative liberal* says in seven.[1] This retort neatly encapsulates the distance between establishment whiggism and classical liberalism in its final Victorian form. The democratic and republican spirit of classical liberalism had taken liberalism away from whig conservatism, socially as well as politically. But what was the difference, if any, between conservative liberalism and liberal *conservatism?*

Liberal conservatism was a very English product, and as such it was quite unlike the compact, reactionary conservatism of the continent. In the first half of the nineteenth century, most continental conservatives were still resisting representative, responsible government and religious freedom, whereas British conservatives were trying to preserve the antiabsolutist settlement of 1688. British conservatism, notes a distinguished modern interpreter, Anthony Quinton, comprehends at least three doctrines. The first is *traditionalism,* the belief that political wisdom is somehow of a historical and collective nature and resides in institutions that have passed the test of time. The second is *organicism,* the idea that society is a whole, not a mere sum of its parts or members, and as such has a value definitely far superior to the individual. The third is *political skepticism,* in the sense of a mistrust of thought and theory as applied to public life, especially with wide-ranging innovative purposes.[2]

As Lord Quinton and many predecessors have stressed, in the British conservative tradition, traditionalism and organicism are both flexible positions. Traditions do not bar adaptive change, and organicism does not rule out the piecemeal modification of institutions and procedures. Most continental conservatives, by contrast, issuing from a rabid revulsion against the French Revolution and its contagion, tended to petrify tradition into a timeless edifice and to see institutions as unalterable. In their attempt to force European society back into the ancien régime after a quarter of a century of political and social change (1789–1815), they were cast into a highly doctrinaire and even visionary attitude, scarcely compatible with the prudent skepticism of establishment conservatives.

Continental reactionaries like Joseph de Maistre (1753–1821),

Louis de Bonald (1754–1840), Friedrich Gentz (1764–1832), and Adam Muller (1779–1829) were great admirers of Edmund Burke (1729–97). Burke was the first outstanding critic of the Revolution in his widely read *Reflections on the Revolution in France* (1790), and he is generally considered the father of English conservatism. Ironically, though, by preaching an uncompromising restoration of hierarchy and autocracy, the French Restoration thinkers and their German counterparts went against the grain of Burke's own principle of legitimacy: *prescription,* authority hallowed by continuity.

The essence of Burke's attack on the Revolution was that the French revolutionaries had wished to erase the past instead of re-vigorate old rights against royal absolutism. Burke's respect for tradition was not always reactionary. Using the same argument in favor of old rights, he had defended the American insurgents 15 years before. Moreover, just as his conservatism was politically liberal, so was it economically modern: no one less than Adam Smith praised him for his perfect understanding of liberal economics. Burke was an establishment whig of the 1770s who had turned tory because in the 1790s the "new whigs," as he dubbed them, were people like Fox, admirers of the Revolution.

It is typical of the conservative bent of Burke's mind that he substituted a historicist emphasis on English tradition for the Scottish Enlightenment's cosmopolitan emphasis on the stages of civilization.[3] He also replaced the Enlightenment whigs' scorn for superstition with a reverence for religion. Again, instead of linking refinement with the rise of commerce, as did the *philosophes,* Burke was one of the creators of the romantic revaluation of medieval faith and chivalry as factors of civilization—a theme soon to be given much glamour in the magic prose of France's leading liberal conservative, Viscount François-René de Chateaubriand (1768–1848).

Burke's penchant for religious orthodoxy and organic society made him a true conservative, since it meant the very opposite of two persistent traits in mainstream liberalism, moral latitudinarianism and individualism. Moreover Burke's nostalgic historical outlook was not balanced by an acceptance of democracy. On the contrary, by placing a wedge between representation and delegation, Burke managed to keep his parliamentary model poles apart from radical and utilitarian demands for democratization of power. This maintained his liberal conservatism at a far remove from classical liberalism, politically as well as conceptually.

Burke rekindled the flame of the "ancient constitution." Nevertheless, he held a rather flexible, adaptive concept of tradition, allowing for *change within continuity.* Probably his most famous epigram still is, "A state without the means of some change is without the means of its conservation," an oft-quoted jewel from the *Reflections.* His defense of the ancient constitution was far more sophisticated than the arguments of those who simply asserted an unchanging set of norms that had presumably been restored in 1688.

The Burkean perspective of change in continuity was used by a whig historian, Henry Hallam (1777–1859), in his influential 1827 *Constitutional History of England,* which covered the period from the Tudor accession to the death of George II in 1760. Hallam deployed the ancient constitution thesis against Hume's popular *History of England* (1754–62). The thought of the paramount whig political historian, Thomas Macaulay (1800–59), also took shape against this Burkean background. By 1830, Macaulay brilliantly saw the need to oppose tory resistance to electoral reform by dealing creatively with the ancient constitution myth. By then, the tories were presenting the Glorious Revolution (originally an antitory movement) as an arrangement for all times. Macaulay undertook to show that it was a solution for *its* time and as such just a stage in a series of wise political adjustments to historical change. Thus, in his hands the Burkean theme of change-in-continuity was in turn subtly changed into the idea of a continuity of change. Against the tory appeal to tradition in order to resist reform, Macaulay asserted *a tradition of reform.* In this perspective, the wisdom of 1688 provided a precedent for the Reform Bill of 1832.

From then on, liberal conservatives often spoke the language of Burke. The jurist Sir Henry Maine (1822–88), together with Catholic historian Lord Acton (1834–1902), are cases in point. Maine's self-appointed task was to demolish Rousseaunian ideas about the state of nature, parading as grounds for a social contract vindicating universal equality. Maine was a conservative liberal, not a conservative, and he shared Macaulay's belief in progress. This showed in his celebrated concept of an evolution "from status to contract," first expounded in his 1861 book, *Ancient Law.* Mankind, wrote Maine, had evolved from a social state in which all relations were ruled by status in a kinship structure to a stage in which modern individualism thrives on personal property. In *Popular Government* (1885), Maine deplored the prospect of a socialist setback in this process of growing individualization. Thus in Maine and others, Burkean arguments serve the un-Burkean end of individualism, wrongly seen as threatened by democracy.

Lord Acton's worries were not very different. A nobleman with a European genealogy, John Dalberg, Baron Acton, was educated as a Catholic under the liberal historian Ignaz von Dollinger and eventually became Regius Professor of History in Cambridge. A Catholic humanist, he fought papal absolutism (which was declared "infallible" by the Holy See in 1870) and condemned "modern confessionalism," together with nationalism, as an illiberal trend. But as a Burkean, he combined religion, liberty, and tradition. His anti-nationalism led him to uphold federalism; he looked wistfully at the medieval Church as a bulwark of liberty in the feudal world. But while for other liberal historians federalism was the very warrant of a *polis*-like political participation, Actonian federalism was ideally put to a very different purpose; for it was to be a check on democracy through a whiggish multiplication of power centers.[4]

Evolutionist Conservative Liberals: Bagehot and Spencer

Not all misgivings about democracy were Burkean. The 1860s and 1870s witnessed another kind of conservative liberalism as well: the utilitarian kind. Such was the position of Walter Bagehot (1826–77), a banker, economist, journalist, and political theorist who edited the *Economist* from 1861 until his death. Bagehot came from a provincial nonconformist banking family and was educated at the Benthamite University College in London. In his *The English Constitution* (1867), he voiced fears that with the coming extension of the franchise (which actually materialized in 1867 and 1884), both parties, conservative and liberal, would bid for the support of workers—something Bagehot envisaged as a definite "danger" to liberty. Like Maine, Bagehot pitted social evolution against democratic progress. He divided his loyalty between innovation and stability, using social Darwinism to brake democracy. Stability, he bluntly said, rested upon invaluable stupidity, on a "cake of custom" formed by complying social habits due to the uncanny prestige of otherwise useless institutions like the monarchy or the Lords (the "dignified" as opposed to the "efficient" parts of the constitution). Why indeed, asked he, should "a retired widow and an unemployed youth" (namely, Queen Victoria and the Prince of Wales) attract so much attention? They did so because England "could not be governed" without the bemusing effect of the crown. Likewise, the ruling classes could linger on the top by shrewd electioneering, manipulating the dignified aspects of the polity in order to extract deference to the powers that be. In *Physics and Politics* (1872) Bagehot gave this cynical Machiavellianism a Darwinist twist: he painted social and national success as instances of the "survival of the fittest" and countenanced the social function of force beside institutional fraud.

This kind of plain-speaking utilitarian conservative liberalism turned rather nasty in the work of Judge James Fitzjames Stephen (1829–94), elder brother of Leslie Stephen and Virginia Woolf's uncle. A great codifier of criminal law, Stephen received a Millian education in Cambridge, imbibing Mill's *Logic* and *Principles of Political Economy*. But he became impatient with Mill's later moralism and disliked Victorian sentimentality, deploring that man was becoming ever "more sensitive and less ambitious." Some of his obiter dicta are good maxims of rugged individualism, like "It is not love that one wants from the great mass of mankind, but respect and justice." But alas, he leaned too heavily to the other side. His anti-Millian essay *Liberty, Equality, Fraternity* (1873) mocked all three by claiming that force, not freedom, rules over social life: men must be coerced into decency by legal retribution of the sternest sort. Stephen criticized Mill for holding too favorable a view of human nature. But Stephen's beastly alternative picture was less a deepening than a pathology of liberalism. After some passionate campaigning for birching at schools and, of course, capital punishment, Judge Stephen (who paradoxically was rather lenient on the bench) ended his days in a mental hospital—a fitting comment on the moral imbalance that was changing utilitarianism from a liberating to a punitive cast of mind.[5]

By far the most influential conservative-liberal position toward the end of the century was articulated by the father of evolutionism as a general ideology, Herbert Spencer (1820–1903). Spencer was born in industrializing Derby into a Wesleyan home, then trained as an engineer. He became a contributor to the *Economist*. All his life he clung tenaciously to a minimalist idea of the state and a maximalist form of liberism. He was also an extreme individualist and a true heir to the Benthamite contempt for aristocratic privilege and spiritual hierarchy. Yet there were at least two stages in Spencer's way of justifying his individualism, his anti-statism, and his liberism.

The young Spencer's *Social Statics* (1850) displays a natural rights theory derived from William Godwin (1756–1836), author of

Political Justice (1793). Godwin is generally considered the father of English anarchism and, as Mary Shelley's father, the grandfather of Frankenstein; his point of departure was the protoanarchism of Thomas Paine, for whom society was good but government an evil. This natural rights doctrine was dismissed by Bentham ("nonsense on stilts"), but Spencer leveled three objections to utilitarianism.

First, Spencer believed that the "felicific calculus," the gauging of the greatest happiness of the greatest number, was an impossible task. Second, he starkly refused Benthamite reformism, since it meant a set of state-made (legal and governmental) change. Third, he asserted the preexistence of rights instead of insisting, as did Bentham, that rights are created by law. Using these assumptions, the young Spencer derived from a "law of equal freedom" private property and laissez-faire, universal suffrage, and a "right to ignore the state"—in fact, an individualist right of withdrawal, all the more reasonable since, as he put it, "as civilization advances, governments decay."

In Spencer's eyes, government has as its sole office the defense of citizens against aggressors, both foreign and domestic. But as he surveyed liberal legislation after 1860, the mature Spencer found that the state had in no way confined itself to this legitimate function. By sponsoring the promotion of well-being through industrial legislation and many other philanthropic measures, liberals had lost sight of liberalism's traditional stand against state coercion. The exposure of this liberal betrayal forms the core of *The Man versus the State*, Spencer's best-seller of 1884.

In Spencer's view, the growth of welfare legislation—"over-legislation," as he called it in an essay of the late 1860s—could only lead to despotism. "Though we no longer presume to coerce men for their *spiritual* good," wrote he, "we still think ourselves called upon to coerce them for their *material* good."[6] Annoyed by the buying of council houses and state ownership of railways, Spencer loudly deplored the prospect of "state usurpation" of all industries, which threatened in his opinion "to suspend the process of adaptation" and its outcome, natural selection. Moreover, the growth of the state brought bureaucracy, and bureaucracy was to him something intrinsically corrupt. On the other hand, welfare statism was also immoral. The modern faith in government was but "a subtle form of fetishism."

On reason's side, by contrast, one found evolution, "the beneficent though severe discipline" to which all life was subject and that operates through the harsh method of the survival of the fittest. As has been often noticed, Spencer's social theory gave quite a twist to Darwinism for it stated less that evolutionary conflict obtains in society as well as in nature than that it *ought* to operate for civilization to advance. In a history of liberal ideas, however, the point is that as Spencer fully embraced evolutionism, he dropped his former equalitarian concern for general freedom and universal suffrage. Now he became a stern critic of majoritarian rule; he called belief in parliamentary majorities the greatest political superstition of the age; and he stated that in the future the function of true liberalism would be to put "a limit on the power of Parliament."

Thus, as social Darwinism completely prevailed over his erstwhile rights theory, Spencer reached a kind of social utilitarianism. But this social utilitarianism procured him precisely the opposite of the Benthamite variety: a distrust of representative democracy. At the end of the century, wherever the widespread influence of Spencer was felt, liberism and liberalism were seen as being at loggerheads with democracy. From the great tycoons like John D. Rockefeller and Andrew Carnegie to liberal intellectuals in Europe and the Americas, the concept of evolution, with the survival of the fittest, was endlessly quoted. Many others, from Victorian poets to Russian populists, nonetheless demurred. One of the fathers of American sociology, Yale's William Graham Sumner (1840–1910), famously declared that for all its harshness, the law of the survival of the fittest was not the work of man and therefore could not be abrogated by man.

Nation-Building Liberalism: Sarmiento and Alberdi

Conservative liberalism—the avoidance of democracy—was also the spirit of many Latin American liberals of the age. But it could also nearly turn into liberal conservatism. This option was most conspicuous in the contrast between two Argentinians, Domingos Sarmiento (1811–88) and Juan Bautista Alberdi (1810–84). Both were liberals in the 1840s, in that they opposed the long dictatorship of the caudillo Juan Manuel de Rosas, who was toppled in 1852.

Sarmiento's great 1845 book, *Facundo: Civilization or Barbarism,* equated the Catholic autocracy of Rosas with ruralism and liberty with urban civilization. *Facundo* presented the Argentinian predicament as a stadial drama, with the violence of agrarian barbarism encroaching upon an age of city progress and refinement. As an exile in Chile, though, Sarmiento was far from supporting the local liberals: in his newspaper, *El Progreso,* he praised the enlightened authoritarianism of the Santiago regime, founded by Diego Portales, and stressed the need for strong, stable government. Neglecting the traditional liberal concern with checks and balances, Sarmiento admired the majoritarian fusion of executive and legislature in Andrew Jackson's administration. A trip to Europe and the failure of 1848 convinced him that democracy was not viable in largely illiterate countries.

But disillusionment with Europe did more than that. After 1848, like Herzen, Sarmiento changed his political model. Discovering urban squalor and rural wealth in industrializing Europe, he toned down his city-country dichotomy and embarked on a Tocquevillian discovery of North America. Unlike Tocqueville, however, Sarmiento found the United States a democracy (in the social sense) but not a republic—a vigorous civilization based on the market and the school.[7] Sarmiento became great friends with the New England educationist Horace Mann (1796–1859). The only way to overcome barbarism, he thought, was to build equality, for equality was not as much the fruit as the condition of progress. His sociopolitical recipe became the homestead frontier society rather than the network of historical towns. Widely distributed landowning, ubiquitous schools, and urban-rural communities ought to provide the backbone of liberty and civilization.

Tocqueville-wise, Sarmiento wished to inject civic virtue into the modern republic. That is why he contemplated giving the franchise to immigrants—the natural agents, in his eyes, of progress in civilization in the Argentinian Pampas. Later in the century, after his own victorious but bitter presidential tenure (1868–1874), he realized that the creole elites had retained an oligarchic hegemony and that foreign labor hadn't acquired any citizenship. He then accepted the principle of a patrician system led by prominent *criollos* and owner immigrants, until the time when central education, his pet civilizing prop, broadened the social basis of the republic. He never foresaw that when prosperity and literacy reached the immigrants' children, as it vastly did early in the next century, they would enter politics in a social scenery strikingly different from the homestead democracy Sarmiento liked so much in the United States. By then, anyway, Sarmiento's ultimate concern seemed to have shifted from civic virtue to the maintenance of order. The self-made fan of Benjamin Franklin had become an admirer of Paine's conservative denigration of the French Revolution. The dreamer of democracy ended up a true conservative liberal, putting authority as high as civic liberty, as close to Bagehot as to Tocqueville.

The other founding father of Argentinian liberalism, Alberdi, was never under democratic delusions. He criticized Sarmiento's education preaching as just a new form of colonial clerisy, the old ecclesiastic bid for herding people into moral guidance from above. He construed rural barbarism as the resentment of old elites displaced by the decline of the colonial economy and resorting in desperation to oligarchic militarism. Above all, he chastized Sarmiento's bookish worship of literacy as a national solution. Sarmiento, quipped Alberdi, wanted to get rid of the consequences of poverty before ending poverty itself. Not schooling, said Alberdi, but objective education in the arts of progress, the daily practice of civilized life, would rescue the Argentine from backwardness and disorder.

Like Sarmiento, Alberdi was impressed by the American achievement. But instead of following Tocqueville, he paid more attention to Michel Chevalier (1806–79), the liberist Saint-Simonian who guessed and gauged the industrial future of the United States. Alberdi had a strong distaste for liberal rhetoric. He derided Latin American revolutions for their "calligraphism," their copycat attitude toward European ideas and principles unapplicable to South America, a society where Independence had misbegotten a clumsy match between the century's progress and a backward Hispanic heritage.[8]

As Natalio Botana has perceptively shown, Alberdi was playing Burke to the immigration tune. According to him, the only way to stop calligraphism and eradicate both poverty and violence was the *transplantation* of right European cultures into Argentina. "To rule is to people," he wrote in his blueprint for the post-Rosas constitution of 1853, the *Bases and Starting Points for the Political Organization of the Argentinian Republic.* Given a proper social and moral environment—a very Montesquieuan idea—the republic would prosper. Unlike Sarmiento's plea for civic virtue, Alberdi's concern was not with a legitimacy of content but with a legitimacy of environment: graft into Argentina the proper social context, and progress will come.[9]

What about liberty? There are two kinds of freedom, said Alberdi, one external and the other internal. External freedom is national independence. Internal freedom consists of personal independence and the right to choose one's rulers. The big problem of postcolonial South American politics lay in its inability to see that the method good for conquering and maintaining external freedom is inept when it comes to the creation of internal freedom. This method, employed by the liberators, was the sword. Their spiritual heirs, the caudillos, acted as armed liberators after independence was won—and the result was unfreedom inside their borders. Alberdi recommended an alternative method, capitalist production: "Only rich countries are free, and only countries where work is free are rich."[10] A good reader of Montesquieu and Constant, Alberdi preferred commerce to conquest.

His liberalism was chiefly a rejection of the patrimonial state. The King of Spain had owned all the land in North America, even before its discovery, but the soil was *res nullius*, nobody's land, available to whoever occupied it and worked on it. Alberdi impugned this "political," statist-patrimonialist notion of property, in which to be rich was to hold a *grant* from the crown or its successors. He wanted to replace it—in social mentality as well as in law—by a Lockean conception of property as a natural right, stemming from individual industry rather than from court favor.

Alberdi's critique of patrimonialism, along with his "two freedoms" concept, figured in a "lecture" given by a mythical character, Day Light, in his 1871 novel *Peregrinación de Luz del Día en América*, subtitled "Travels and Adventures of Truth in the New World"—actually a sharp satire on Sarmiento's presidency. As should be expected from such a "Lockean" stance, Alberdi set great store by civil society. Indeed, Botana is right in stating that the first rule of Alberdian legitimacy is that civil society is more important than the state—something hard for civic-minded Sarmiento to swallow. Alberdi wanted to people Argentina with disfranchised settlers. Civil freedom should be wide open, he thought, but political liberty highly restricted. To a large extent Alberdi was less the legislator of 1853 than the mentor of fin de siècle undemocratic progress in the Pampas.

At the center of Alberdi's feud with Sarmiento was the difference in their sociopolitical models after midcentury. As we saw, after 1848 Sarmiento embraced an American model. Alberdi, by contrast, was under the spell of the French Second Empire and its illiberal progressivism. He accepted—even wanted—authoritarian politics, provided it brought about unimpeded economic activism. Forced to choose between liberty and progress, says Mariano Grondona, Alberdi would opt for progress, for he equated the former with the latter.[11] This is the classical script of liberal conservatism, or perhaps one should say, of liberist conservatism, trying to withstand the democratic tide.

All in all, Alberdi emerged as a kind of Burkean Saint-Simonian: a constitutional elitist, keenly aware of the roots of authority, yet deeply enamored of economic progress in the age of industrialism. For like Macaulay and Maine, Alberdi was no true conservative: there was in his heart no love for the past, no organicist romance, no reverence for established religion. A political authoritarian and a social conservative, Alberdi was utterly free from cultural conservatism. But by preaching centralism, Alberdi was giving hostages to the future. For when the immigrant masses became literate (in a belated triumph for Sarmiento's pedagogic utopia), their demand for citizenship and patrician resistance created factional conflict of a concentrated nature—exactly what the Madisonian strategy for a federal republic sought to prevent.[12] Unfortunately, the resumption of serious political contest after the collapse of the "conservative order" in 1916 tended to reproduce factional, internecine conflict—except that this time the antagonists were social rather than regional forces.[13]

To understand this long process of political decay in a country that was one of the prize promises of 1900 and 1930, one must turn to the Sarmentian/Alberdian crossroads. Alberdi wanted to deny citizenship to his future immigrant masses; the latter obliged by retaining their (mostly Italian) nationality. In Argentina, a country where the foreign percentage was much larger than in the United States, immigrants were not co-nationals and were not enfranchised. In a country largely devoid of the liberal institutional fabric of Anglo-Saxon lands, the noncitizen immigrants that swamped the country made the native bourgeoisie quite uneasy. The age of liberal reform, under the "radicals" of Irigoyen (1916–30) extended the franchise but left the bulk of the working class without political representation—and therefore available to demagogic mobilization by Perón's left fascism.

Toward the end of World War II there was a failure of nerve among export oligarchies. They had ruled undemocratically since the 1930s Depression, and they were now no longer assured of a protected market in Britain. Local elites became afraid of class struggle. On the other hand, in Argentina labor had a de facto union strength, even before Perón, that had no counterpart in either Brazil or Mexico. The resulting scenario included both a return to protectionism under Perón (this time industrial and corporatist containment of the working class) and a veto power unofficially vested in the unions long after the first downfall of Perónism (1955). Although unable to rule, labor was able to prevent other classes from implementing economic reforms. The thoughtful study by Carlos Waisman, *Reversal of Development in Argentina,* spells out the mechanics of this crippling stalemate, which now constitutes the main challenge of postpraetorian democracy.[14]

While it would be grossly unscientific to lay all the blame at the doorstep of ideology, it seems pretty obvious that a number of strategic options made a century ago by a liberist but illiberal patriciate foredoomed the whole political culture. Interestingly enough, liberal institutions have long failed in Argentina not because the state is strong (though *statism* has been) but because, in the words of political scientist Guillermo O'Donnell, social forces have been "colonizing" state action instead of allowing for a modicum of social contract to work.[15]

The Second French Liberalism: Rémusat to Renan

French liberalism, meanwhile, remained deeply *historical* because it was first and foremost a dialogue with the ghosts of the French Revolution. The French liberals smiled at 1789 and snarled at 1793—they blessed the conquest of civil equality, but cursed the Jacobin Terror as a return to despotism and a veiled threat to property. In the wake of the February 1848 Revolution and the subsequent drift toward authoritarian bourgeois rule, the liberal interpretation of 1789–94 turned national-populist in the exuberant pages of Jules Michelet's *History of the French Revolution* (1847–53). An opponent of the Second Empire, Michelet (1798–1874) fought on two fronts in his writing. His populism set him against Anglophiles like Guizot, who represented the Orléanist plutocracy. But his liberalism clashed with socialist neo-Jacobins like Louis Blanc (1811–82), a leader of the Left in 1848. The new wave of liberal ideologists who came of intellectual age after 1848 did not quite follow the left liberalism of Michelet, but neither did they simply stay in the whiggish positions of most of their predecessors.

The evolution can be measured by a look at the youngest "doctrinaire," Charles de Rémusat (1797–1875). Toward the end of the Restoration, as a leading voice in the liberal Saint-Simonian newspaper of Pierre Leroux, *Le Globe*, Rémusat praised neither the ancien régime nor the Revolution. At the time, even Constant seemed to him too lenient to the Enlightenment and therefore of little use to the modern generation and its spiritualist, romantic leanings. Throughout Louis Philippe's reign (1830–48), Rémusat tried to make his former fellow "doctrinaire" Guizot liberalize the politics of the "bourgeois king." But he failed and drew closer to his friend, Adolphe Thiers (1797–1877), liberal historian of the Revolution and chief rival of Guizot. In 1840, as a minister in Thiers's short-lived cabinet, he ordered the imprisonment of Napoleon's restless nephew, Louis-Napoléon, who had staged a putsch.

After Thiers succeeded in turn in toppling Louis Philippe and Guizot in 1848, Rémusat headed a momentous ideological shift. For the first time among French liberals, he accepted the republican principle as a historical form of national sovereignty. After all, he argued, responsible representative rule was the thing, regardless of its (preferably) monarchic dress. So the republic, with its democratic potential, became acceptable to mainstream Orléanist liberalism in France. This started a development that eventuated in the dissociation of the republic from Jacobin illiberalism. Rémusat was a key figure in the liberals' transition from constitutional monarchy to liberal republicanism.

The republic itself collapsed. Bourgeois panic after the June 1848 riots doomed the new regime and cleared the way to imperial dictatorship. But Louis-Napoléon was far from sharing the reactionary creed. He was keen to put Bonapartist glory at the service of the new political faith—nationalism. So in 1859 he decided to give his upstart throne a sheen by helping Cavour (but not Mazzini) unify Italy, adding Nice and Savoy to France in the process. In 1860 he had Michel Chevalier sign a free-trade treaty with Britain, thereby placating London's alarm at the new activism of France on the continent. Soon Catholics and others joined liberal pressure for making the regime parliamentary. As a result, the political arena became conspicuously more lively, in the last decade of the empire, with many a liberal intervention.

The wily Louis-Napoléon was quick to realize that religion was a powerful cement of conservative support. Accordingly, he allowed the Church to make a bid for the control of education. His dash at imperialism in Mexico, which ended in fiasco in 1867, was meant to please the Catholics. Since the very beginning, the Second Empire had been under attack from *liberal* Catholics. Count Charles de Montalembert (1810–70), who fought the ultramontane, or papist, party both in parliament and at the prestigious Académie Française, pointed out that the rule of one man who would act and think for everybody was a pagan idea, embodied in the Roman caesars and obviously incompatible with Christian freedom (*On the Catholic Interests in the XIX Century*, 1852). Rémusat, also an *académicien*, pointed out that socialism seemed to thrive not in Protestant lands but in countries like France, where the state enforced Catholic orthodoxy. This amounted to updating the de Staël-Constant thesis, that religious freedom was a prop of general liberty. Rémusat closed his political life as a foreign minister during the brief presidency (1871–73) of his crony Thiers, the savage victor of the red Paris Commune in the spring of 1871.

The modernization of the liberals' political formula fell to the legal scholar Edouard Laboulaye (1811–83), whose 1863 program book, *The Liberal Party*, adapted liberalism to universal suffrage.[16] Laboulaye was no political Anglophile. Rather, he belonged to the American school, accepting presidentialism in a separation-of-powers system and warmly recommending decentralization. A claim destined to a brilliant future in rhetoric, if not the practice, of the Third Republic (1871–1940), local self-rule was to be quickly enthroned by an influential work—*La France nouvelle* (1868)—written by one of Thiers's disciples, Lucien Prévost-Paradol (1829–70).

The most thoughtful historiographic work of those years (besides Tocqueville's *Ancien Régime*) was entitled *La Révolution Française*, which was published by a liberal exile, Edgar Quinet (1803–75), in 1865. A victim, like his friend Michelet, of imperial repression, Quinet challenged the then-prevalent view of French modern history as the triumphant march of the bourgeoisie. Embittered by the new spell of authoritarianism under Napoléon III, Quinet wanted no liberating monarchy. Sure, he remarked, the nobility had lost their rights, but the people had received none. Worse, he noted, the French Third Estate had damaged democracy, by allying itself to the absolutist crown, making the crown illiberal from the start. Quinet shattered the historiographical myth of the bourgeoisie and left liberalism ready for new, less class-ridden vindications, in the bulk of republican thought.

But French "second liberalism" turned conservative in the Attic prose of one of the century's most-read thinkers, Ernest Renan (1823–92). Born into a humble family in Brittany and trained as an orientalist, Renan almost took holy orders but lost his faith. Then, having treated Christ as a man, a charming guru, in his 1863 *Life of Jesus,* he was expelled from his university chair, only to become a hero of intellectuals and freethinkers.

Renan is sometimes described as a positivist, but all he shared with Comte (whose style he disliked) was a denial of the supernatural, a cult of science, and a three-stage view of civilization. Renan found Comte a reductionist unfaithful to "the infinite variety of human nature" and grievously ignorant of history and philology.[17] His historical ladder ran from an age of faith followed by one of criticism to a final epoch of "synthesis" that was at once scientific and religious. Renan's key problem was to ground belief after the ebbing away of traditional religion. He veered between skepticism and nostalgia, with nothing of that fervent secular faith typical of Comte's "religion of humanity." His *Prayer on the Acropolis* (1876) was a classic of Victorian humanism, exalting ancient Greece as the cradle of reason and beauty. But in *The Future of Science,* written in 1848 but published 42 years later, he described science as a new religion of learning that was replacing old dogmas in the heart of modern man.

In 1848 Renan sympathized with the republicans. But France's humiliating defeat by Prussia in 1870 and, even more, the red Commune threw him into a despondent mood. The Commune was a "hideous parody of the Terror," he wrote, apparently oblivious that the real violence had been that which the *white* terror employed in decimating the communards. Then he decided to exchange dejection for inspection and identified the roots of French decadence. The result was a short book, *Intellectual and Moral Reform* (1871), widely read as a gospel of national regeneration.

Renan named two main causes of decline: democracy and materialism. France had fallen because she was growing selfish and cynical, just as Rome had succumbed to the barbarians for want of something for Romans to love. The country was sailing toward mediocrity. Renan had two criticisms of democracy. First, he denounced its revolutionary pedigree as an "abstract" right, innocent of history; like the reactionaries, he wanted to put an end once and for all to "the fetishism of 1789." His second line of attack amounted to a moral criticism of the revolutionary-democratic tradition, using the racial idiom that was so common at the time. Insisting on the Celtic substratum of the French stock, he claimed that the Gallic race—unlike the German one—abhors ranking. The

Germanic taste for conquest and sense of ownership was being replaced west of the Rhine by the leveling forces of socialism (springing from selfishness) and democracy (stemming from envy). Democracy, however, "neither disciplines nor brings moral improvement," so it was no wonder that French morale as well as French morals were sapped. Germany, by contrast, had been living nobly for science and war.

This gibberish was topped by Renan's musings on the two types of society he found prevalent in the age. While American society, young and historyless, was based on liberty and property, Prussia thrived on science and ranking.

By the end of the decade Renan, now at the Académie and much honored by the anticlerical establishment of the Third Republic, had come to terms with democracy. But the 1878 dialogue marking his lukewarm reconciliation, "Caliban," showed that he still saw the people as the mob and the mob as a monster, in a manner not very different from the elitist bias of the collective psychology concocted by Gustave Le Bon (1841–1931)—which was a racialist attempt to blast "the democratic myth." The difference was that now Renan believed the masses could be tamed, so that the future lay in the republic but not in the revolution. Therefore, the limitation of the suffrage that he had explicitly urged in the *Reform* could be toned down. His famous Sorbonne lecture of 1882, "What Is a Nation?," also moved away from the near-hysterical racialism of the *Reform*. Refusing to accept the German concept of the nation as a racial community, Renan—even without endorsing the Rousseaunian idea of the nation as a political unity based on the general will—defined it as "a plebiscite of everyday," a large instance of tacit consensus.

Democracy, meanwhile, still left his heart cold. He prefaced his *New Religious Studies* (1884) by acknowledging that the progress of basic education was undermining superstition and fostering the rise of a scientific mentality—yet he gave no credit for this to the democratic endeavors of the Third Republic, a schoolteachers' regime if ever there was one.[18] On the whole, Renan's image remained imprisoned by his implausible severance of liberalism from democracy, at a time when many French liberals were prepared to take an enlarged view of political freedom. Possibly the greatest artist of French nonfictional prose since Chateaubriand, Renan's ideological legacy was as shriveling for liberalism as the politics of Guizot. Fortunately, French liberalism in the last quarter of the century largely bypassed or ignored his obsessions.

Semi-liberalism:
From German *Rechtsstaat* to Max Weber

Two concepts of German liberalism have already been mentioned. One is Humboldt's idea of "limits of the state," originating the noninterventionist notion of the state as "night watchman" (*Nacht-wächterstaat*). The other is freedom as individual autotely, or self-determination—a Kantian concept that Humboldt welded into Weimar humanism in the form of the *Bildung* idea, the principle of self-cultivation. The political philosophy of the great post-Kantians, notably Fichte and Hegel, moved away from liberalism, so we have to go back to Kant in order to grasp the seeds of German liberal thought in the mid-nineteenth century.

The key concept here is the *Rechtsstaat*, the "law state,"[19] a German alternative to the rule of law. For just as English liberals had been mainly economists and moral philosophers (like Smith, Mill, and Bagehot), and French liberals mostly historians (like Guizot and Tocqueville), German publicists of liberal leanings were principally jurists.

Although the term was coined (by Karl Welcker) in 1813, the *Rechtsstaat* idea belongs to the age of Kant. It denotes at least four things: a constitutional arrangement able to provide security and endowing the legal system with regularity; the enshrinement of subjective public rights in positive law; a depersonalization of law, supplanting the old identification of law and ruler by the acknowledgment of law as a norm bounding both the ruler and the ruled; citizens' participation, however indirect, in the law-making process.[20] The *Rechtsstaat* so conceived involved two basic liberal tenets: individual rights and constitutionalism in the sense of the rule of law.

The rise of the concept of a "law state" was a reaction against the idea of the *Polizeistaat*, the "police state" (in the classical sense of "police," that is, civilized, polished). The *Polizeistaat* was the "moral state" of enlightened absolutism or of Hegelian constitutional monarchy, both being states explicitly committed to the happiness of their subjects. Early liberal thinking strongly opposed this paternalistic view. Constant made a famous demand that the state just saw to it that order and security were provided while the citizens of a free society would make it their business to be happy ("*nous nous chargerons d'être heureux*").[21] There was a clear kinship, therefore, of the "law state" with the night-watchman state of early liberalism on both sides of the Rhine.

The father of *Rechtsstaat* theory was Robert von Mohl (1799–1875), a Heidelberg jurist very active in liberal politics. (He was minister of justice during the brief Frankfurt Parliament rule in the 1848 revolution.) Mohl divided state law into two branches, constitutional and administrative, thereby making room for the concept of a rights-based "law state." In 1859 he stated that "the individual is as little absorbed by the whole as the human being by the citizen."[22] Mohl was not altogether happy with Kant's individualism because in his view the great philosopher had downplayed the political dimension of individual rights.

The liberalism of the *Rechtsstaat* concept was criticized by Friedrich Julius Stahl (1802–61), a conservative theorist who was teaching in Berlin. Stahl, too, was for constitutional rule, but he claimed that by means of law, the state had a right to determine and secure the scope and limits of governmental action as well as the free sphere of its citizens—in that order. This could only mean an attack on the liberal *Rechtsstaat*, an attack whose political meaning became all too clear when Stahl, in his anti-Hegelian *Philosophy of Right* (1846), took pains to dissociate the "law state" from "the popular state of Rousseau and Robespierre," an "aberration" in which people think their standards are not "restricted by any legal barrier."

Strengthening the scope of political liberty within the "law state" was the aim of the southern German liberals Karl von Rotteck (1775–1840) and Karl Welcker (1790–1869). Their jointly edited *Political Dictionary* (1834–48) became the most prestigious corpus of German liberalism. Rotteck and Welcker were constitutional liberals who lost both their Heidelberg chairs by virtue of their demand for modern representative government. German authoritarian conservatism was so strong that more often than not the southern liberals, holding anti-Prussian views like Mohl's, had to fight reactionary measures instead of putting forward comprehensive liberal reforms.[23]

With the rise of the Prussian-dominated Second Reich, German liberalism became hard to distinguish from liberal or not-so-liberal conservatism. Stahl's main challenger, Rudolf von Gneist (1816–95), dean of the Berlin law faculty, is a case in point. In his classic treatise *Der Rechtsstaat* (1872), he rebuked the French parliamentary system for entailing a triumph of politics to the detriment of legal consciousness. France, claimed Gneist, had enslaved the executive to the national assembly, and the slave in turn dealt despotically with the citizenry; thus, paradoxically, the sovereign people lived under an arbitrary administration.[24] Gneist fought in two fronts: to his right, against the conservatism of Stahl, and to his left, against western liberalism. He exalted Bismarck's reforms as a third way between the feudal privileges of the Junkers and elective local government western style. Gneist's defense of the German system, deprived of parliamentary power but with administrative courts, was resumed by a younger scholar, Heinrich von Treitschke (1834–96). Treitschke defined *liberty* as freedom *within* the state, not *from* it, discarding emphatically the night-watchman concept.

In all this development there was one conspicuous casualty: the autonomy of individual rights. The strongest legal school in the second half of the nineteenth century, the legal positivists, rose in full decline of the citizen concept. A leading figure of Wilhelmine legal positivism, Strassburg's Paul Laband (1838–1918), simply denied the existence of subjective public rights—the very notion that had motivated the creation of the *Rechtsstaat* principle. The greatest name in the Wilhelmine theory of the state, Georg Jellinek (1852–1911) of Heidelberg, distinguished between two kinds of personal rights. There are rights having the nature of a *licere* (from Latin for "to allow") and there are rights amounting to a *posse* ("to be able, to have power"). The former are private rights, whereas the latter are public rights inherent in the status of the individual. Unlike the *licere*, which remains altogether at the discretion of the person, *posse* rights are at the same time rights and duties—and the assertion of these rights does *not* entail a recognition, in natural law fashion, of absolute individuality. Here the ghost of Hegel obviously prevailed over the shadow of Kant and Locke. German juridical liberalism, fraught with much reticence before individualism, turned out to be at most a semiliberalism.

In the post-Bismarckian age (1890–1918) a new generation of liberals began to question the political status quo. In terms of post-humous world influence, none of them surpassed the sociologist (trained as a legal historian) Max Weber (1864–1920), who became the brightest star in Heidelberg's academic firmament after the turn of the century. One of Weber's first shots in the political fray was a study of the economic and political ineptitude of the Junker class east of the Elbe. His critique of the "feudal" Junker mentality and oligarchic status contained an option for both capitalism and liberalism. More generally, he challenged the authoritarian structure of the Wilhelmine Reich from an advanced national-liberal position. In an inaugural lecture delivered at Freiburg in 1895, he upbraided all social classes for their political immaturity in regard to the further-ance of Germany's interests as a power state. In a series of wartime articles, *Parliament and Government* (1917), he advocated a parliamen-tary regime as a means for selecting real leadership and suggested that Bismarck's autocratic rule and its institutional frame had de-prived Germany of good political breeding. Unlike Tocqueville and Mill, Weber was very much a "power liberal," standing unabash-edly for rule, elite domination, and national hegemony.

Although Weber did not overlook the fact that even the most creative leaders need social support and have to operate in a class context, a Nietzschean element in his thought made him see leader-ship as a prop for ranking ways of life. To him, as to Nietzsche, value-creation implied hierarchy and dominance. His historical out-look was a mild brand of *Kulturpessimismus.* Modernity was the realm of rationalization—the continuous, widespread growth of in-strumental rationality (the "end-means" optimum in social action), as contrasted with behavior ruled by absolute values, tradition, or sentiment. In Weber's eyes, modernity also meant a growth of *for-mal* rationality, an increasing number of rules whose application requires qualified skills. This sort of norm-expertise was, as much as efficiency, the soul of the vast social process of *bureaucratization.* Weber entertained serious misgivings about the march of rationaliza-tion because it might establish a domination of means over ends, while bureaucracy might entangle modern society in an "iron cage" of bondage.

Against this icy prospect, Weber envisioned two antidotes: vo-cation (a calling) and charisma. Robert Eden, in a very perceptive inquiry into Weber's political thought, believes that his emphasis on calling was a response to Nietzsche's demonic individualism.[25] The concept of vocation was of course an old Lutheran notion, but We-ber gave it a novel glamor by using it to sketch a dialectic between individuality and the rise of professionalism in our time. This also enabled him to reenact the ascetic ethos of the heroic age of the bourgeoisie, so well portrayed in his best-known work, *The Protes-tant Ethic and the Spirit of Capitalism* (1904).

In his late political writings, calling and charisma are blended, as in the stark admonition of "Politics as a Vocation" (1919): "there is only the choice: leadership-democracy [*Führerdemokratie*] with the [party] 'machine,' or leaderless democracy—that is, the domination of 'professional politicians' without a vocation, without the inner charismatic qualities that alone make a leader." The only way to avert "uncontrolled bureaucratic domination" was a politics of charisma, best exemplified by leaders like Gladstone and Lloyd George. Weber longed for elective Caesarism, plebiscitarian leadership; and in the constitutional debate at the onset of the Weimar Republic, he prescribed a strong presidency stemming from universal suffrage.

Weber's liberalism contained no theory of natural rights and no love for democracy. He rejected socialism because, regardless of revolution (which, in the case of the German social democrats, he sensed was more rhetoric than threat), socialism would beget extensive social planning and therefore more bureaucracy, no matter how democratic its intentions. Democracy itself, in his view, would bring no real distribution of power, only a decline of local chiefs and a rise of the plebiscitary leader, owing to the emergence of large party machines in order to cope with mass suffrage.[26] Weber was impressed by the demonstration by Moisei Ostrogorski and Robert Michels (his Heidelberg pupil) of the role of party oligarchies in large modern democracies like Britain and the United States. This realization made him less sanguine about Parliament as a leader selector, although he remained convinced of the Chamber's role in the control of the administration and the protection of civil rights.

Weber could be a very shrewd analyst of political conjunctures and sociopolitical structures, as shown in his comments on the Russian Revolution of 1905, in his conceptualization of the state, and in his pioneering approach to patrimonialism in his magnum opus, *Economy and Society.* But his place in the history of liberalism is rather marred by the absence, both in his sociological and in his political writings, of any perspective that links the legitimacy of regimes and rulers to the actual plight *of the ruled.* Always anxious about the freedom of cultural man, Weber seems to have often overlooked the concrete range of social freedom.[27] He offered, in short, no view from below. But if liberalism is to be loyal to its concern with power control, it must remain mindful of the underdog's viewpoint. This alone classifies Weber's leadership liberalism as a conservative liberalism indeed. While his individualism and his distaste for the Wilhelmine state saved him from the half-liberalism of the *Staatslehre* jurists, including his Heidelberg colleague Jellinek, his fundamental lack of democratic instincts put him behind the wisdom, and not just beyond the hopes, of the classics of liberty.

Croce and Ortega

In his historical sociology as a whole, Weber can be said to be the man who made peace between German historicism, with its passion for the meaningful uniqueness of social and cultural phenomena, and positivism, as a search for causal explanation in social science. Weber's leading contemporary in Italy, the philosopher and historian Benedetto Croce (1866–1952), had a very different attitude toward the positivist tradition. Oddly enough, the southern Italian Croce was much closer to the standard neglect of causal explanation in *Historismus* than the Prussian Weber. Historicism was all for interpretation and actually evolved the dualist conception of knowledge, according to which the logic of the humanities is essentially alien to the quest for regularities that characterizes natural science. Coming from a school of thought openly neoidealist, the southern Italian Hegelians, Croce was proudly steeped in antipositivism and in this vein made his debut by blasting the more deterministic versions of Marxism (in *Historical Materialism and the Economics of Karl Marx*, 1900).

Positivism, to Croce, was part of a larger picture of intellectual error, harking back to natural law thinking and the rationalism of the Enlightenment. In Croce's view, eighteenth-century reason had been too abstract and rigid and was definitely inferior, as a grasp of all things human, to the concrete *historical* reason forged by the 1800s. Against the Enlightenment *philosophes*, Croce pitted the counter-Enlightenment of Giambattista Vico (1668–1744), who had been rediscovered by romantics like Michelet.

Croce extolled the Risorgimento itself as a wonderful romantic interlude between two negative stages—the Enlightenment (Jacobinism, freemasonry, and equalitarian bigotry) and the sad age of positivism in the late nineteenth century. Croce's own fin de siècle swarmed with virulent antipositivist currents, but the truth is that Croce himself included democracy among those principles most contaminated by "the positivist phraseology" and its "profoundly mistaken" views on man and society. He tended to disparage the most romantic wing of the Risorgimento—the school of Mazzini, which, Croce was glad to say, had never penetrated into Naples. His anti-Mazzinianism, soon to be shared by the fascists, showed his little sympathy for left republicanism—for the democratic component of the liberal heritage. To Croce, the democratic spirit of equality was as simplistic as it was "abstract," and he sided with the

Central European empires in the Great War because they held much sounder historico-political beliefs.[28] The postwar arrival of political democracy, accompanied as it was by an embattled spell of class struggle, could only sharpen Croce's misgivings about democracy.

Thus, as heir to the right wing of the Risorgimento (*"la destra storica"*), Croce was as little fond of democracy as Weber. But like Weber, he came to accept if not properly love the interplay of democratic mechanisms. In 1923, two years before he launched a manifesto of antifascist intellectuals, Croce followed the conservative elite theorist Gaetano Mosca (1858–1941) in a defense of liberal institutions.[29] The new stance was bound to reflect in his own brand of liberalism. Croce wrote two remarkable works on the century of his birth and formation, a *History of Italy from 1871 to 1915* (1925) and a *History of Europe in the Nineteenth Century* (1932). He wanted to write philosophical history as "the story of liberty" from an "ethico-political" viewpoint—an Actonian program, as it were. But he also wanted to show why liberalism eventually failed to generate a successful resistance to fascism, a dictatorship that, after some hesitation, Croce decided to resist. He thought that in its heroic days liberalism, in order to defend itself against ideological oppression from traditionalist quarters, launched the view that values are subjective and facts are value-neutral. But the trouble was that in so doing, liberalism undermined its own moral conviction in the long run.[30]

Croce was the living symbol of anticlerical thought among Italian nonsocialists. Nonetheless, he seemed to imply that some moral consensus in lieu of faith ought to fuel the liberal flame if it were to ignite a political movement as it had the Risorgimento. Also, out of his haughty contempt for materialism in ethics Croce introduced a conceptual wedge between liberalism and *liberism*, his own term denoting "economic freedom." In *Ethics and Politics* (1922) and other texts of the 1920s, he insisted that liberalism should not be equated with the ephemeral age of laissez-faire or more generally with economic practices and interests. In his essay "Liberalism and Liberism" (1928) he stressed that while liberalism is an ethical principle, liberism is just an economic precept that, if unduly mistaken for a liberal ethic, degrades liberalism into a low utilitarian hedonism.

Croce became the best-known liberal opponent of Mussolini's regime. His European fame after the publication of his *Aesthetics* (1902) forced fascism to respect him. The main fascist intellectual was his former friend, the philosopher Giovanni Gentile. As Mussolini's minister of education (a job Croce himself had previously occupied under the foxy liberal prime minister Giolitti), Gentile appropriated the Hegelian concept of the "ethical state" with a clear anti-individualist animus. He also tried to prove that the historical right—traditional Italian liberalism—had also been anything but individualistic, so that fascism was a true continuation of genuine Italian liberalism.

Croce had the good sense to refute fascist hocus-pocus about the "ethical state" by drawing honest attention to the element of coercion inherent in all states. In this he followed Treitschke (whose *Politics* he had translated) and kept close to Weber's celebrated definition of the state as the monopoly of coercion within a given territory. Equally, he reminded the fascist political romance of Machiavelli's awareness of politics as a sphere of force and conflict.

On the negative side, however, Croce evinced a basic indifference to the liberal concept of power and state limits, ending up with a quasi-mystical, providentialist notion of liberty. He spoke of liberty as the unfolding of the Spirit in concrete history—something hardly less foggy than its Hegelian original and scarcely conducive to an empirical-minded analysis of freedom and unfreedom.[31] In order to avoid the irrationalist voluntarism of Gentile (even before they fell apart on fascism), Croce collapsed his "absolute historicism" into a lay theology of freedom, a "religion of liberty" ultimately untranslatable—as charged by a Crocean marxist, Antonio Gramsci[32]—in the down-to-earth language of real praxis. Croce's worthy opposition to fascism and his defense of moral individuality in the face of authoritarian holism placed his liberalism, for all its conservative aspects, at a clear distance from the liberal conservatism of Vilfredo Pareto (1848–1923), with Mosca the founder of elite theory. His liberal historiography as an epic of the "moral life" of the modern West exudes a spirit not to be found in anything written by the "neo-Machiavellian" Mosca, for all his belated acceptance of liberal institutions.[33] But in the end, Croce's inspired "historicism of liberty" was not much of a theoretical gain, whereas his exorcism of liberism sounds rather inadequate in our age of economic liberalization.

In Spain, hegemonic influence of the kind exerted in Italy by Croce belonged for a long time to José Ortega y Gasset (1883–1955). Ortega is best known in political theory as the author of *The Revolt of the Masses* (1929). Analyzing modern society, Ortega claimed that for the first time in recorded history, civilization had come to reject the

principle of the elite. Mass society is inhabited by self-satisfied creatures, though psychologically they are a little lost in the midst of
technology. Their general human type leads to an assertion of the
rights of mediocrity. Seven years before, in his pamphlet *Invertebrate
Spain*, Ortega chided his own country for its "aristophobia," its
avoidance and disparagement of the best. After its traumatic defeat
by the United States in the Cuban war of 1898, Spain had been
swarming with soul-searching diagnoses of the "national disease";
decadence became a leitmotiv of Spanish high culture. Ortega
wished to go as far as possible in a more radical approach: the quest
for ancient roots of the Spanish malaise.

He began by taking a snipe at democracy. The democratic ideology, said he, is wont to ask, what must a society be? But the real
problem is to ascertain, in what does a society consist? What constitutes it—or rather, how can a society *be?* This *constitutive* problem-
atic was typical of the neo-Kantians, under whom the young Ortega
had studied at Marburg immediately before the war. Now, Spain
had once been a great state; a state, like Rome, capable of creating
integrative systems ever more comprehensive, from the Seven Hills
to the Latium and from Italy to the whole Mediterranean. Such
states are not based on force alone; for a state to be so integrative,
there must be a "suggestive project of life in common"—like the
long struggle of Castile against the Moor. Hence the energy with
which Spain, from the close of the Reconquista, undertook the conquest of Italy and especially America.

Yet every such endeavor requires an aristocracy, said Ortega, a
leadership that has the assent, nay the enthusiastic following, of the
people. Without aristocracy, there could be no state-formation or
state-expansion—not even national reassertion. Spain, after Phillip
III, had grown diffident, conservative, and narrow minded. Particu-
larisms had arisen everywhere—in government, in the regions, in
the social classes. In a flight of racial fantasy not unworthy of
Renan, Ortega mused at the weakness of the Visigoths, the Germanic tribe that had settled in the peninsula. Unlike the Franks, he
claimed, the Visigoths had been contaminated by Roman decadence. Above all, they lacked the Frankish instinct for following
vigorous leaders in conquest and domination. It was a pity Spain
never had a proper feudalism, he said. Ortega didn't stoop to explain how such poor stock had come to invent the "suggestive
project" of both the Reconquista and the Conquista. He even
mocked the Reconquista, asking how one could call a conquest an

enterprise when it had taken so long (eight centuries) to succeed. He concluded that the "Visigothic" ascent of 1500 had rested on an artificial strength—and therefore it was no wonder that decline had set in so quickly, already by 1600. Spain remained a peasants' nation, loath to guidance by the *aristoi*, the best: it was an aristophobic society that had produced as few great men as Russia. Significantly, its best art was folk art—crafts, dance, the popular lot.

The Revolt of the Masses writ aristophobia large. Mass man, Ortega said, was mediocrity trying to impose a mediocracy, a nihilistic leveling in the name of democratism. The world of mass man was on the point of being ruled by "childish people" like the Americans and the Russians; the former only masked their primitivism behind the latest inventions. For a moment, Ortega defined *barbarism* as a lack of norms. But he also told us that while Greece and Rome failed because they lacked principles, we the moderns are failing because we lack men—the *aristoi*, of course.

Ortega was by no means a *social* elitist. He took pains to explain that his plea for elites was a *cultural* stance, not a social prejudice in favor of the upper classes; the new elites, he specified, should be based on excellence, not on money. Then why all the rage against democracy? Ortega's answer is a tautology, for it seems to lie in his largely implicit equation of democracy with an allegedly sapless civilization, the Victorian culture of reason and progress. In his most original book, *The Modern Theme* (1923), Ortega applied a Nietzschean critique to European culture. Nietzsche had discovered the autonomy of "life" values in and against a civilization given to culture-worship. Culturalism was to him a godless Christianity, for in the eyes of the bourgeois (those whom Nietzsche immortally dubbed the "culture Philistines"), the realm of culture enjoyed the same transcendental status earlier ascribed to the Christian deity. *The Modern Theme* was a clarion call to break with culture bigotry for the sake of a "vital reason"; and this ratiovitalism, preaching "the need to subject reason to life," became Ortega's philosophical banner.

Ortega's great predecessor in Spanish essayism was Miguel de Unamuno (1864–1936), a central if solitary figure in the 1898 anti-decadent generation. Unamuno had decried the "Sancho Panzaism" of modern civilization: its positivism, its naturalism, its empiricism. Between Unamuno and Ortega, there was a personality gulf. Ortega detested the older man for his strident romanticism; the sophisticated upper-middle-class philosopher, a darling of Madrid high society, couldn't conceal his contempt for the harsh, uncompromising provincial humanist who was exiled by the military dictatorship of Primo de Rivera (1923–30) in the last throes of the Spanish monarchy. Instead of Ortega's hopeful if elusive synthesis, "ratiovitalism," Unamuno offered a downright misology, an open revulsion against rationalism. Ortega, by contrast, insisted on the value of science and technology and scorned Unamuno for pitting Saint John of the Cross (that is, Spanish mysticism) against Descartes (the rationalism of modern thought). Also, Unamuno was a radical individualist, wanting to make of Spain "a people of I's" (*un pueblo de yos*). This obviously clashed with Ortega's dreams of national projects.[34]

But *The Modern Theme* is not just a critique of culturalism. It also questions in no uncertain terms the utopian cult of revolutionism. In his early articles, Ortega was not above quoting the saying of his Marburg master, Hermann Cohen (1842–1918), that revolutions are "spells of experimental ethics." But in the 1920s one of his liveliest essays, "Mirabeau or the Statesman" (1927) sharply separated statesmanship from revolutionism. The statesman is more than a man of action, said Ortega. Unlike the intellectual, the statesman must be a man of action, but one with a vision. Yet the statesman's is a highly realistic and pragmatic vision, not a bit like the intellectualist blueprint of the ideologist. The revolutionary, on the other hand (like Robespierre, whom Ortega called a "jackal"), is a fumbling fellow who ends up getting exactly the opposite of what he intended. Here one must wonder whether Ortega's aprioristic antirevolutionism matches the historical record. I, for one, can't think of Lenin as one who got the opposite of what he wanted—rather, the other way around. But in more general terms and in the long run Ortega's observation that the cult of revolution went against the grain of modern western culture turned out to be an undeniably prescient view.

Ortega's actual politics underwent a curious evolution. In his youth he had been attracted by the ethical socialism of his neo-Kantian teachers, and he wrote sympathetically on the anti-individualist and anti-utilitarian line of the English "new liberals." His heroes were reformist socialists who endorsed the state and the nationality principle, like Ferdinand Lassalle (1825–64) and Eduard Bernstein (1850–1932).[35] Then, beginning perhaps with his review of Georg Simmel's 1908 book *Schopenhauer and Nietzsche*, the young Ortega started to tread a virtually undemocratic ground.

At first Ortega tried to hold together his socialism and his Nietzscheanism. In his 1913 essay "Socialism and Aristocracy," he declared, "I am a socialist out of love for aristocracy." Since capitalist power was faceless and materialistic, devoid of inner glow, socialism should shine as a moral improvement of mankind. But during the 1920s Ortega's positions took on increasingly conservative hues. He flirted with the republic, but chiefly from a rightist standpoint,[36] then exiled himself from the beginning of the civil war until the end of the world conflict. Afterward, during his last decade, he refused to act as a focus of liberal resistance, as Croce had in fascist Italy. Like Weber and unlike Croce, he was a nationalist. Again like Croce, his patrician bourgeois outlook saved him from complacency with the plebeian politics of mobilization in fascism, just as their agnosticism separated them from the rightist clericalism that blessed both the unbeliever Mussolini and the pious general Franco, "caudillo of Spain by the grace of God."

Ortega knew how to prevent his cultural elitism from degenerating into political reaction. He once said that while every democratic interpretation of a living order other than the sphere of public law is plebeism, every nondemocratic conception of public law is tyrannical. The same thinker who, in *The Dehumanization of Art* (1925), located an "aristocratic" element of modern art in its willful *ludic* obscurity thought, as he put it in *Mirabeau,* that "the actual historical reality is the nation and not the state"—a normative rather than a descriptive axiom. The brilliance of *The Dehumanization* comes logically (and not just chronologically) between *The Modern Theme* and *The Revolt of the Masses:* for while the ludic nature of modern art makes it a symbol of life values against Victorian culturalism, the hermeticism of modernist forms represents a deliberate insult to the vulgar, demotic mind of mass man. So in the end Ortega's way of being hostile to fascist statism implied both the traditional liberal concern for a social as opposed to the political sphere and the revulsion of the cultural elitist against populist politics—less because they are illiberal than because they are plebeian.

Conclusion

Classical liberalism unfolded into a set of different conceptual discourses. Liberal theorists spoke the languages of natural rights (like Locke and Paine), civic humanism (like Jefferson and Mazzini), stadial history (like Smith and Constant), utilitarianism (like Bentham and Mill), and historical sociology (like Tocqueville). With such discourses, classical liberalism advanced from whiggism—the mere demand for religious freedom and constitutional rule—to democracy, or self-rule with a broad social basis.

By contrast, the conservative liberals from about 1830 to 1930 were generally intent on *slowing the democratization* of liberal politics. In this regard, they signaled a return to whig positions. Whig liberalism was essentially a liberalism of limited, restrictive representation. Whigs would normally agree with Kant, the republican and constitutional liberal, that "the domestic servant, the shop assistant, the laborer, or even the barber are . . . not members of the state, and thus unqualified to be citizens,"[37] on the grounds that such people live by selling their labor and therefore, being without a property basis, are not independent enough for the exercise of political rights. Census democracy, for all the incongruity of the phrase, remained the standard assumption in whig liberalism—and this was precisely what, from Paine and Bentham to Tocqueville, classical liberalism surpassed.

The conservative liberals were *neo-whigs.* They differed from conservatives, liberal or not, in their faithfulness to basic traits of the liberal worldview, like individualism and moral latitudinarianism, and in their rejection of holism and religious authority. But they coincided with the conservatives in their bias against democracy. Thus, the cautious broadening of the franchise devised by whig reformers like Macaulay had less-than-democratic scope and significance; and subsequent Burkean liberals such as Maine and Acton tried to use liberism (Maine) or federalism (Acton) against the democratic tide. Nor were utilitarian evolutionists like Bagehot, Stephen, and Spencer democrats; rather, they wanted to harness democracy to undemocratic purposes (Bagehot) or to resist it in the name of ensuring the survival of the fittest (Stephen and Spencer). Equally, the evolution of the second French liberalism, from 1830 to 1870, looked, from a Tocquevillian stance, like an involution, for if Rémusat's acceptance of the republican principle was a considerable step toward democracy (like Laboulaye's acknowledgment of universal suffrage), Renan's equation of democracy with decadence took the opposite direction. His reactionary move was undone only in part by his eventual lukewarm surrender to the democratic course of the Third Republic. The semiliberalism of the German jurists, with its rights-under-control motif, was still another instance of the conservative slowing-down within liberalism, and so was the primacy of order over liberty in Alberdi's nation-building formula. Finally, early-twentieth-century conservative liberals such as Weber, Croce, and Ortega were all reluctant or ambivalent in the face of democracy. Their dislike of mass politics or egalitarian culture landed them in positions less liberal-democratic than those of Tocqueville, Mill, and Mazzini, at the close of classical liberalism. For where Mill wanted a qualified democracy just because he dreamed of a quality democracy, the conservative liberals tended to quarrel with the democratic principle itself, which they were prepared to espouse at most out of reason, not as a true preference.

The net result of the conservative inflection of liberal doctrine, then, was an open or inner, overt or covert retreat from liberal democracy. In its discursive complexion, three further modes were added to the set of liberal discourses: the Burkean idiom, as in Macaulay, Maine, Alberdi, Renan, and Acton; the "Darwinian" language, as in Spencer; and the historicism, of elitist roots, of Weber and Ortega. For while Croce's focus on the odyssey of western moral life (*"vita morale"*) still dimly resembled the old progressive, stadial view of liberal historicism, Weber's plea for charisma and Ortega's yearning for cultural aristocracies were rather complex cases of the modernist revolt against modernity—the curious allergy of modern intellectuals vis-à-vis modern society.

5

From New Liberalisms to Neoliberalisms

The Claims of Social Liberalism

According to Albert Dicey (1835–1922), the liberal jurist who penned the classic *The Law of the Constitution*, legal reform in England knew two stages during the nineteenth century. From 1825 to 1870, its goal was primarily the furtherance of individual independence. Thereafter, it aimed at social justice. Dicey, a conservative liberal friend of Sir Henry Maine, deplored the shift from laissez-faire to "collectivism." Others shared his account of change without endorsing his valuation of it. They were the "new liberals" of 1880, convinced that the "older individualism" was no longer valid in the social context of late industrialism. They started what one of them, Francis Charles Montague (1858–1935), called the "revolt against negative freedom"—the very thing still so central in the libertarian liberalism of Mill.[1]

Theorists like Montague rejected the evolutionist outlook of the Spencerians, the use of Darwinism as an elegy on the threatened value of individualism. In *The Limits of Individual Liberty* (1885) Montague mounted a skillful refutation of the analogy on which social Darwinism was predicated. Free competition, he claimed, left the weak powerless. But in society the weak are far from being the worst. At any rate, unlike what happens in nature, in society evolution's victims are not eliminated altogether but linger on as a dead weight on the social body. So why not help them, especially as their degradation ends up harming the whole?

Montague's case for social liberalism was far from anti-individualistic. He thought that in modern times people differ in their personalities (if not in their attire) more than people did in the past; in the Middle Ages their different accoutrements covered much more uniformity—knight, burgher, and peasant tended to share the same inner life or lack of it. It is not true, argued Montague, that modern society is so organized as to leave little room for individual freedom. What is unfortunate is that society is organized for money-making, but unorganized for every other end. The same individualist faith inspired the famous *Lectures on the Principles of Political Obligation*, delivered in Oxford by Thomas Hill Green (1836–82) in 1879 (published posthumously in 1886). Green's premature death did not prevent his redefinition of liberalism from becoming very influential before the Great War. The son of a Yorkshire clergyman, Green embraced Hegelianism in mid-Victorian Oxford. But his was a rather peculiar Hegelianism. For while retaining the master's notion that history is a long struggle for human perfection, he put a Kantian accent on individual autonomy. Both in ethics and in political theory Green stressed the absolute value of the person as the *fons et origo* of human communities.

The new liberalism was as individualistic as Mill's. Nevertheless, it also involved a critique of Millian philosophical assumptions. Like Montague, Green objected to a picture of the human in which knowledge is ultimately reduced to sensations and morality to impulses, and that sees society as a bunch of individuals. This was a clear attack on the empiricism, the utilitarianism, and the atomism of the Bentham-Mill tradition, an attack conducted in the name of German-like idealism.

Green insisted that rational action is dictated by will and choice in a way that goes beyond merely following desire or passion. He was at a far remove from the Humean basis of utilitarian ethics (and Hume's famous dictum, "Reason is and ought to be the slave of passions"). For Green, the rational ends of conduct imply the realization that when we speak of freedom as something invaluable, we think of a positive power to do or enjoy worthy things. Therefore liberty is a positive and substantive concept, not a formal and negative one. In this sense, the idealism of the new liberalism was indeed a revolt against negative freedom in the Lockean-Millian meaning, based on the Hobbesian notion of freedom as absence of impediment. Green was moving from a preoccupation with *freedom from* to a rekindled appreciation of *freedom to*.

What about his views on the state? Classical liberalism had put the burden of justification on state interference. Normally, the state should leave the citizenship free to go about their business. Its interference was legitimate only for the sake of the individuals' security, as a guarantee of the free determination by society of the greatest happiness of the greatest number. Green was not that minimalist. The function of the state, he taught, ought to consist in the "removal of obstacles" to human self-development. This was also a German idea, deriving from Humboldt.[2] The state could never substitute itself for the human endeavor toward *Bildung*, or self-cultivation, but it could and should "promote conditions favorable to moral life."

Green believed that in its classical form, liberalism was becoming "obstructive" insofar as its minimalist political recipe became increasingly obsolete due to the growing penetration of law into society as civilization advanced. In his eyes the Maine-Dicey-Spencer fears of such a trend missed the point, which was the *quality* of state interference, not the fact of it. "Removal of obstacles" through enlightened reforms that enabled more individuals to enjoy higher freedoms, he thought, is a good thing. One should be prepared to violate the letter of the old liberalism in order to be faithful to its spirit—the fostering of individual freedom. This required enhancing access to opportunity.

Crane Brinton called Green a savior of liberalism.[3] And so he was inasmuch as he changed assumptions and wanted to alter practices without reneging on the basic values of the doctrine. For instance, though he was no laissez-faireist, he did not drop liberism. He deemed private property to be an essential prop of character development, and he resisted the socialist belief that capitalism is the root cause of poverty. Convinced that economic independence breeds self-reliance, he wished to convert workers into small property owners; and as a sincere admirer of the Quaker liberist John Bright (1811–89), he held an emphatically non-whig antiaristocratic view of English history.[4]

At bottom, Green's idea of social improvement was that the middle classes would dutifully help the poor become good, conscientious bourgeois—not so far from Mill's own civic elitism. Like Mill, Green underscored political participation as a moral obligation. His modern interpreters are right: Green gave liberalism a new lease on life by coupling the stock values of individual rights and liberties with a new stress on equality of opportunity and the community ethos.[5] In so doing, he lent late-Victorian new liberalism no socialist inflection. This was to come a little later, in Belle Époque social theory on both sides of the Channel. But with his high-minded idealist philosophy Green wrote the moral prologue to the social liberalism of 1900. The original charter for the British welfare state, drawn up by the liberal William Beveridge (1879–1963) at the Reform Club (where else?) in 1942, may be said to reflect a Greenian concern to balance social security with individual liberty. Green fathered the greening of liberalism in modification rather than negation of the classical creed.

In France, the ethical transformation of liberalism in a social-liberal though not socialist direction (that began in Britain with the spell of Green's *Lectures*) took the form of *republicanism*. Claude Nicolet, in his remarkable book, *L'Idée républicaine en France*, discerned three kinds of republican thought around 1870.[6] First, there was the romantic republicanism of the spirit of 1848. This was subdivided in turn into several political positions: neo-Girondins like Quinet; neo-Dantonists like Michelet and Victor Hugo (1802–85), the ex-*légitimiste* poet turned fierce enemy of the Second Empire; and neo-Jacobins like the socialist Louis Blanc. Second, there were spiritualist republicans like the academics Étienne Vacherot (1809–97) and Jules Simon (1814–96), who lost their chairs because they refused to take an oath of loyalty to the imperial regime.[7] In 1859 Vacherot published *La Démocratie* (meaning the republic) and Simon *La Liberté*, two bibles of left liberalism at the time. Beside Vacherot and Simon, one can put Charles Renouvier (1815–1903), a prolific nonacademic philosopher. Renouvier emerged from the battles of 1848 with a philosophical stance that shared many ethico-political tenets if not metaphysical assumptions with the spiritualist republicans. Last, as a third group, there was the positivist republicanism of Jules Ferry (1832–93) and Léon Gambetta (1838–82), republican leaders of the infant Third Republic.

From the viewpoint of liberal theory, the most interesting cases in this motley republican set are those of Simon, Renouvier, and Ferry (apart from the reinterpretations of the French Revolution by Michelet and Quinet). Simon preached universal suffrage, responsible government, and local freedoms. He was deeply hostile to revolutionism and Jacobinism, pitting the republican ideal against the insurrectional communism of Auguste Blanqui (1805–81). As for the economy, he favored competition over the *dirigisme* of Louis Blanc. Legitimate state power should be kept on a level of "least action." Though he was the author of *Radical Politics* (1868), Simon called himself a "profoundly moderate republican." Governmental power, he wrote, ought to be "strong but restricted, strong *because* restricted."

Like Simon, Jules Ferry served as a minister in the first decades of the Third Republic. Having blasted the financial dealings of Napoléon III's famous mayor of Paris in a series of articles for *Le Temps* (wittily collected as *Les Comptes fantastiques d'Haussmann*, a pun on the well-known opéra-comique *Les Contes fantastiques d'Hoffmann*), Ferry was himself appointed mayor of the capital after the fall of the empire. But his great job was what he accomplished as education minister in the 1880s, implanting the impressive network of lay schooling that, in Eugen Weber's phrase, made peasants into Frenchmen. Stemming from a Protestant bourgeois background, Ferry was an anticlerical liberal for whom state action on the social problem should be "hygienic" rather than "therapeutic": the government ought to encourage social security arrangements but without trying to remedy social needs directly.[8] He conceived of the republic as a lever of progress, moral as well as material. The republic was both an order and an ideal predicated not on natural rights but on the evolution of mind and society, as in Comte's positivism. But Ferry replaced Comte's utopia of scientific rule with liberal politics; and he conceived of the republican ethos as a sense of mission, civilizing modern society.

Ferry was more of a statesman than a theorist. Renouvier, by contrast, was nothing but an intellectual. He was born at Montpellier like Comte (and studied under him at the École Polytechnique) and died the same year as Spencer, but his cast of mind could not have been more different from either's. Renouvier was a free Kantian who believed that ethics is a matter of obligation and that duties are more important than rights. In his youth he composed a *Republican Handbook* (1848), a socialist catechism for schoolteachers. Having withdrawn from politics during the Second Empire, he published *The Science of Morals* (1869). In his view, rational man was bound to sign (so to speak) two contracts: one with himself, establishing an "inner government" of conduct; the other with his fellow moral agents, based on justice as Kantian respect—that is to say, as an obligation not to reduce others to mere means to one's own ends. In this context, socialism came to mean a rational *telos* but not a principle of social organization. In a work of political fiction, *Uchrony* (1876), which described the saga of humankind as it might have been, Renouvier equated human happiness with the wide-spread recognition of individual freedom. He fought the Catholic clericals and praised Protestantism for its emphasis on individual conscience. In his *Outline of a Systematic Classification of Philosophical Doctrines* (1886), he distinguished two kinds of philosophy: the philosophy of the thing—infinitist, naturalist, and necessitarian—and the philosophy of consciousness—finitist, personalist, and libertarian. The last two adjectives encapsulate the gist of Renouvier's ethical liberalism. It was a theorization fairly akin to the spirit of Green's idealism in England.

While in Britain the new social-minded liberalism of 1900 was spurred by civic-service institutions such as Toynbee Hall, in France the local equivalent of social liberalism—ethical republicanism—was powerfully catalyzed by the human-rights campaign launched through the Dreyfus affair (1896–98). Intellectually speaking, though, the role that Oxford philosophy played in Britain was played in France by the rising discipline of sociology. As in the English case, individualism, a mainstay of liberal thought, was far from dead in France. One might even say that it was actually strengthened in a few dimensions before it was eventually neglected in French social theory. Early and midcentury French liberals had often been indifferent to liberism, except for economists like Jean-Baptiste Say (1767–1832) and Frédéric Bastiat (1801–50), a friend of the Manchester free-traders, but it now got a wider audience. A classic of fin-de-siècle liberism, *The Modern State* (1890) by Paul Leroy-Beaulieu (1834–1916), became a best-seller.

The clash between republican intellectuals and reactionary forces in French society over the fate of Captain Dreyfus caused a split in national opinion that led many a thoughtful spirit to meditate on the moral state of modern society. The founder of the French sociological school, Émile Durkheim (1858–1917) was an upholder, not a detractor, of individualism; but as an analyst of anomie, the condition of normlessness, the moral drift in urban-industrial civilization, Durkheim sought to protect society by bolstering professional associations and more generally by extolling sundry forms of social solidarity. In the shift from Renouvier's personalism to Durkheimian solidarism, the ethic glow of late-19th-century liberalism was well preserved. The passage into socialism, if defined in terms of state control, was once more avoided, but the profile of social liberalism got neater.

The favorite politics among the Durkheimians was the liberal

socialism of Jean Jaurès (1859–1914), a Dreyfusard for whom socialism was a completion, not a denial, of individualism. But at least
one prominent member of Durkheim's school, Célestin Bouglé
(1870–1940), openly tried to put sociology at the service of liberalism. His 1902 essay "The Crisis of Liberalism" was a clever account
of the ideological situation. He realized that rightist onslaughts on
liberty on the one hand and the anarchist upsurge throughout the
1890s on the other were driving the liberals into unity-angst. Bouglé
wanted to prevent a liberal surrender to too much state authority by
showing that the social roots of modern freedom were as strong and
healthy as they were manifold. He saw in modern society a process
of value-differentiation, of end-multiplication ("polytelism"), as
much as a growing division of labor. But the proliferation of ends
did not jeopardize social unity, because many different goals could
be reached through the same means.[9] At the same time, the growth
of liberty as freedom of choice rested on a significant expansion of
equality, as Bouglé showed in a perceptive 1899 study, *Egalitarian
Ideas*. With this kind of insightful arguments, Bouglé resisted Durkheim's own concern over the alleged lost unity of modern—that is,
liberal—society. But as sociological theory as a whole took a very
different path from his liberal-democratic temper, his level-headed
sociological defense of liberalism remained largely unheeded.

One may legitimately connect Durkheimianism with liberalism,
regardless of labels, because of the school's general loyalty to individualism as the modern value matrix. At the height of the Dreyfus
affair, Durkheim himself, while taking pains to dissociate the message of sociology from the narrow, "commercialist" individualism of
Spencer, reasserted in no uncertain terms individualism as the lawful faith of modern society.[10]

Another bridge between sociology and the liberal tradition was
the Durkheimian attitude toward the state. Indeed, the reply to the
German glorification of the state was mainly due to another inde-
pendent Durkheimian, the legal theorist Léon Duguit (1859–1928).
While rejecting the master's notion of a collective consciousness,
Duguit used Durkheim's focus on civil society associations to dis-
mantle the mystique of national sovereignty and its statist aura.
Like Durkheim, he criticized Rousseau and Kant for overlooking the
social cradle and framework of individual autonomy. But in his
Treatise of Constitutional Law (1911) he inveighed against German
Staatslehre for its talk of the state as a legal subject endowed with a
higher personality. Duguit's concept of the state substituted the

function of public service for the *imperium* of sovereignty. His influence among civil servants and the moderate left in the interwar years was enormous.[11] By giving "solidarism" a legal face, he landed French republican thought in the border between social liberism and communitarianism. Perhaps a tentative label—*fringe liberalism*—would aptly describe his position, which was of great moment in the history of the intertwinements of political theory and legal philosophy.

The Cambridge legal historian Maitland may be said to have reached a similar point of arrival through a very different route. Maitland broke with the pious whig legend that corporate rights (association law, in Duguit) were linked to the premodern world of tradition and prescription.[12] Maitland learned from Gierke that this was not so. Small self-governing units were not "Teutonic" antiques—they were the creatures of modern commercial society. The conservative liberal Maine believed that corporateness was an ancient notion, reeking of *Gemeinschaft* and therefore nonindividualist. But Maitland, in studies like *Township and Borough* (1898), showed that the corporation was a much more recent concept. In so doing he helped establish a juridical basis for the institutional props of social liberalism, like trade unions and associations.

Social liberalism proper blossomed in the first years of the new century chiefly thanks to "the two Hobs," John Hobson (1858–1940) and Leonard Hobhouse (1864–1929). Hobson was a prolific essayist, writing freelance high journalism. He belonged to the left of the British liberal party, and in a defense of positive liberty not unlike Green's, he wanted government to create equal opportunity. But he grounded new liberalism in evolution instead of in Hegel, emphasizing organic growth. In *Work and Wealth* (1914) he acknowledged the evolutionary method "in all organic processes," from acorn to oak, from savage noises to the symphony, and from the primitive tribe to the modern federal state.[13] Also, in Hobson's opinion Green still had too benign a view of capitalism. Hobson, by contrast, saw the market as a source of waste and unemployment—evils for which thrift by itself was no solution. Hobson's critique of the market has often been construed as a harbinger of Keynesianism. But in fact (as Lionel Robbins noticed long ago and Peter Clarke has recalled), for Keynes the trouble arises when savings cease to become investments, whereas for Hobson the real difficulty is that investment can become excessive in regard to consumption.[14]

Hobson inherited the concept of underconsumption from a

liberist tradition harking back to Say, Ricardo's contemporary in France. In his best-known book, *Imperialism* (1902), written in reaction to the Boer War, Hobson rekindled the old liberist, Manchesterian condemnation of aggressive foreign policy and military intervention. But he also revised the Manchesterian's diagnosis. While for Cobden and Bright militarism sprang from aristocratic ambition, Hobson pointed out another cause: bad income distribution. Excessive wealth and savings led to underconsumption and therefore to imperialism as an outlet. Before the Boer conflict, Hobson and his friend Hobhouse, as new liberals, shared the collectivist outlook of the Fabians (the Webbs and Shaw). When the Webbs, like other reforming liberals such as Asquith and Haldane, came out in favor of imperialist action in South Africa, the two Hobs parted company with them.[15] Hobson's anti-imperialist protest had a streak of *Kulturpessimismus* about it—he deplored the workers' betrayal of the intellectuals in the opposition to war and the force of jingoism in advanced industrial society.

In Hobson's view the remedy was at hand: Get redistributive taxation, and you shall have consumption and justice at home together with peace abroad. His 1909 essay "The Crisis of Liberalism" was written in defense of social reform (Lloyd George's embryonic welfare state). Hobson's plea was for some public ownership of the soil, allowing for decent housing; public transport; no monopolies; a national network of public schools (in the continental sense); and a fairer legal system. Fiscal redistribution of income would do the trick, in a way not remotely like revolution; while capitalism, once regenerated and regulated, was certainly not to be replaced by an altogether different economic system.

Faithfulness to liberalism was eventually even greater in the case of the other Hob. Like Green, Hobhouse was the son of a county parson. Unlike Hobson, he was an academic and founded the first chair of sociology at the London School of Economics and Political Science in 1907. He was a "mind" evolutionist—one, that is, who stressed the emergence of higher forms of existence rather than the harshness of the survival of the fittest. Like the Saint-Simonians and the more humane anarchists, notably Kropotkin (1842–1921), he was keen to demonstrate that society advances by dint of human cooperation and the ultimate prevalence of altruism over egoism.

Hobhouse's 1911 book, *Liberalism*, became the gospel of the new dispensation by giving positive freedom in the Greenian sense an evolutionary foundation. His ideal was an organic society that provided "a living equality of rights" with plenty of chances for individual self-development to most of its members; the main institutional machinery, as in Hobson, was social welfare agencies financed by social-minded taxation. Hobhouse believed that the worst of the class struggle was over since late-Victorian wealth could afford ample distribution while responsible trade unions evinced an increasing ability to practice democracy.

As in all new liberalism, Hobhousian rights were granted by society, yet their function was to help the growth of individuality. He occupied a halfway position between Green and Mill, sensitive to the former's concept of liberty as one's right to yield "the best of oneself," yet willing to recognize that when it comes to deciding who is to be the judge of it, the only reasonable liberal way to deal with the problem is to ensure personal freedom in the Millian sense. Hobhouse tried to devise an evolutionary ethics as a basis for a free collectivism. But in fact, he showed some ambivalence toward the unions since they could act out of particularist interests instead of fostering the common good. Like Green, he saw the common good itself as a norm higher than individuals' goals, but it was not to be equated, Durkheim-wise, with any suprapersonal will. In wartime London, hearing the sound of German bombing, Hobhouse angrily took Hegel to task and wrote an entire volume, *The Metaphysical Theory of the State* (1918), as a refutation of Bernard Bosanquet (1848–1923) and other British Hegelians' tribute to the "common self."

In practice these distinguos, indicative though they were of the ability of empiricism to survive the Millian synthesis, did not amount to very much. But the conceptual path opened by Hegelian concepts like the higher self of the "ethical state" could host perfectly illiberal implications. Francis Herbert Bradley (1846–1924), the leading neoidealist, wrote a very influential essay, "My Station and Its Duties" (collected in his *Ethical Studies,* 1876), that reduced the moral self to a social self feeding on the awareness of one's humble function within the social organism. Bonsanquet, under Bradley's spell, stated that "the deepest and loftiest achievements of man do not belong to the particular human being in his repellent isolation" (preface to *The Philosophical Theory of the State*)—which was no doubt anti-individualism with a vengeance. Hobhouse's exorcism of Hegel's ghost was a timely reassertion of liberal verities.

Green and Hobhouse shared a social version, as it were, of the German concept of freedom as autotely, which as we know is compatible with but different from freedom as (political) autonomy. But Hobhouse, as the moral leader of liberalism in the Belle Époque, underwent a subtle evolution. Unlike Hobson, he did not live to see the outbreak of World War II. But after 1918 he began to fear the growing powers of the state and moved closer to both liberism and traditional political liberalism.[16] Accordingly, the German idea of liberty lost some significant ground in his thought as he made a qualified return to the Millian blend of human improvement with the classical English and French concepts of freedom as personal independence and as collective self-rule. Thus "new liberalism" drew close to classical liberalism.

All in all, the new liberalism, including the social liberalism of the two Hobs, was not very un-Millian in outlook. The new liberals wished to implement the potential for individual development that Mill had cherished after Humboldt, and in so doing they thought of law and the state as enabling institutions. This concern with positive liberty led them to go beyond the minimalist state. But they were by no means hostile as a matter of principle either to individualism or to liberism; and their civic-mindedness was already present in Tocqueville and Mill. They certainly got rid of early liberal statophobia, but they were no statists. With the benefit of hindsight, Belle Époque social liberalism looks more like classical liberalism than it does mainstream socialism—at least before socialism consciously turned into social democracy.

From Kelsen to Keynes: Left Liberalism between the Wars

In France the voice of radicalism as left liberalism was a contemporary of the two Hobs, Émile Chartier, known as Alain (1868–1951). Alain had a long career teaching philosophy at lycées, deliberately avoiding the Sorbonne. A Dreyfusard, he fought in the Great War but then became a fierce critic of bellicose nationalism, one of the Right's standard positions. In the 1920s his dislike of the republican establishment dictated books such as *Le Citoyen contre les pouvoirs* (1926) in which the singular ("the citizen") is typical: for Alain's blend of left liberalism was not, as in the two Hobs, a modulation of individualism into social concern. Rather, it was a moral attack on corrupt parliamentarianism, as the republican Chamber disgraced itself in scandal after scandal. Alain's was a rugged individualism bordering on anarchism. Democracy to him was not the noble end result of a pedagogic republicanism, as it was in Simon and Ferry; it was, more immediately, an anti-elitist strategy, a weapon against both military and political despotism. Alain's essayism offered more rage than political theory, but it was highly influential in the inter-war period and a key reading for the generation (born at the beginning of the century) of Sartre, Simone Weil, and Raymond Aron.

In Italy, left liberalism was less moralistic and more historical-minded. The early death (as an antifascist exile) of Piero Gobetti (1901–26) deprived the liberal left of an imaginative leader. In 1924, two years after the fascist March in Rome, the young Turinese Gobetti collected a few essays under the title (already given to a weekly) *The Liberal Revolution*. His historical verdicts were harsh enough: the Risorgimento had been a failure, and corrupt parliamentary politics under Giolitti, in the Belle Époque, a mere preface to fascism. As for the present, liberals and republicans—the "historical right"—were out of tune with the new times. Socialists were impotent and Communists bureaucratical, while the nationalists fell prey to an empty rhetoric. Like the Marxist Gramsci, Gobetti dreamed of an Italian social revolution, the undelivered promise of the Risorgimento. But he envisaged an Italian revolution that, unlike the French one, would be popular rather than bourgeois and yet—unlike the Russian one—liberal instead of communist.

Almost the same age as Gobetti, Carlo Rosselli (1899–1937) also died young—murdered by fascist thugs in France. His aim, as stated in *Liberal Socialism* (1928), was to rescue socialism from marxism. While Marxism had opposed socialism to liberalism, Rosselli insisted that socialism could overcome its defeat before fascism only by acting as the true heir of the liberal idea. Socialism should have liberation as a goal, and the liberal state—improvable but not relinquishable—as a means. This liberal-socialist trend nourished the ephemeral Partito dell'Azione, founded in 1942 by the academic philosopher Guido Calogero (b. 1904). It was to be the political cradle of young Norberto Bobbio, whose work we shall discuss at the close of this chapter.[17]

In the German world, left liberalism meant first and foremost a political doctrine suitable to the Weimar Republic—that fragile institutional order born of the defeat of the Wilhelmine Reich and the crushing of red socialism. The greatest name in Weimar political and juridical theory was that of an Austrian, Hans Kelsen (1881–1973), who ended his days as a professor of law at Berkeley after codifying the Austrian republican constitution (1920) and serving as justice in his country's Constitutional Court. A scion of a Jewish family from Galicia, he was teaching at Cologne when Hitler rose to power. When Kelsen published his *Reine Rechtslehre* (*Pure Theory of Law*, 1934), the dean of the Harvard Law School, Roscoe Pound, called him "unquestionably the leading jurist of the time." At the very least, he was most influential, from England to Latin America and Japan.

Kelsen restructured the tradition of legal positivism. Legal positivism brushed aside natural law by recognizing the contingency of the link between law and morality. But having severed law from ethics, the older legal positivists collapsed norms into facts, reducing rights and obligations to chance events. Kelsen, on the contrary, stressed the *normative* nature of law. In order for a demand to qualify as lawful (to be unlike, say, the command of an armed thief), such a demand has to be authorized by a legal norm based in turn upon a whole chain of further norms.

How does Kelsen's legal philosophy apply to the political sphere? The crucial concept here is that of the state, for a vital dimension of the state lies in its being an edifice of norms. In 1900, Jellinek had appropriated the neo-Kantian taste for a dualism of fact and value to propose a split-state theory: a *Rechtslehre* would deal with state as a body of law, whereas a *Soziallehre* would concern itself with the state as a social institution. Kelsen rejected this duality. In its stead, he proffered a purely juristic notion of the state: the state equated with the legal order. The reigning neo-Kantian in the interwar years, Ernst Cassirer, had taught the distinction between substance concepts and function concepts. Thus the atom, said Cassirer discussing modern physics, is not, properly speaking, any substantial core—it is just a *Funktionsbegriff,* a functional concept used by scientific analysis. Likewise, the Kelsenian state is simply a useful logical idea: the concept of the unity of the legal system.

Kelsen made much of epistemological modernization: he tried to ground his legal and political theory on new approaches to knowledge. After the 1880s Austrian epistemology, thanks to Ernst Mach (1838–1916), was recommending the replacement of causal concepts by *Funktionsbegriffen.* Kelsen saw Marxism as a causalist, naturalistic program for social science, all the more dubious because of its Hegelian historicist inheritance. Marxism compounded the anachronism of postulating causal essentialism with a mystique of historical prophecy. This much was suggested by Kelsen in a powerful critique, *Socialism and the State* (1920). Marxists mistook the relations between state and society in two ways. First, they reduced the state to the expression of social forces, thereby making a paradox of their famous plea for the eventual abolition of the state. Secondly, Marxists erred in claiming that there was a contradiction (*Widerspruch*) between state and society. For society is to the state what a broader concept is to a narrower one, like "mammal" to "man." The relationship, therefore, is of distinction and implication, not of contradiction: it is a *Gegensatz*, not a *Widerspruch*.

Kelsen also fought the views of the antiliberal right, notably the writings of the Rhenish jurist Carl Schmitt (1888–1987). Schmitt detected an overlap between state and society. In his 1931 work *Der Hüter der Verfassung* (*The Guardian of the Constitution*, 1931), he claimed that while the liberal institutions of the nineteenth century were unchanged, the actual sociopolitical situation had been deeply altered. A major change was precisely that one could no longer discern the political from the social. Society had become state as the modern state increasingly acted as an economic agency, a welfare state, a source of culture, and so on. From the absolutist state of the seventeenth and eighteenth centuries and the "neutral state" of the following century, there had been a shift, in European politics, to the "total state." In Schmitt's eyes, the total state, in turn, ought to be totally politicized, with few liberal-constitutional boundaries.[18]

For Kelsen, by contrast, the state is and remains a specific group within society, the association for domination (*Herrschaftsverband*). But as a *lawful* system of rule, the state reflects the nature of a legal order that, as positive law, regulates its own creation. The legal system as state denotes a process whereby norms grow more and more concrete, ending up in specific instructions issued by authorized individuals (the state agents). In a paper published in 1922 in Freud's journal *Imago*, Kelsen availed himself of psychoanalysis's mass psychology in order to stress that Freud rightly distinguished between the primitive, transitory mass, which blindly followed chieftains (like the primal horde in *Totem and Taboo*, 1912), and the artificial, stable masses, which replace the leader by an abstract principle. For Kelsen, the state presupposes the second, *institutional* kind of mass and corresponds to a full normative specification of its leading principle.

Nomogenesis—the process of norm making—is crucial to Kelsen. In 1920, the same year he first published *Sozialismus und Staat* (*Socialism and the State*), he printed a classic among modern statements on democracy, *Von Wesen und Wert der Demokratie* (*Of the Essence and Value of Democracy*). Democracy, according to Kelsen, is a particular kind of nomogenesis: harking back to the Kantian distinction between autonomy and heteronomy, Kelsen singled out the way constitutions regulate the production of norms in a given state or legal system. When the addressees of such norms take no part in their elaboration, the system is heteronomous. When they do, the system is autonomous. Politically, heteronomy means autocracy, and autonomy means democracy. Democracy, insofar as it implies the principle of self-rule, is a process of autonomous nomogenesis.

In the 1920s, Kelsen also made clear that liberal democracy is the fruit of a relativist outlook. Political pluralism implies a modicum of recognition of perspectivism, of less-than-absolute beliefs, he argued. Pluralist democracy is the proper polity in a culture marked by what Weber famously called "the polytheism of values." Thus Kelsen—the left liberal for the troubled Weimar years—added an epistemological argument to his enlightened juridical defense of the democratic state.[19]

Woodrow Wilson (1856–1924) is a name not normally entered in encyclopedias of political thought, but he changed the temper of American liberalism. The founding fathers had conceived of the republican social contract as a means of solving or composing reasonable conflicts of interests. Wilson may be said to be the first great American leader who became dissatisfied with this sensible ideal of utilitarian consensus. As a prominent academic, he introduced into American politics what campus ideology would so cherish half a century later: the ethics of conviction, the politics of principle. His dream of leadership democracy cleared the ground for the patrician reformism of the second Roosevelt.

Wilson's actual program, "The New Freedom," which was formulated with the help of Justice Louis Brandeis and earned Wilson the White House in 1912, avoided the attack on capitalism by concentrating its fire on the big trusts. Wilson lambasted the "special interests" of big business and promised laws for the rising men against those already on the top—a fine political reprise of the American Dream, without the harshness of class conflict that was still present in the Populist movement. Even the utopianism of his international stance at the Versailles peace conference was at one with the ultimate traditionalism of his political views: for as Richard Hofstadter has seen, just as the Wilsonian prospect of competition without monopoly reverted to midcentury capitalism, his pacifism after 1918 was aimed at restoring the world power balance disrupted by the war.[20]

On a strictly theoretical plane, the leftward shift in American liberalism owes more to another contemporary academic, John Dewey (1859–1952). An outstanding educationalist, Dewey moved to the newly founded University of Chicago in his early thirties and there launched his famous Laboratory School. At the beginning of the century, he went to Columbia. He was a trial-and-error pragmatist for whom perfecting rather than perfection was the goal, and an eloquent if sometimes facile critic of philosophy's remoteness from the world of action. He transformed the occasional dalliance of classical liberalism (like Mill's) with socialist tenets into a stronger sympathy. His books, notably *Democracy and Education* (1916) and *Freedom and Culture* (1939), helped leftists like Sidney Hook to get rid of Marxist dogma without dropping socialist leanings.

The theory of impulse in *Human Nature and Conduct* (1922), a treatise on social psychology, was the summit of Dewey's pragmatism. For Dewey, truth is efficacy. All reality is relative to man, and all human ends are immanent, with no beyond and no absolute. He designed his pragmatism as an "instrumentalism" in order to emphasize that conduct and knowledge are but instruments of adaptation to experience, and of transformations thereof. Reading Hegel taught him a sense of interrelatedness as well as a highly dynamic view of reality. Dewey set out to challenge the "classic tradition," from Plato to the modern syndrome of empiricism and utilitarianism. The classic tradition assumed the universe to be essentially fixed and changeless, while in knowledge it privileged individual contemplation. Yet for Dewey "criticism," meaning the application of the sense of adaptation to problems of conduct, consisted in a process of inquiry by which one chooses the kind of action able to transform a troubling situation into an integrated condition. Criticism is thus preeminently a social activity, a sustained method of intelligent exchange.[21]

Morals and politics are therefore as social as they are experimental. The highest human good is the growth of such collective adaptation. Human nature is social from the start, though by no means less individualized for that. Dewey's 1930 book *Individualism Old and New* scolded the "pecuniary culture" of our age as a "perversion" of perfective individualism; thus he maintained the value of individuality while rejecting its antithesis to society. It is easy to see why, if morals and politics are so conceived, liberal democracy of a strong reformist cast of mind became the most legitimate polity for Dewey. What Kelsen came to value in the name of value pluralism, Dewey extolled as the regime best suited to the reality of change.

In 1938 he put his healthy instrumentalism to good use in a short polemic with Trotsky. Early that year, the great Soviet exile wrote an essay entitled "Their Morals and Ours." It was, among other things, a belated defense of Trotsky's much-criticized attitude during the 1921 Kronstadt rebellion. There are no moral criteria, argued Trotsky, outside history and independent of social man. Unless one sticks to religious, otherworldly absolutes, one must acknowledge that morality is a product of social development. But this does not license a vulgar Machiavellianism. On the contrary, not *every* end is legitimate. Rather, it has to be justified itself. Therefore, the conclusion of Trotsky's essay was devoted to claim the superiority of the marxist end—the liberation of mankind.

Dewey accepted Trotsky's starting point—the rejection of absolutist ethics, religious or not. In his reply, "Means and Ends," published in the same journal, *The New International*, Dewey stressed that the end, in the sense of consequences, provides the sole criteria for morals. But if means are justified insofar as they lead to proper ends, it is all the more necessary to examine each means very carefully in order to fully determine what would be its consequences. And this was exactly what Trotsky had failed to do. Extolling class struggle and even revolutionary terror as a means to human liberation, Trotsky had *prejudged* the means in an aprioristic way. For there is no self-evident reason for declaring class struggle the only means to achieve the substantial betterment of the human plight.[22] Dewey's reply was a quiet logical victory of pragmatism over revolutionary dogma.

With the coming of the war, the central figure in left liberalism for the English-speaking world was neither Dewey nor Kelsen, but John Maynard Keynes (1883–1946). Not the philosopher-educationalist and not the jurist but the economist redesigning political economy became the main reference of liberalism rebuilt. In his *Essays in Persuasion* (1931), Keynes wrote that "the political problem of mankind is to combine three things: economic efficiency, social justice, and individual liberty." The last tenet shows the survival strength of Millian concerns even after half a century of social-liberal qualifications. The second just proved that Depression new liberals were not to relinquish the humane, humanitarian, and humanistic preoccupations of the Hobhouse-Duguit-

Dewey generation (the social liberal masters who had been born around 1860). But the first element—economic efficiency—was a bitter lesson from the traumas of world war and world depression.

Keynes gave orthodox liberism its quietus with his 1926 book, *The End of Laissez-Faire*. But already in 1919, as the chief representative of the British Treasury at the Paris Peace Conference, he came radically to disagree with the Allied policy of overburdening Germany; he stated in *The Economic Consequences of the Peace* that Victorian capitalism had been only a special case, capitalism being normally fragile and unstable. By the midtwenties, Keynes realized that Leninist power was historically out to destroy capitalism (in spite of the compromising tactics of the NEP) and that fascism sacrificed democracy in order to save capitalist society. There remained a third option, which was to save democracy by refurbishing capitalism. It came to be known and practiced as "Keynesianism."

Keynes's economic revisionism stemmed from something larger than economic and political considerations: it was deeply connected with a revolution in morals. John Maynard belonged to a brilliant generation of Cambridge scholars (he was taught by the great economist Marshall and by A. C. Pigou) determined to embark on a daring denial of Victorian morals. They looked at themselves as "immoralists" and inspired the so-called Bloomsbury group, the London literary circle of Virginia Woolf and E. M. Forster.

At the dawn of the century, in Cambridge, the philosopher G. E. Moore (1873–1958) had undermined traditional ethics. In his influential *Principia Ethica* (1903), he stated that "good" bears no definition short of various forms of a "naturalistic fallacy." He then suggested that bliss is to be found in "certain states of consciousness . . . as the pleasures of human intercourse and the enjoyment of beautiful objects." As Keynes's mate, Lytton Strachey, was quick to notice, this threw by the board classical ethics and Christianity, along with Kant, Mill, Spencer, and Bradley, to say nothing of conventional sexual morality.[23] Like Strachey, the young Keynes was not above locating "the pleasures of human intercourse" in homosexual adventures. In full reaction against the Victorian ethos, they downgraded conduct and exalted exactly what their ascetic, philistine ancestors, who had been stern Protestant dissenters, had dutifully avoided: personal relationships and aesthetic experiences. Virginia Woolf's grandfather, Sir James Stephen, had been a typical Victorian; he was said to have once tasted a cigar and found it so delicious that he never smoked it again. Now the Cambridge and Bloomsbury immoralists decided to indulge in sinful pleasure with a vengeance.

Keynes's socialist contemporaries, the Fabians like the Webbs and George Bernard Shaw, blamed social evils on capitalism. Keynes blamed to a psycho-cultural cause, the Puritan ethic. His *General Theory of Employment, Interest and Money* (1936) addressed the problem of unemployment by subverting economic doctrine. Keynes basically accepted Marshall's microeconomics, but he complemented microeconomics—value, or price theory—with a new degree of attention to general levels of income, output, and employment. Influenced by Marshall's idea that in explaining booms and slumps monetary analysis has to be separated from other areas of economics, he took the level of income, as a dependent variable, as the crucial issue. Challenging the conventional equation of saving with investment, he showed that saving, apart from being often less important to investment than credit, could stay in excess regarding the need for investment.

At the core of classical economics was Say's Law, which stated that supply creates its own demand. Translation: All income is spent; money not spent on consumer goods is saved yet not hoarded, since no rational owner of savings would wish to hold balance yielding no income. Keynes, however, showed that in some circumstances money is hoarded, if only because it is not just a medium of exchange but also an amount of value for speculative purposes (a means of acquiring assets in the future). Thus, left to itself, the savings rate would not mean high investment, bringing about the reduction of unemployment. Therefore, Keynes proposed "the euthanasia of the rentier" and "a somewhat comprehensive socialization of investment," as capitalism's creative response to the socialist insistence on the socialization of production. As has been noticed, Keynes's prescription was for the state to control expenditure and demand rather than ownership and supply. Besides, focusing on aggregate demand did much to defuse class struggle, since a vigorous demand would lead to both high profits and full employment with rising wages.

Keynes's diagnosis was very British indeed. The peculiarities of the situation—the key role of money, the near absence of investment and capital accumulation—were British traits. It has been said that although Keynes liked to think of himself as having buried Ricardian economics, he was merely adapting it. What Ricardo had mainly done was to analyze how the outcome of the rivalry between landowners and industrialists determines the rate of capital accumulation. Anti-City Keynes replaced the landowner by the financier and focused on the level of employment instead of on the rate of accumulation.[24]

But Keynesianism projected Keynes's short-term analysis (his theory was lacking in trade cycles and lags) into a long-term recipe for growth and development, resting on doubtful assumptions about demand and consumption. Keynes himself overrated the rationality of economic policies enacted by democratic governments—he overlooked, in a word, what Samuel Brittan has graphically called "the economic consequences of democracy," the many distortions brought about by interest-group pressures able to prevail, or to block, in the democratic political market.[25] Keynes did not want government to invade the microeconomic sphere. But so it did, often in his name, acting directly on wages and prices. Keynes traced slumps to the hoarding instincts of a rentier class. Yet Milton Friedman, scrutinizing the monetary history of the United States between the victory over the Confederates and the Eisenhower years, found that instability had been chiefly connected with zigzags in the money *supply*—hence with governmental behavior rather than anything else.

Keynes's paradox is this: while they had been earning incredible profits, Victorian capitalists had invested rather than consumed; and when workers were most miserable, they had complied instead of revolting. None of this subsists, as a rule, in modern, post-Keynesian capitalism. Self-restraint is over. Nowadays the public sector itself, with its bureaucratic armies, lobbies for increased governmental spending, further fueling the "fiscal crisis of the state." Ironically, the recipes of Keynes the anti-Puritan worked only as long as the Puritan ethic—meaning asceticism and forbearance—was a living force in capitalist society.

Karl Popper and a Few Postwar Liberal Moralists

Technically, Sir Karl Popper (b. 1902) is not a political philosopher but a stern critic of political philosophies associated with a particular belief—*historicism*. Historicism may be broadly described as the theory of the logic, or global meaning, of history. Popper, however, defines it as an approach to social science whose goal is *prediction*. Such an approach he finds intellectually untenable and morally repellent. The dedication of his 1957 monograph, *The Poverty of Historicism*, reads: "To the countless men and women of all creeds or nations or races who fell victims to the fascist and communist belief in the Inevitable Laws of Historical Destiny." Popper himself, the brilliant son of well-to-do Lutheran Jews from Vienna, had been a maverick member of the so-called Vienna Circle of logical positivists led by Moritz Schlick (1882–1936) and Rudolf Carnap (1891–1971) when he fled Austria shortly before the Nazi *Anschluss*. Already the author of a classic of modern epistemology, *The Logic of Scientific Discovery* (1934), he spent the war in New Zealand, and in 1945 joined the faculty of the London School of Economics and Political Science.

In *The Poverty of Historicism*, as in his previous lengthy contribution to social theory, *The Open Society and Its Enemies* (1945), Popper tried to establish a link between historicism and totalitarianism. He saw marxism, in particular, as an economic historicism providing the worldview for a totalitarian utopia. Popper's point was that the totalitarian revolutionisms of our century, for all their claims to radical novelty, are at bottom political monsters based on deeply archaic intellectual roots. The *Logic of Scientific Discovery* painted critical rationalism as the readiness to stick one's neck out, facing the risk of *falsification*. Unlike the Vienna neopositivists, Popper deemed falsifiability, not verification, to be the criterion of scientific knowledge.

The "open society" is the social analogon of this intellectual daring. It is a free-thinking culture, highly individualistic, in which people bear responsibility for each other's decisions. Popper's open society is in fact a more individualistic version of Dewey's "criticism" as a way of life. The opposite of the open society is *tribalism*, the social spaces dominated by dogma instead of scientific testing. The projection of the tribalist spirit onto thought breeds false beliefs like historicism, which Popper holds to be false because it asserts general laws about a phenomenon—the whole historical process— that is unique by definition.

Inasmuch as the Popperian critique harbors a justification of a certain kind of society and politics, it is patently a consequentialist defense of liberal democracy—something not very far from Mill's position in *On Liberty*. Fighting totalitarian "final solutions," Popper preached "piecemeal social engineering." But the reformist bent of Popperian politics is unmistakable, even if his cautious tone conveys a note or two of disillusioned prudence. Thus he constantly writes of the need for eliminating misery instead of the vain attempt at maximizing happiness. His is a humanitarian minimalism, frustrating the generous scope of Benthamite democracy. But in fact Popper's caution is more epistemological than social. There is nothing in the essence of the open society to prevent wide-ranging social reform, provided one proceeds with a neat cost-benefit consciousness. The oft-quoted quip that Popper is a revolutionist in science but a shy reformist in society seems to me groundless.

It is true, however, that Popper keeps his idea of democracy too close to a narrow procedural notion, not unlike Joseph Schumpeter's famous redefinition (democracy is less a method of self-rule than a competitive struggle for the people's vote). Popper's democracy is above all a means for changing power without violence. And just as we should try to minimize misery rather than maximize happiness, we should ask, not how can we get good rulers, but rather how can we minimize the damages rulers may cause. Popper also highlighted the "paradox of democracy"—the fact that democracy can commit suicide by electing tyranny, as it did at the sad end of the Weimar Republic.

Popper remains chiefly an epistemologist, a theorist of science and (in his later work, like *Objective Knowledge*, 1972) of evolution, both natural and human. His work has little to offer by way of an analysis of the structure of politics or the nature of authority. Some critics have pointed out that his scientific analogy for dealing with social problems is weak, since social issues, unlike scientific queries, normally don't exist in isolation and therefore cannot be dealt with in a spirit of detached objectivity.[26] Criticism may also be directed against the core of Popper's position, his claims about historicism and totalitarianism. Lord Quinton has done just so. Reassessing the three main enemies of the open society according to Popper—Plato, Hegel, and Marx—Quinton finds that none of them was a totalitarian (at most Plato and Hegel were authoritarians); that Plato was only very marginally a historicist; and that though Hegel definitely was one, his authoritarianism does not derive from his historicism.[27] All these points seem to me rather well taken.

The same year Popper published *The Open Society* (1945), there also appeared *Animal Farm*, the first political fable by George Orwell (1903–50), the pen name of Eric Blair. It told the story of a good animals' revolution that is ghastly betrayed by Stalinist pigs. Although he reached a larger public with this book, Orwell had been polemicizing with the Left—and *within* the Left—for almost a decade.

Born in India into what he called "the lower-upper middle class"—that is, the upper middle class without money—Orwell had an Etonian upbringing but failed to get into the Oxbridge world. He was a policeman in Burma until 1927, which only made him into an anti-imperialist. Thereafter he led the life of an impecunious free writer, taking several menial jobs and living occasionally among tramps, including a spell in a Parisian slum. The book portraying these experiences, *Down and Out in Paris and London* (1933) showed his genius for fiction journalism and for the moral grasp of social predicaments. *The Road to Wigan Pier* (1937) painted the plight of unemployment and announced his conversion to socialism (between Burma and his lumpen years he had described himself as a tory anarchist). Then Orwell went to Spain at war, on the republican side. He came back with a book—*Homage to Catalonia* (1938)—that openly defied the Stalinist bid for domination of the Left. During World War II he maintained this independent leftist position, helping Aneurin Bevan edit *Tribune*. In *The Lion and the Unicorn,* he exalted a radical tradition of patriotism, only too happy to steal the Union Jack from conservative and imperialist hands.

But Orwell's world fame rests on his blasting of Communist cant. His second political fiction, *Nineteen Eighty-four* (1949), became the classic modern dystopia, the perfect cautionary tale about totalitarian tendencies operating in the name of Communist redemptionism. In particular, Orwell's debunking of Newspeak—the unabashed intellectual dishonesty involved in the party's "noble lies"—remains unforgettable, a wonderful feat of *Ideologiekritik.* And his essays took up many liberal themes: censorship, violence, obfuscating language.

Orwell believed that the "destruction of the Soviet myth" was of the utmost importance. Did it make him a liberal? Here we have a problem of self-definition. The mature Orwell always thought of himself as a democratic socialist, in those very words. His views were much akin to D. H. Lawrence's revulsion against modern industrial civilization, certainly a serious departure from the world-view of mainstream liberalism. On the other hand Orwell never had traditionalist leanings. All his life he wrote as an egalitarian libertarian, much closer to the popular liberalism of William Cobbett than to anything belonging either to the conservative or whig patrician ethos or to the new technocratic elitism of the Fabians. He was above all a fierce lifelong critic of all elitisms—including, of course, the elitism of radical intellectuals.[28]

In one vital aspect Orwell was very much a liberal: his love of unbridled individualism. In *Inside the Whale* (1941) he wrote that the novel is practically a Protestant form of art because it is the product of the autonomous individual. It was from such a standpoint—a central value shared by Locke and Mill, Hobhouse and Keynes—that Orwell's crystal-clear prose displayed his irresistible moral criticism of socialist ideocracy. The typical socialist, wrote he, is "a prim little man with a white-collar job," usually a teetotaler and a vegetarian. The point was not, of course, to suggest that self-righteousness is endemic to socialists but to show how priggish the mentality of some self-appointed liberators of mankind can be. Predictably, several of them tried to downgrade the mature Orwell as a prejudiced cold warrior and a decadent bourgeois—and this kind of exercise surfaced opportunistically in 1984.[29] Perhaps the best reply to such bouts of bad faith among radical-chic intellectuals is quietly to recall the unflinching popularity of Orwell in Eastern Europe. All in all, Orwell was no theorist and formally not a liberal—but liberalism cannot dispense with the ethical verve of his libertarianism.

Also crystal clear was very much of the prose of the novelist, playwright, and essayist Albert Camus (1913–60), the French pendant to Orwell as a liberal-minus-the-label moralist. A *"pied noir"* (a colonial French from North Africa), Camus spent a fatherless childhood in a working-class district of Algiers. But during the Occupation, the bright young man was already writing for the Resistance newspaper *Combat*.

In 1942, Camus published a long essay, "The Myth of Sisyphus," exhorting modern, godless man to face the challenge of the absurd. The core of the absurd was of course mortality, and Camus, on account of this and his outstanding novel *The Stranger* (1942), was soon classified among the existentialists. Yet his was less an existentialism like Sartre's, stressing the ceaseless if futile restlessness of human consciousness, than a return to pagan morals. Camus extolled the Midi, the spirit of the Mediterranean: lucidity and sensuousness, a sense of tragedy and a taste for measure. "No man is a hypocrite in his pleasures," wrote he in his last, posthumous novel, *The Fall* (1956). Death and the sun—such was Camus's existential arena. In 1957, at 44, he became the youngest Nobel Prize winner since Kipling.

In the 1950s, in what he himself called his second cycle, the moralist in him, not unlike Orwell, engaged a polemic against marxism, which was by then the tidal wave in French intellectualdom. Camus saw Marxist historicism as an alibi, a pseudoscientific escape from the burden of freedom. In "The Rebel" (1951), his second major essay, he declared that Plato had been right, against Nietzsche. For history has no conscience, and consequently we have to look elsewhere if we are to find criteria for the humanity of our actions and institutions. Stalinists and Sartrean existentialists seemed to him all prisoners of history—which led to a bitter quarrel with the group of *Les Temps Modernes*, Sartre's prestigious journal. The rift was soon compounded by the impact of the Algerian tragedy. Sartre and his followers supported the root-and-branch anticolonialism of writers like Franz Fanon (1925–61); Camus, torn between "justice and his mother," personal loyalty and democratic principle, eventually chose a silence self-righteously condemned by the Parisian left.

Camus gladly acknowledged Marx's role in stirring up our social bad consciousness. But he warned that no true dialectic could ever assert either an end of or an end to history. Revolutionary idealism led to slogans and hence to Terror, indifferent to human suffering. Better to have *revolt* than revolution: the clean, undeluded effort to say no to the absurdity of life and the evils of society. This was what "solar thought" recommended, instead of the mist of revolutionary faith. Octavio Paz, the great Mexican writer, later resumed and enriched this antithesis between the historicism of revolution and the presentist ethics of revolt. Camus was indeed Orwell-like in his longing for an independent left position and above all in his gift for seeing through the rhetoric of revolution. In his remarkable 1950 play *Les Justes* (*The Just Assassins*) the revolutionaries are bourgeois characters who seek not so much justice as self-justification. We still need this kind of moral realism.[30]

The Latin world in the postwar decades counted at least one more distinguished liberal moralist: Salvador de Madariaga (1886–1978). Much older than Camus and even Orwell, Madariaga was a prolific Spanish man of letters who helped establish the League of Nations. A moderate republican, he published in 1937 a political essay, *Anarchy or Hierarchy*, that offered the historical wisdom of a disillusioned conservative liberal. In older European times, thought he, the state had been like a plant. But the modern state, the child of the English, American, and French revolutions, was grounded on the principle of contract. The problem was that democracy, to be stable, needed to be organic: not just the sum of fleeting opinions but the ripe fruit of a living together. As for plebiscites, they were wrong because they rest on the mass, not on the organic nation—and also, no doubt, because liberal don Salvador was horrified by their abuse in fascist hands. Madariaga's political testament was *De la angustia a la libertad* (*From Anguish to Freedom*, 1955). It criticized the excessive reliance of Victorian liberalism on the eventual natural harmony of individual egoisms. The fascist furies and the Communist bulldozers took advantage of the resulting vacuum. Therefore, one should drop universal suffrage and build a general federalism in its stead, a pyramid of associations both local and industrial. It was organicism again, in a rather wistful mood.

Britain's liberal moralist was not British born. Oxford's Sir Isaiah Berlin, born in 1909, comes from a Jewish family from Riga that settled in England in the aftermath of the Russian Revolution. In the war years he served at the British Embassy in Washington, where his reports drew the attention of no less than Churchill. In 1946, posted in Moscow, he left the foreign office to lead a long and distinguished academic life at All Souls College. His work in the history of ideas, especially on thinkers like Marx, Vico, Herder, and Herzen, is a performance of its own. Berlin helped rescue Oxford philosophy from the hair-splitting of linguistic analysis; he was not afraid of asking some big "metaphysical" questions again.

In 1953 Berlin gave a famous lecture on historical inevitability.[31] The brunt of his attack was not very different from Popper's antihistoricist stance: the search for predictive laws in history seemed to him misleading, and believing in historical destiny resulted in an atrophy of the sense of responsibility. While Popper had stressed the epistemological flaws of historicism, Berlin—writing a few years before the publication of *The Poverty of Historicism*—stressed the moral side of the problem. His best-known contribution to political theory is another lecture, "Two Concepts of Liberty" (1958), which codified for the Anglo-Saxon world the distinction between *negative* and *positive* freedom, or freedom *from* and freedom *to*.[32] As we saw in Chapter 1, Berlin equated negative liberty with absence of coercion and positive liberty with the pursuit of rational ends—which in his view opens the way to a fateful further equation, that of freedom with reason.

Berlin claimed that from Plato to Marx there prevailed in Western thought the notion of the universe as an intelligible whole ruled by a single principle, with the implication that man should order his life, social as well as personal, in agreement with such unitary cosmic structure. Berlin pointedly questioned such value objectivism. Like Weber, he thought that ultimate meanings are not *there;* they are given—or imposed—by man on the world. Moreover, the universe is irredeemably plural; hence the second mistake of the Western philosophical tradition—its *monism*. Rejecting this moral monism predicated on a hierarchy of values, Berlin preferred to enlarge on Machiavelli, who had faced the impossibility of reconciling the pagan ethic of *virtù* and *fortuna* with the Christian morality of otherworldliness. Value pluralism, insisted Berlin, is unavoidable—and therefore so are conflict and choice. In his view the trouble with "positive liberty" conceptions is that by trying to redesign all values as aspects of a given "rational freedom," they lapse into moral monism—and often, in its name, into authoritarian practices, no matter how noble their original purpose.

Berlin is an eloquent libertarian. Like Popper, Orwell, and Camus, he has little to say on the institutional side of liberty. Looked at in historical perspective, positive liberty in the general sense of freedom *to* deserves a kinder judgment than it gets from Berlin. To Sir Isaiah, the long, massive modern "pursuit of happiness" is at bottom "a hankering after status and recognition" distinct from (though not unrelated to) either of the two freedoms. Yet who would deny that the conquest of increasing entitlements, the multiplication of life chances, and the breakaway from tribal and traditional bounds have been largely experienced by millions as an enjoyment of freedom? In historical practice, the hunger for recognition is almost inseparable from both the sense of personal achievement and the feeling of getting rid of fetters.[33] If this is so, there is a sociological account of freedom that defies Berlin's antithesis.

Interestingly enough, the most remarkable work of liberal ethics since Rawls, Joseph Raz's recent *The Morality of Freedom* (1987), restates value pluralism, stressing the incommensurability of value so emphasized by Berlin. Yet Raz's treatise, in a very un-Berlinian move, combines the approval of value pluralism with a cogent defense of autonomy, of *positive* freedom. Raz finds autonomy precious because many different ways of life are worth living, as Mill and Berlin, deep admirers of human variety, both knew. Raz's distinguished contribution to this school of moral thought consists in severing the praise for variety based on autonomy from too individualistic a view of human skills and achievements, and in severing the advocacy of civil liberty from its Millian utilitarian premises. For the historian of ideas, Raz's work gives an ironic twist to Berlin's pet ideas. What Berlin kept wide apart—value pluralism and positive liberty—Raz has ingeniously united.[34]

Neoliberalism as Neoliberism:
Mises to Hayek and Public Choice Theory

According to Walther Rathenau, the end of old Europe in 1914–18 meant that thereafter "the economy became fate."[35] In the interwar years, there were two main reactions to the threat of economic institutional hegemony: one was state socialism, which tried to put an end to the "anarchy of production," and the other was fascism, an attempt to harness capitalism into the spell of nationalism or racism. Yet in the long run the economy prevailed. Half a century after the rise of Hitler's and Stalin's autocracies, conquering states either perished or fared distinctly worse than *trading* states.[36] Politics, of course, does go on, but it does not throttle the autonomous thrust of economic forces.

The earliest theoretical challenges to the antieconomic reaction were due to an Austrian, Ludwig von Mises (1881–1973). His 1922 book *Die Gemeinwirtschaft* (*The Communal Economy*; translated as *Socialism*) provided essential ammunition against the fashionable trends favoring an overregulation of the economy. Mises was attracted to economics by the works of Carl Menger (1840–1921), a founder, with Jevons, Walras, and Marshall, of the neoclassical school. The young Mises attended the antebellum seminar of Eugen von Bohm-Bawerk, a formidable critic of Marx. The core chapter of Mises's *Socialism* was a fierce critique of the socialist utopia of economic calculation, dispensing with the market. In 1927, Mises published a volume entitled in German *Liberalismus,* but whose essence is best conveyed by the English translation: *Liberalism in the Classical Tradition*. It was very hostile to Mill. In his scholarly treatise on money, Mises coined the term *catallactic* to denote exchange phenomena—the soul of the market.

Mises's disciple, Friedrich August von Hayek (b. 1899) transformed the catallactic into a worldview. But he went explicitly beyond Mises by stressing (in his preface to *Socialism*) that it was not "rational insights into its general benefits that led to the spreading of the market economy." This is pure Hayek: like Adam Ferguson and Adam Smith, he thinks that progress derives from man's actions but not from man's design.

Born in Vienna, Hayek attained a chair at the London School of Economics in 1931, thence to Chicago in 1950, and eventually to Freiburg in 1960. In 1974, already retired, he was awarded the Nobel Prize for economics. His *Pure Theory of Capital* (1941) reflected the anti-Keynes animus of LSE economics (where, curiously enough, political science at the time was under the leftist spell of Laski). In 1944 Hayek, swimming against the current, published *The Road to Serfdom*, in which he indicted planning and the welfare state as leading to tyranny. Keynes declared himself in "broad sympathy" with the sentiments animating the book, which only shows how little had he departed from the liberal faith. But Hayek's prognosis was obviously far-fetched. Ironically, his own later strictures against democracy can be read as a refutation of *The Road*'s thesis. If unimpeded democracy, as he now thinks, militates against the market, at least it obviously survived rather than perished during the long growth of the welfare state.

Hayek's full book on political theory came out in 1960 under the title *The Constitution of Liberty*. A treatise in the classic form, it openly defied the analytic tabooing of political philosophy. It set market and progress into an evolutionist framework. Hayek went on to present the market as an unrivaled system of information: prices, wages, profits high or low are mechanisms distributing information among economic agents otherwise unable to know, since the colossal mass of economically significant facts is bound to escape them. State intervention is bad because it makes the information network of the price system emit misleading signals, besides reducing the scope of economic experimentation. As for progress, it obtains through a myriad of trial-and-error attempts by humans, for social evolution proceeds by "the selection by imitation of successful institutions and habits."[37] Generalizing his insight on the role of the market, Hayek held that human problems as a whole are too complex and changing to be mastered in a "constructivist" way by the human intellect. Such rationalism is a big mistake, though it has been fostered since the French Revolution by so many blueprints for the perfect society. Like the liberal conservative Michael Oakeshott, his contemporary at the London School,[38] Hayek put *cosmos*, or spontaneous, crescive order, well above *taxis*—the willed arrangements of rationalist utopias.

In the 1970s Hayek reinforced these views in an impressive trilogy, *Law, Legislation and Liberty* (1973–79), "a new statement of the liberal principles of justice and political economy." Hayek's summa harbors many good things, including a fascinating attack on Kelsen apropos the concept of justice. It contains a hearty reassertion of liberism. The only two functions of legitimate government are, according to Hayek, "to provide a framework for the market, and to provide services that the market cannot provide." This, by the way, shows that Hayek, for all his determinate dismissal of "the mirage of social justice," did not just go back to pure laissez-faireism or to the night-watchman state.

Law, Legislation and Liberty also reasserted what came to be known as the thesis of the indivisibility of liberty, thanks to another Chicago star, economist Milton Friedman (b. 1912). The claim is that unless you get or keep economic freedom, the other freedoms—civil and political—vanish. In *Capitalism and Freedom* (1962), Friedman argued that by dispersing power, the play of the market offsets concentrations of political might. Now, the liberist state shuns by definition every trend to put economic power in the state's political hands. The lesson is clear: Liberism may not be a sufficient condition, but is certainly a *necessary* condition of global liberty—such is the great Chicagoan message.

I was privileged to be present at the Reform Club's centennial dinner. (In its rooms, let it be said in passing, Lord Beveridge drew his famous report, the Magna Charta of the British welfare state, something far more liberal in the original conception than in its present state.) The board of directors of our venerable institution, the social home of Macaulay and Gladstone, had the brilliant idea of choosing as speaker a distinguished member who in fact was himself commemorating 50 years of membership that very summer. He was, of course, F. A. Hayek, sprightly as ever at 84. He began by telling us how big a part of his intellectual efforts in his Vienna youth had consisted in freeing himself from the spell of Marx and Freud.

Indeed, the third tome of *Law, Legislation and Liberty* ends with a critique of the constructivism of Marxism and of the latent anarchism of Freudianism. In regard to the latter's impact (despite Freud's own misgivings in later essays like "Civilization and Its Discontents"), Hayek worries about the thoughtless undoing of repression in the name of psychological health, ending up in our permissive age with "non-domesticated savages who represent themselves as alienated from something they have never learnt, and even undertake to construct a 'counter-culture.' "[39] In Hayek's view, in order to create and maintain a social order susceptible of constant growth and frequent improvement, people not only must submit to instinctual sacrifices, but also have to drop "many sentiments that were food for the small band," such as innate tendencies to act together in pursuit of common goals. For civilization, says Hayek, is an "abstract society," resting far more on learned rules than on pursuing common objects. The working of its best embodiment on an evolutionary account—the market—implies a respect for rules, but not any spontaneous solidarity.[40]

The macrohistorical meaning of this stands all too clearly: primitive man must be seen as *oversocialized*—a chummy fellow, but too gregarious, no matter how violent—and as such, unfit for the cold manipulation of rules that distinguishes members of the abstract society. Therefore, the march of civilization presupposes, besides instinctual control, a good measure of distance from "tribal" feelings, from community and commonality, in sum, from *Gemeinschaftslust.*

Hayek is the ultra of liberism among the post-Keynes neoliberals. His scathing criticism of egalitarian dreams and his quixotic repudiation of majoritarian democracy (replaced by a qualified version, "demarchy") are generally thought to put him in the company of conservative liberals. Yet Hayek does not see himself as a conservative. An epilogue to *The Constitution of Liberty* bears precisely the title "Why I Am Not a Conservative." Liberalism, warns Hayek, "is not averse to evolution and change," while conservatism is too fond of authority, generally lenient on coercion, often ignorant about economics, too nostalgic, and antidemocratic rather than antistatist.

The last point has its own irony, since Hayek himself became less than wholehearted about democracy in his old age. But taken together, this brilliantly summarizes real differences between liberalism and its alternatives. They tend to be blurred because of the custom (much encouraged by socialist propaganda) to see conservatism, liberalism, and socialism as points along a line. No, says Hayek, this is an optical illusion: the conceptual truth bids us to see them rather as the corners of a triangle.[41] Then the discrepancies between conservatism and liberalism become as clear as those separating liberalism from socialism.

As Samuel Brittan has perceived, there is a gulf between two strands in Hayekian thought. One strand is the classical liberal appreciation of limited government, free markets, and the rule of law. The other is a Burkean mystique, often claiming rather than proving the hidden wisdom of long-existing institutions. Now this represents quite a problem, for if, in his Burkean evolutionism, Hayek defends progress and the market because they possess a kind of inbred wisdom, on what grounds can one deny it to the long-existing institutions that Hayek so abhors, like rent control, price control, and progressive taxation? Might not their abolition upset a whole society?[42] Moreover, is it not true that most welfare states have *not* been set up on the basis of a comprehensive conscious planning? In other words, are not they, too, the outcome of many unforeseen evolutions?

Such are just a few of the queries raised by Hayek's blind bet on the wisdom of evolution as tradition. If evolution is a cosmic tradition, everything—even what hampers the market and thereby indirectly undermines freedom—is eligible to be blessed by its criterion. On the other hand, if evolution is *selection*, why all the fuss about social experiments that, according to this theory, will be dropped anyway? No wonder Hayek has been sharply criticized for the contradiction between his evolutionary fideism and the role that he assigns to critical reason.[43]

Hayek is, of course, an upholder of moral individualism and therefore of value pluralism. His view is that, except for well-circumscribed ambits, there need be *no* agreement about ends: "we do not enforce a unitary scale of concrete ends," wrote he, "nor attempt to secure that some particular view about what is more and what is less important governs the whole society."[44] This sounds like Berlin—libertarian individualism at its favorite sport, the dismissal of large substantial definitions of the common good. Instead, Hayek goes for *nomocracy:* what we need is rules of the game rather than shared values and ends. When all is said and done, freedom for Hayek is at bottom an instrument of progress; the supreme worth of the Hayekian individual is to be a contributor (unawares) to social evolution. This view undercuts Hayek's claim to be a liberal in the same league as Locke and Humboldt.[45] Neoliberism as neoevolutionism ends up by undermining the very soul of liberal ethics.

In the liberist literature, we often find much praise for Hayek in the texts of the so-called public choice theory. The leading name here is James Buchanan, author (with Gordon Tullock) of *The Calculus of Consent* (1962) and of *Cost and Choice* (1969). As an economist, Buchanan's influence on the liberist revival is second only to that of Milton Friedman. Under the inspiration of the work on public finance built by Scandinavian neoclassic economist Knut Wicksell (1851–1926), Buchanan has focused on *politics as exchange.* In *Liberty, Market and State,* a recent selection of his papers, Buchanan stressed the role of public choice as "a *perspective* on politics that emerges from an extension-application of the tools and methods of the economist to collective or non-market division-making." The result is a crucial insight on the causes of governmental failures (basically owing to the tendency on the part of elected politicians and Parkinsonian bureaucracies to crate budget deficits), a realization as significant to political science as the theory of market failures has been to economics. Buchanan often quotes Hayek, but he is a liberist who has no qualms about devising "rules for a fair game," including a sober view of taxations of transfers and public education as moderators of social inequality.[46]

Other liberist books of note comprehend the works of two Frenchmen, Henri Lepage (*Tomorrow, Capitalism,* 1978) and Guy Sorman (*La Nouvelle richesse des nations,* 1987), as well as the fine 1986 work by sociologist Peter Berger, *The Capitalist Revolution—Fifty Propositions about Prosperity, Equality and Liberty.* Mises's American disciple Murray Rothbard (*Man, Economy and State,* 1970; *Ethics of Liberty,* 1982) has been by far the most insistent advocate of liberism on libertarian grounds.[47]

Sociological Liberalism:
Aron and Dahrendorf

Sociology has often been deemed rather inimical to liberalism. In the United States, Robert Nisbet has forcefully underlined the affinities between classical sociology and conservatism, insofar as both trends, the discipline and the ideology, were reacting *against* the disruptive effects of industrialization and secularization, two phenomena generally upheld by mainstream liberalism.[48] Yet we saw that the towering figure of Weber, a conservative liberal, belongs at the same time to the *Grunderzeit* of sociology and to the central line of German liberalism.

At least one of Weber's peers as a founding father of sociology, Georg Simmel (1858–1918), deserves to be reckoned as a liberal (though a rather apolitical one), while in the French sociological school sired by Durkheim we have the interesting case of Bouglé, whom we've already discussed. In postclassical American sociology Talcott Parsons was a moderately conservative liberal (and was criticized as such by the late Alvin Gouldner[49]), and Robert Merton is a liberal too, while Daniel Bell exchanged his youthful leftism for liberal positions. In today's France, Raymond Boudon and, increasingly, Alain Touraine can be so described, though only Boudon, I think, would accept the label. Here, however, in a short survey of liberal thought since the war, I shall limit my discussion to two more militant intellectuals, Raymond Aron and Ralf Dahrendorf. Probably because of their deeper involvement in politics (Dahrendorf literally, and Aron by way of decades of political journalism) they were led to unfold their sociological work into some essays openly professing the liberal creed, to which both of them have made very distinguished contributions.

Raymond Aron's (1905–83) position in the history of liberal thought is a curious one. A sociologist, he was highly critical of what he called *sociologism*, the neglect of the specifics of politics in theories asserting social determinisms. By contrast, Aron stressed that the main differentiation of modern societies rests on the polity. All industrial societies, he pointed out, are very much alike on the cultural level and the type of productive forces. It is in their system of government that they differ.[50] Aron never forgot the alternative underlined by his hero Tocqueville: that democratic societies can be ruled in either a free or a despotic way.

Writing as a Montesquieu of industrial society, Aron displays superb comparatist skills. After a remarkable youthful work in philosophy of history (*Introduction to the Critical Philosophy of History*, 1938), he first made his mark on the international scene with a shrewd critique of "progressive" ideology. In *The Opium of the Intellectuals* (1955) he attacked four myths: the myth of the left, the myth of the revolution, the myth of the proletariat, and the myth of historical necessity. But he was soon to exchange *Ideologiekritik* for a probing analysis of modern industrial society. This was the object of his famous Sorbonne trilogy, begun with *Eighteen Lectures on Industrial Society* (delivered in 1955–56, printed in 1962).

He saw industrialism as a cluster of four basic processes: an increasing division of labor; capital accumulation for investment; rational accountancy and planning; and the separation of the enterprise from family control. One can easily recognize the theoretical sources: Durkheim for the first, Marx the second, Weber the third, and Schumpeter the fourth. Add private ownership of the means of production, the profit motive, and a decentralized economy, and you get capitalism. But as a good sociologist, Aron also noticed some shortcomings of classical social theory, as when he chided

Tocqueville for letting his concern with the equality overlook industrial hierarchy.

Aron's political sociology starts from a conceptual crossroad where Tocquevillian questions fuel a kind of analysis inspired by Elie Halévy (1870–1937) and Max Weber. Halévy's intellectual testament, *The Era of Tyrannies* (1938), bequeathed Aron the theme of modern despotism (fascist or Communist), whereas Weber, the knowledge of whose work he pioneered in France, offered him fruitful perspectives on power, the state, and status groups. Thus equipped, Aron saw through the trimmings of representative democracy, often initiating pathbreaking assessments of the power interplay between parties and governments on the other hand, with social forces like unions and the intelligentsias on the other.

The main purpose of Aron's Sorbonne lectures was not so much the sociology of industrialism per se as an inquiry into the different kinds of polity within the industrial world. The conceptual kickoff of Aron's triptych on industrial society was his realization that contrary to their self-image the Bolsheviks, far from representing the workers, were a new ruling class. In other words, Mosca and Pareto (the ruling class, the circulation of elites) gave the lie to Marx. As Robert Colquhoun, his thorough and able commentator, has seen, this Pareto/Marx confrontation and the theory of economic growth elaborated by Colin Clark and his French disciple, Jean Fourastié, were the two main strands in Aron's theoretical basis for the *Eighteen Lectures* and their sequel.[51]

Aron's trilogy really reaches its logical conclusion at the end of the third tome, *Democracy and Totalitarianism* (1965; delivered in 1957–58), where he presents a dichotomy of industrial polities. On one side, the constitutional-pluralist regimes have a constitution, party competition, and acknowledged social pluralism. On the other, in the ideocracies, there is a monopoly of power, revolution instead of a working constitution, bureaucratic absolutism, and the party-state. Then follows a typology of liberty, with the position of each main industrial polity toward the types of freedom. Thus, the constitutional-pluralist regimes guarantee freedom as security, freedom of opinion, and political freedom but concern themselves less with freedom in work and social mobility. By contrast, the party-state regimes violate the first three kinds of freedom quite often. In short, free politics are only moderately egalitarian, but ideocracies are really nasty.

Another dimension of the Aronian oeuvre—also known for its

outstanding contribution to international politics—consists precisely in a careful reflection on liberty in itself. Two books stand out: *An Essay on Freedom* (1965) and *Political Studies* (1972). In the latter collection, Aron among other things criticizes Hayek and Berlin in the name of sociological realism. Both volumes contain a defense and illustration of what Aron calls "the liberal-democratic synthesis"— an amalgam of traditional civil and political rights with modern *social* rights, which he depicts as "credit" claims (*droits-créances*). Aron's point is that in our time the rule of law cannot possibly exhaust the functions of the state; Hayekian nomocracy has to allow for the unavoidable welfare tasks and infrastructure-providing attendant on the modern state.

In his old age, shaken by the resurgence of ideological irrationalism in 1968, Aron returned to an old concern of his: the phenomenon of "ideocracy," the totalitarian thrust of radical regimes. He tended to reject the leftist view of Leninist dictatorship as a "deviation" owing to Russia's social and political backwardness. Instead, he correctly traced the roots of Soviet authoritarianism to Marx's own distrust of money and the commodity, a distrust that his dogmatic followers put in practice to burst the institutional autonomy, and hence the resilience, of the economy. One of his last books, *Plaidoyer pour une Europe décadente* (1977), is a subtle conceptual polyphony between the decline of the East-West détente, the depression of the 1970s, the nature of Marx's thought, and the role of marxism as a state ideology.

Aron was an outstanding scholar doublé of a masterly political journalist. He left a huge rambling work, seminal in at least three areas: foreign policy, philosophy of history, and political sociology. His lucid, often caustic liberalism, only too conscious of the contradictions of modernity, marks a worthy reprise of the best element in the tradition of French liberalism: its grasp of history, its ability to interpret and assess the broad structures of change. Long victimized by ideological bigotry in his own country, branded by Sartre and the Communists as a servile Atlanticist, he became, toward the end of his life, the patron saint of the remarkable liberal revival in France.[52]

Ralf Dahrendorf once said that Raymond Aron "inhabits his pantheon." The pantheon is indeed a respectable one: it also includes Humboldt, Tocqueville, Weber, Keynes, Beveridge, and Schumpeter. We shall see what common inspiration Dahrendorf derives from such a pleiad. Born in 1929, young Dahrendorf earned a stay in a concentration camp for being too naughty as an anti-Nazi schoolboy. As a student at the London School of Economics, he listened to Popper and sociologist T. H. Marshall, whose *Citizenship and Social Class* (1950) told the story of the modern progress of rights: civil rights conquered in the eighteenth century, political ones won in the nineteenth century, and social ones were established in our century. Dahrendorf, always a good social liberal, was active in politics, in Germany, and the European Economic Community, from 1965 to 1974, when he became a brilliant director of the London School of Economics for a whole decade. He is now warden of St. Anthony's College, Oxford, and has been recently knighted.

Dahrendorf's first book, *Class and Class Conflict in Industrial Society* (1955) was meant to provide the unwritten chapter in Marx's *Capital:* the one on class. Dahrendorf gladly accepted the Marxian stress on class struggle, but he showed that the antagonic classes need not be economic groups. Rather, economic conflict is just one species of a genre: the fight for power. At the time, thanks to Parsons's and other influences, the talk of mainstream sociological theory was all social cohesion and value-sharing. No, said Dahrendorf: conflict is endemic, because of differences in access to power. The *quality* of such differences changes; the fact of power asymmetry doesn't. To a large extent, Parsons had been veiling what Weber knew: how much power does shape society.

But while Weber had had a few Tolstoyan ecstasies that led him to demonize power, Dahrendorf relished, if not power, at least conflict (which hinges on power). In a 1962 paper on "Uncertainty, Science and Democracy,"[53] he develops the highly Popperian argument that the only adequate response to uncertainty is the need "for maintaining a plurality of decision patterns, and an opportunity for them to interact *and compete*" (my italics). Yet conflict, to be fruitful, requires a modicum of social homogeneity. In Weimar Germany the elites weren't able to articulate this healthy kind of competition. All they could muster together was a cartel of anxiety, utterly undermining the democratic game. Such was the thesis of Dahrendorf's *Society and Democracy in Germany* (1965).[54]

Following the protest waves of the late 1960s and the OECD slump after the first oil crisis in 1973, Dahrendorf embarked on a persistent attempt to analyze the new plight of modern industrial democracies. He somehow sees himself taking over from Aron's scrutiny of postwar industrialism, and in fact few other social scientists have kept so abreast of a deeper intelligence of recent trends.

Three books in particular encapsulate the later Dahrendorf's views: *The New Liberty* (1975), *Life Chances* (1979), and *The Modern Social Conflict* (1988). *Life Chances,* a collection of essays, includes one on the demise of social democracy. Dahrendorf downplays conflict and regrets the loss of "ligatures," of roots that give meaning to individual "options." There is a distrust of growth and of rapid modernization. The tone is not far, as noticed by John Hall, from the later Daniel Bell's "postindustrial" ethos; though Dahrendorf is more emphatic on the role of initiative in the "improving society" he envisages as a cure for late capitalist ills.

The Modern Social Conflict both elaborates on and refines the diagnosis of the present. Dahrendorf describes the modern social conflict as one between the advocates of more choice and those demanding more rights. The key opposition is between "provisions" and "entitlements." Provisions are "the supply of alternatives in given areas of activity." They are "things," liable to increase or diminish; it is an economic concept. Entitlements, on the other hand, are entry tickets, rights of access to whatever goods or walks in life. Dahrendorf borrows the concept from Amartya Sen, the Oxford poverty and famine expert, who demonstrated that most famines happened not because of lack of food but because of lack of *access* to food. Unlike provisions, which are incremental, entitlements draw lines and barriers. As entry tickets, either you have them or not. The Industrial Revolution generated a revolution of provisions, whereas the French Revolution was a revolution of entitlements. The 1970s were a period of entitlement policies, while the 1980s witnessed a shift to provisions, to choice rather than access. The Keynesian reforms centered on sustaining entitlements—basically, the state-fostered right to work; in the 1980s, by contrast, Schumpeter got the upper hand, for these were years of the conquering entrepreneur, of Schumpeterian animal faith in credit and innovation.

Armed with these two basic concepts, Dahrendorf depicts contemporary Western society. (He doesn't say much about Japan.) He rightly worries about "casino capitalism" (in Susan Strange's apt phrase) and the stubborn presence of a minority "underclass," more visible in the United States and Britain than in Europe, yet painfully unintegrated everywhere. He sees many people as given to "two addictions": easy money-making and drugs. He warns against nationalist fundamentalisms and "their attack on the civilizing forces of citizenship in the name of minority rights or cultural, religious, ethnic autonomy." He wisely reflects on the anomic conflicts of our society, fraught with violence and corruption: of nations where inner cities have "no-go areas" and of social culture that now also exhibits "symbolic no-go areas," like the acquittal of the guilty and the unabashed law-breaking rife among youth.

Dahrendorf does not moralize about all this. Rather, he writes as a concerned late-twentieth-century *Aufklärer,* eager to understand and improve. His essay on the 1980s fully restored his sense of social conflict without dropping the cultural alarm of his writings of the 1970s. Stressing once again that "conflict is liberty [and] also a condition of progress," he blames the corporatism of the 1970s for having "turned entitlements into sectional interests, thereby stifling the process of expanding provisions."[55]

Above all, Dahrendorf keeps a good grasp of structural trends. He is very deft, for instance, in thinking about unemployment. He shows unemployment to be in large part the effect of deep techno-economic change. In Germany alone, while the GDP grew fourfold from 1950 to 1986, the amount of work per capita, after increasing until the late 1950s, plummeted: thus a vast new wealth was produced with far less human effort. In the age of Keynes, procuring work seemed the best way to roll back both economic depression and social misery. Today, however, as stated in *The Modern Social Conflict,* "work is no longer the obvious solution to social problems, but a part of the problem itself."

The world Dahrendorf describes so well is no longer, except residually, an arena of class struggle in the traditional sense. The tensions between "the majority class"—the dominant salariat, blue and white collar—and the underclass do not beget aligned conflict. The adversarial picture became "one of a dominant social democratic mood represented by many different political parties, and episodic attempts to break out of the great consensus either by innovation and entrepreneurship, or by fundamental democracy and alternative life styles."[56] Briefly, there is the ingrained welfarism of the majority class, its Thatcherite challengers, and the counterculture: the yuppie party and the neohippie party.

Dahrendorf is unhappy with these options. He dreams of a "radical liberal alternative," enacting much-needed "civil societies in the classical sense of the term" as steps to a *world* civil society, able to cope with the gulf between North and South. As he sees it, the 1990s threatened to be a quarrelsome spell, a protracted pitched battle over new citizenship claims, contrasting with the apparent social calm of the 1980s. Never mind, says Sir Ralf the Agonistes— better to accept and contain conflict than to deny or ignore it.

This radical liberalism will have to be something rather ambitious in scope and scale, something definitely beyond Popper's "piecemeal social engineering." Mindful of his pantheon, Dahrendorf suggests that political innovation could come, as it did with Keynes and Beveridge, as radical specific recipes offered within a general conservative or nonrevolutionary framework. What is essential is to change the system, not to break it and thus invite retrogressive consequences. Anyway, "the liberal who ceases to seek new opportunities ceases to be a liberal."[57]

The Neocontractarians: Rawls, Nozick, and Bobbio

The main idioms of liberalism since the war have been the critique of historicism (Popper), antitotalitarian protest (Orwell and Camus), the ethic of pluralism (Berlin), neoevolutionism (Hayek), and historical sociology (Aron). By 1970, with the air still full of the romantic voluntarism of the student revolts, there was room for a further kind of neoliberal discourse: the idiom of rights and social contract. Its sound, in the mammoth treatise of John Rawls, *A Theory of Justice* (1971), was greeted as the new gospel of liberals—especially in the American sense of the word. And no sooner had Harvard's quiet Rousseau made his splash than its liberal formula was loudly contested, in the name of libertarian individualism, by Robert Nozick's theory of rights. Meanwhile, in Europe, the head of the Turin School, Norberto Bobbio, reached an international audience with his long intercourse with the classics of contractarianism.

Born in Baltimore in 1921, John Rawls was 50 when his great book became the talk of academe. Having studied at Princeton, he had already been at Harvard for a decade. His grand return to normative ethics boldly broke with the timid minutiae of the linguistic approach to moral philosophy. And *A Theory of Justice* was no less daring in aim: nothing short than a full-blown alternative to utilitarianism. The contractarian nature of Rawl's enterprise showed on a procedural plane, for it was in the techniques he employed for deriving principles of justice that Rawls adopted a social contract standpoint. All the same, it was a social contract very different from that of the early modern tradition, since its purpose was not the establishment of legitimate authority and obligation, as in Hobbes, Locke, or Rousseau, but the laying down of rules of justice.

Rawls's chief claim is that we can reach sound principles of social justice by thinking of what rules we would adopt, as rational beings, in a hypothetical "original position." In such an imaginary situation, people would not know their place in society, nor their own talents and skills: rather, they would have to act under a "veil of ignorance." This must be in order to ensure "justice as fairness." For in such a predicament, as I wouldn't know whether I am rich or poor, male or female, white or black, clever or stupid, I ought to feel bound to be prudent and therefore to choose principles that do not advantage any group at the cost of others. People in the original position are no altruists—all they know, owing to the veil of ignorance, is that their interests may clash in a world where scarcity tends to prevail. Besides, they also know that some "primary goods"—a few rights and freedoms, powers and opportunities, a modicum of income and self-respect—are necessary means to a decent, desirable life.

Given this situation, two principles of justice are likely to be chosen by the pactarian: (1) each one is to have an equal right to the maximum of liberty compatible with a similar extent for others; and (2) social inequalities are to be allowed only insofar as they benefit the least advantaged members of society—what Rawls dubs "the difference principle," as against the identity-of-freedom range obtaining in the first.

According to Rawls, individuals in a social limbo ought to prefer such principles because they would follow a "maximin" criterion: being utterly uncertain about the consequences of their choice, they will normally minimize the danger of being damaged. Hence they will consider a hypothesis of *maximum* risk, making sure that each inequality benefits the *least* advantaged among the pactarians. The "maximin" is therefore an insurance policy.

Rawls is on familiar liberal ground both in the first principle (in which liberty is defined as freedom as independence plus political rights) and in giving the first principle priority over the second, for all the egalitarian spirit of the latter. In the second part of *A Theory of Justice*, which deals with institutions, this typical American liberal balance is quite noticeable, as Rawls envisages a constitutional democracy and a free economy—yet allows for a liberal socialist regime.

The left was not amused. Rawls was charged with superficial

egalitarianism, well below the true levels of distributive justice.[58] Other radicals saw in the Rawlsian contract a reflection of the spirit of consumerism.[59] At the time, Ronald Dworkin, the legal philosopher, was almost alone in the "progressive" camp to salute Rawls's "original position" as the foundation of the right to "equal respect and concern."[60]

Criticisms are not missing from the liberal side either. Daniel Bell, the Harvard sociologist, wrote an admiring comment but deplored that Rawls was seemingly postulating a stationary economy.[61] Generally speaking, the avoidance of risk in Rawls's hypothetic social contract looks too remote from a modern, individualistic society to provide a relevant rule. Naturally it would hardly be fair to blame Rawls for the lack of realism of his avowed *Gedankenexperiment*. But sociologists cannot help asking about the degree of applicability of such principles to societies as complex as the industrial ones. In his later work, Rawls considerably historicized his theory, assigning his "primary goods" to Kantian moral agents, able to comply with social justice while pursuing their own ideals of the good.[62] He maintained his antiutilitarian stance because the scions of Bentham would admit of just one good, happiness.

Robert Nozick, the youngest major liberal theorist discussed here, was born in Brooklyn in 1938. He studied at Columbia and Princeton and was appointed to Harvard in 1965. Like Rawls, he is the author of a single text, *Anarchy, State and Utopia* (1974). Nozick praises Rawls for having accomplished "a great advance over utilitarianism." But thereafter they part company in crucial ways. The second part of *A Theory of Justice* sketched a consideration of individual talents and their fruits as social assets and contemplated the legitimacy of wide-ranging wealth distribution. As a radical libertarian, Nozick disagreed. According to him, every single soul is "entitled" to keep his own—unless it was unjustly acquired—and whatever may accrue to it in future. He starts with a state of nature, but in the fashion of Locke rather than Hobbes. In part 2 of the book, which as in Rawls's treatise is an institutional charter, Nozick defended a "minarchist" idea of the state. A state there must be, but only protective and in particular, with no right to tax. (Nozick likens income tax to forced labor.)

Nozick is convinced, as he says right from the outset, that "the fundamental question of political philosophy, one that precedes questions about how the state should be organized, is whether there should be any state at all." The purpose of *Anarchy, State and*

Utopia is to deploy a defense of the minimal state on two fronts. Against anarchists, who would have no state whatsoever, Nozick is set on demonstrating that there *can* be a legitimate state compatible with freedom. Against antiindividualists, on the other hand, he wants to show that the good state need not curtail natural individual rights.

Nozick is a master of conjectural reasoning. Suppose, he asks, that in a given society, half the population has two eyes, whereas the other half just got none. Is it not outrageous to think (assuming eye transplants are no problem) that each person belonging to the first half ought to lose one eye in favor of each person of the eyeless lot? Now, as everyone has a right to the integrity of one's body, so it should be with whatever is made or produced by it: let each person keep his own and whatever property they can legally come by. Nozick opposes "patterned theories" of justice, stipulating the distribution of wealth or income according to people's characteristics (like Rawls's "least advantaged"). Suppose, he writes, that everyone in an egalitarian community decides to give the famous sportsman Wilt Chamberlain a quarter of a dollar to make him play basketball. This would give Chamberlain a huge fortune—but how to keep the pattern without thwarting individual freedom?

Political legitimacy, indeed the legitimacy of all social arrangements, rests for Nozick on an absolutist demand for voluntary consent. As he writes paraphrasing Marx, "from each as they choose, to each as they are chosen." Or with a little more elaboration, "from each according to what he chooses to do, to each according to what he makes for himself (perhaps with the contracted aid of others) and what others do for him and choose to give him of what they've been given previously . . . and haven't yet transferred."[63] The cardinal rule is always free individual consent. One is obviously not entitled to a pretty wife or a handsome husband just because one needs one; therefore why on earth, asks Nozick, should one feel entitled to a subsistence income just because one needs it—if, in order to get it, the freedom of others has to be curtailed? So much for the old arguments about need and desert, as well as for the traditional social liberal stress on the conditions for freedom as self-development. No wonder this kind of short shrift incensed liberal intellectuals in the United States.[64] For Nozick, utopia could only be (as he explains in part 3) a libertarian state of affairs, with each individual choosing his or her form of life.

Norberto Bobbio (b. 1909) is an outstanding political theorist.

Widely translated in Germany, Spain, and Latin America, his books are now beginning to receive the attention they deserve in France and the Anglo-Saxon world as well. Preaching a widening democracy to sundry areas of social life, Bobbio states that the "passage from political democracy into social democracy" should be deemed something better, and more viable, than radical proposals for supplanting representative democracy by direct democracy. Accordingly, he writes, "the current problem of democratic development can no longer address just the question of *who* votes but rather *where* one votes."[65] Democratic decision-making outside politics and parliaments is seen as a welcome complement to today's liberal democracies.

Bobbio warns against making a fetish out of direct democracy. For neither referenda nor popular assemblies nor the imperative mandates of Rousseaunian ancestry would fare well in our modern setting. Referenda couldn't possibly cope with the bulk of the complex legislation of a technobureaucratic society; popular assemblies are ruled out owing to the demographic scale of most modern countries. Revocable mandates might play into the hands of authoritarianism, and imperative ones already exist in the shape of parliamentary party discipline—to the detriment of democracy. Therefore Bobbio agrees with old Kautsky's attack on "doctrinaire democratism": in modern society, the noble but impracticable ideal of the government of the people *by the people* turns out to be a "reactionary utopia."

In *The Future of Democracy* (1984), Bobbio lists three obstacles to democracy: the increase of political problems requiring technical expertise for their solution; the spread of bureaucracy, prompted by popular demands as expressed through the ballot; and the very pressure put by such ever-rising claims upon the ability of governments to rule. In short: technification of rule, bureaucratic hypertrophy, and the fall of governmental output.

These obstacles, in turn, prevent modern democracy from delivering its originally intended goods: transparent self-rule based on autonomous citizenship. Hence the "unfulfilled promises" of democracy. To begin with, nowadays the politically relevant actors are no longer individuals but groups (like parties and unions). While individual participation in the choice of representatives is but a shadow of the liberal precept, representation itself mirrors the play of interest groups *and no longer has a predominantly political character.* Finally, the actual practice of political liberties fell short of the

Millian dream of education through democracy: apathy, rather than inspired civics, became widespread, largely inculcated by the mass media and cultural industry.

Bobbio insists on spreading as much democracy as possible throughout the social fabric. This combination of realism about the limits of democracy and the search for new democratic spaces has led some critics, notably the neomarxist Perry Anderson, to misconstrue his position as a cryptoconservatism.[66] But it is this very emphasis on democracy that gives Bobbio's own brand of liberalism a very different flavor from previous Italian incarnations of the liberal idea, like the economic liberalism of Pareto and the ethical liberalism of Croce. Bobbian liberalism is definitely on the left, like that of Gobetti, Rosselli, and Calogero. But unlike all of them, Bobbio gives pride of place to a "rights" liberalism akin to the Anglo-Saxon tradition. Above all, Bobbio displays something quite new, in depth and scale, in regard to the age of Gobetti and Rosselli: a sustained polemic with Marxism.

The first chapter in *Quale socialismo?* (1976) confronts the absence in Marxism of a theory of socialist state and of socialist democracy. Why does Marxism lack a theory of the state? Bobbio can think of two reasons. First, the *primacy of the party*. The historical truth is that the workers' movement turned out to be more interested in the conquest of power than in its subsequent organization and exercise. As a result, there was much attention to the revolutionary party, but practically none to the state-to-be. Writes Bobbio, "If the state is destined to wither away, the new state arising from the ashes of the destroyed bourgeois state—the dictatorship of the proletariat—is just a transitional state. If the new state is transitional, and therefore ephemeral, the problem of its best functioning becomes far less important."[67] Finally, Bobbio stressed that the way power is conquered cannot be indifferent to its future exercise.

In 1954 Bobbio clashed with Galvano della Volpe (1895–1968), the Marxist epistemologist and commentator on Rousseau, over the concept of liberty. Della Volpe had urged the need for a socialist "greater liberty" well beyond the civil freedoms of bourgeois origin, which he branded as mere "class values." Bobbio convincingly protested this "identification of the liberal doctrine of the state with a bourgeois ideology of the state." Insisting that to reduce civil rights to bourgeois privileges was to commit a genetic fallacy, Bobbio stated that the liberal theory of the limited state—limited by both individual guarantees and institutional controls—was a check not only on absolute monarchy "but on whatever form of government"; and that inasmuch as it was also a theory of the *representative* state, the liberal creed meant the possibility of an access to power open to all social groups.[68]

The gist of Bobbio's political thinking is a constant dialogue with the classics, from Plato, Aristotle, and Cicero to Weber and Kelsen. The classical classics as well as the early modern classics like Machiavelli and Bodin, Althusius, and Harrington are found in his pages as often as Tocqueville and Mosca, Schumpeter, Dahl, and Macpherson. Yet in Bobbio the constant commerce with the ancients of political theory is never a revulsion against modern society, as it was, for example, in Leo Strauss. This classical framework is especially visible in *Stato, governo, società* (1985), the nearest thing we now have to an ideal modern compendium of political theory. In it, Bobbio appears as a great, subtle codifier of many insights of political thought throughout Western history.

Bobbio has been rightly praised for having "reoriented Italian political theory from its traditional nearly exclusive concern with power games [the Machiavellian lineage] into a closer scrutiny of the state as an institutional complex."[69] But he is also very much alive to the *societal* distribution of power. He incorporates Mosca's remarks, at the end of his *History of Political Doctrines* (1933), on the resilience and desirability of regimes where political, ideological, and economic powers are separate from one another; and he notices that monocratic party rule of the Leninist type evinces no distinction between *regnum* and *sacerdotium*.[74]

The good state, according to Bobbio, exhibits five characteristics. First, it lives in a *polycratic* environment. That is to say, its only power monopoly is the use of legitimate force—for the rest, as a liberal state, it resigns itself to having lost the monopoly of ideology and of the economy. Second, besides knowing these "limitations *to*" state power, it also has, it goes without saying, "limitations *of*" its power: the constitutional checks and balances, the set of inviolable civil rights, and so on. Third, from a public law point of view, it is a state whose subjects participate (no matter at what remove) in its norm making; in Kelsen's Kantian language, its *nomogenesis* is *autonomous*, not heteronomous. (For Kelsen, it will be remembered, this is the meaning of democracy.) Fourth, it is also democratic in the minimal sense that it has a broad citizenship and that its citizens can actually choose between political teams competing for temporary office. And fifth, it is a state respectful of substantial civil and civic rights, including, of course, minority rights and the free voicing of opposition.

Bobbio is not only a political thinker but a very prominent legal philosopher—a true successor of Kelsen and an equal to H. L. A. Hart. Before teaching political philosophy in Turin, he taught law for many years (1938–72) in Siena, Padua, and again Turin. *Teoria della norma giuridica* (1958) as well as *Dalla Struttura alla funzione* (*From Structure to Function*, 1977), among others, are landmarks of modern legal thought. *From Structure to Function* is a bold departure from the structuralist approach of Kelsen and Hart with a view to understand the new role of law within a social landscape dominated by the mixed economy and the welfare state.

As an expert in full command of the conceptual weaponry of classical social theory, Bobbio has scrutinized the history of the idea of civil society from the early modern natural law theorists to Hegel and Gramsci. Bobbio's application of the concept to modern trends starts from the now-familiar (and very Marxian) antithetical usage: civil society versus state. In *Stato, governo, società* he contended that the contemporary world witnessed a true *statification of society* owing, inter alia, to the growth of the welfare state. On the other hand, the rise of interest groups and mass organizations able to put pressure on the state and often to participate in its decisions *a latere* brought about an equally forceful *socialization of the state*. Bobbio's philosophical comment is impeccable. Contrary to Hegel's prediction, he argues, it was not the state as an ethical totality that took over a fragmented civil society. Rather, to a large extent, it is the social forces from below that have permeated the higher sphere of state authority.[70]

The upward element, the social invader of the modern state, often has a contractual nature. This inspires one more, particularly cogent Bobbian "juridical" insight, this time playing on the *public-private* dichotomy, so prominent in law. Weber had seen that there are, so to speak, two chief ways of reaching collective decisions. If the parts can be assumed to be basically equal at the starting point, majority rule obtains. If not—as in the medieval *Ständestaat*—then the interest groups tend to strike a compromise, avoiding the zero-sum game of contests settled by majority rule. With an eye on Italian parliamentary politics, Bobbio states that this logic of agreement and (crypto)contract holds true for many party systems today, most notably between governments and social forces.[71] The soul of welfare-state rule is social contract.

A whole essay in *The Future of Democracy,* "Contract and Contractarianism in Today's Debate," elaborates on the increasing intertwining of the "privatist logic of contract" and the "publicist logic of domination." But at the same time Bobbio refuses to iron out the differences between old and new contractarianism. *Our* social contracts, warns he, can never forget the individualist basis of modern society—a basis, he hastened to add, no longer "bourgeois." He also points out that the upward drive of the modern social contract idea implies a much wider social basis then was ever allowed by the *rapports de force* prevalent at the time of castles, guilds, and estates.

Both the legal and the political dimensions of the Bobbian oeuvre are bathed in a modern kind of social liberalism. Of all the living neoliberal contractarians, Bobbio comes closest to combining a search for justice and a taste for equality with a robust sense of institutional structures, types of regime, and their respective value, empirically assessed. He shares none of the rabid "statophobia" of other neoliberals, older (Hayek) or younger (Nozick) than he. The question Bobbio addresses to the left in general—What are the rules of rule?—cannot be avoided by true friends of liberty. For, as one of his ablest interpreters, Celso Lafer, remarked, no commitment to collective liberation, however valuable, can ever solve automatically the vexing question of the *constitutio libertatis*—the nature and structure of state power.[72] Some kinds of state contain institutional controls of power; others simply do not. It is because he fully realizes this that Bobbio asserts that *"every genuine democracy is necessarily a liberal democracy."*[73]

Bobbio's liberalism does not cover all the main issues in the new liberal agenda. If one wants to ponder the role of the market or the intricacies of the international power game, one should rather turn to Hayek or to Aron. But Bobbio has done something invaluable: He has powerfully reasserted the link between liberalism and democracy. "The practice of democracy," says he, "is a historical consequence of liberalism . . . all existing democratic states were originally liberal states." And he rightly sees the current rediscovery of liberalism "as an attempt of vindication of existing liberalism against existing socialism."[74]

While in the postwar years mankind compared the many defects and deficiencies of the liberal order with the sunny moral and material promises of the socialist program, 40 years later it has become impossible not to take into account the ugly consequences of state socialism and the shortcomings of social democracy. In the late 1940s, socialisms sat in judgment; in the late 1980s, they themselves are on trial. Moreover, while the postwar comparison was a thought experiment (since one of its terms was purely ideal), ours is bound to be largely an assessment of existing alternative regimes. Says Richard Bellamy, Bobbio does tackle "the question of what institutional arrangements are needed for people not only to change their social set-up but to choose to do so."[75] His insistence on real democracy, his realization of the changed historical position of socialism may irk many radicals, but they remain the only chance for the survival of liberal socialism as a meaningful proposition.

In the meantime, Bobbio's left liberal concerns add to the theoretical resistance to the new forms of conservative liberalism. The essay from which we took our last quote, significantly entitled "Old and New Liberalism," is actually a short critique of conservative liberalisms, Victorian (Spencer) and contemporary (Hayek). Bobbio contends that by denying the state even the smallest social purpose, Spencer performed an arbitrary reduction of public law to criminal law. Now for Bobbio, as for Hegel, any shrinking of public law is a sign of political decay, actual (as in the early Middle Ages) or intellectual (as in Spencer's social theory). As for Hayek, Bobbio takes him to task because of his tacitly cyclic idea of history—his naïve dualism of good and bad stages (good, as the state withdraws; bad, whenever it grows). Unlike Rawls, Bobbio's neocontractarianism openly challenges the conservative neoliberals.

Conclusion

The new liberalism of 1880 or 1900 consisted of three essential elements: a stress on positive freedom, a concern with social justice, and a wish to replace laissez-faire economics. This cluster of new aims and assumptions led to a new liberal political vision, whereas the old claims about individual rights had made room for more egalitarian demands. In the interwar period, this modified liberalism got a new lease on life thanks to influential thinkers like Kelsen and Keynes.

By contrast, the triumphant "neoliberalisms" around 1980 had a very different message. Hayekian neoliberals tend to mistrust positive freedom as a license for "constructivism," think social justice a meaningless concept, advocate a return to liberism, and recommend a minimal role for the state. As for the neocontractarians who rose to fame in the 1970s, some of them, like Rawls and Bobbio, are close in spirit to the egalitarian leanings of new liberalism, whereas others, like Nozick, are rather akin to the neoliberals. The liberal sociologists can also be read as responding to the new liberal-neoliberal dichotomy. While Aron was essentially a critic of totalitarianism, sharing many a liberal assumption or prescription, Dahrendorf's writing on liberty grew in reaction to the neoliberal neglect of egalitarian claims.

Conclusion

A survey, even one as necessarily sketchy as this one, of the three-century-old story of the liberal idea shows above all the striking *variety* of liberalisms: there are several historical types of liberal creed and, no less significant, several kinds of liberal discourse. Such diversity seems chiefly derived from two sources. In the first place, there are different obstacles to liberty; the bugbear of Locke—absolutism—was obviously no longer that of Mill or, again, that of Hayek. Second, there are different concepts of freedom, allowing a periodical redefinition of liberalism.

This book has tried to depict the outlines of the main historical idioms and positions of liberalism. We began by recalling some formative elements, best named as *protoliberalisms* and harking back to the early modern age or even, in a few cases, to the Western Middle Ages, such as the notion of rights and the claims of constitutionalism, or to Renaissance humanism, as in the civic ideology of early republicanism. The culmination of the early modern age, the Enlightenment, contributed a secular, progressive view of history, while the subsequent romantic movement stressed the value of the individual.

Classical liberal thought established the doctrine by building the theory of modern liberty (Constant) and by specifying the structure of the free polity, thanks to the American founding fathers and their redefinition of the concept of republic in terms of large-scale representative government. Meanwhile, classical economists from Smith to Ricardo legitimized economic freedom—another main theme of liberalism in its classic form. Furthermore, the classical liberals added two new focuses: they started the theorization of democracy, from Bentham to Tocqueville, and they developed the libertarian concerns of liberal individualism, most notably in the work of John Mill.

By the mid-nineteenth century, an important inflection in liberal theory had occurred, as the dread of democracy led many prominent thinkers to argue for a distinctly *conservative liberalism.* This was the prevalent position from Bagehot to Spencer. It comprehended most German views on the *Rechtstaat,* as well as the later impact of the influential Latin philosophers Croce and Ortega. Broadly speaking, conservative liberalism produced an elitist version of the liberal idea.

The final years of the nineteenth century witnessed a second major shift from the classical paradigm, this time toward the egalitarian claims of the *new liberals,* as asserted by prestigious thinkers such as Green around 1880 and Hobhouse by 1910. Much of their stance was preserved by the great left liberals of the interwar spell, like Kelsen in Europe, Keynes in England, and Dewey in the United States. The postwar years saw the rise of a liberal critique of totalitarianism (to be distinguished from the conservative critique) in the writings of Popper and of moralists like Orwell, Camus, and Berlin.

The last two decades have evinced a strong revival of liberalism. There has been a bold reprise of the contractarian discourse of rights, as in Rawls, Bobbio, and Nozick. A very different school of thought challenged the social-mindedness of new liberalism by articulating a powerful *neoliberal* defense of the market and a cogent critique of bureaucratism.

Insofar as the neoliberal onslaught means a return to liberism if not to laissez-faire, it seems rather well entrenched in an age of widespread liberalization, as ours has become. However, as the glorious events in Eastern Europe in 1989 have made abundantly clear, the contemporary will to freedom is a comprehensive move and seems to value political and civil liberty as much as the higher standards of living contingent on large amounts of economic freedom. Nor does the rise or rebirth of more economic freedom—the *liberist* trend—necessarily sound the death knell of egalitarian drives, either in argument or in practice. As noticed by some distinguished liberal sociologists like Aron or Dahrendorf, our society remains characterized by a continuous though changing dialectic between the growth of freedom and the thrust toward greater equality—and liberty seems to come out of it enhanced rather than weakened.

Chronology

1688	Glorious Revolution in Great Britain.
1689	Locke, *Letter concerning Toleration*.
1690	Locke, *Second Treatise*.
1748	Montesquieu, *The Spirit of the Laws*.
1762	Rousseau, *Social Contract*.
1775–1783	American Revolution.
1776	Smith, *The Wealth of Nations*.
1787	United States holds Constitutional Convention.
1787–1788	*The Federalist Papers*.
1789	Storming of the Bastille; French Revolution begins. Bentham, *Principles of Morals and Legislation*.
1791	Bill of Rights adopted in the United States. Paine, *Rights of Man*.
1795	Kant, *Perpetual Peace*.
1799	Coup of 18 Brumaire in France; rule of Napoleon I begins.
1810–1816	Argentina's struggle for independence begins.
1814–1815	Congress of Vienna creates German Confederation.

1815	Napoleon defeated at Waterloo. Constant, *Principes de Politique.*
1817	Ricardo, *Principles of Political Economy.*
1818	De Staël, *Considerations on the French Revolution.*
1820	James Mill, *Essay on Government.*
1821	Napoleon dies at Saint Helena; Mexico gains independence from Spain.
1828	Guizot, *Histoire générale de la civilisation en Europe.*
1830	Simón Bolívar dies.
1832	Reform Bill passed in Great Britain.
1834–1848	Rotteck and Welcker, *Political Dictionary.*
1835–1840	Tocqueville, *Democracy in America.*
1837	Victoria accedes to British throne.
1847–1853	Michelet, *Histoire de la Révolution française.*
1848	France's revolutions of 1848; Second Republic begins.
1850	Herzen, *From the Other Shore.*
1852	Reign of Napoléon III begins. Humboldt, *On the Limits of the State* (posthumous).
1853	New constitution established in Argentina.
1855–1861	Macaulay, *History of England.*
1859	John Stuart Mill, *On Liberty;* J. Simon, *La Liberté.*
1860	Mazzini, *The Duties of Man.*
1861	John Stuart Mill, *Representative Government.*
1867	Reform Bill passed in Great Britain. Bagehot, *The English Constitution.*
1868	Isabella II abdicates and a constitutional monarchy is established in Spain.
1871	Unification of Germany.
1884	Reform Bill passed in Great Britain. Spencer, *The Man versus the State.*
1885	Dicey, *The Law of the Constitution.*

1886   Green, *Lectures on the Principles of Political Obligation.*

1899   Bouglé, *Egalitarian Ideas.*

1900   Jellinek, *Allgemeine Staatslehre.*

1903   Renouvier, *Personalism.*

1906   Acton, *Lectures on Modern History.*

1909   Hobson, *The Crisis of Liberalism.*

1911   Hobhouse, *Liberalism.*

1914–1918   World War I.

1917   Weber, *Parliament and Government.*

1919   Treaty of Versailles signed.

1920   Kelsen, *Of the Essence and Value of Democracy.*

1924   Gobetti, *The Liberal Revolution.*

1927   Mises, *Liberalism;* De Ruggiero, *History of European Liberalism.*

1928   Rosselli, *Liberal Socialism.*

1929   Stock market crashes in the United States. Ortega, *The Revolt of the Masses.*

1930   Dewey, *Individualism Old and New.*

1931   Keynes, *Essays in Persuasion.*

1932   Croce, *History of Europe in the Nineteenth Century.*

1933   Hitler comes to power in Germany.

1936–1939   Spanish Civil War.

1939–1945   World War II.

1945   Popper, *The Open Society and Its Enemies.*

1951   Camus, *The Rebel.*

1958   Berlin, *Two Concepts of Liberty.*

1960   Hayek, *The Constitution of Liberty.*

1962   Buchanan and Tullock, *The Calculus of Consent.*

1965   Aron, *An Essay on Freedom.*

1971   Rawls, *A Theory of Justice.*

1974   Nozick, *Anarchy, State and Utopia.*

1979   Dahrendorf, *Life Chances.*

1984   Bobbio, *The Future of Democracy.*

1987   Raz, *The Morality of Freedom.*

Notes and References

CHAPTER 1

1. Cf. D. J. Manning, *Liberalism* (London: Dent, 1976), 9.

2. Montesquieu, *Spirit of the Laws*, bk. 19, ch. 27.

3. Cf. John Plamenatz, *Consent, Freedom and Political Obligation* (1938; reprint, Oxford and New York: Oxford University Press, 1968), 125. For an empirical-minded analysis of freedom within social interaction, see Felix Oppenheim, *Dimensions of Freedom: An Analysis* (New York: St. Martin's Press, 1961), especially ch. 6.

4. John Plamenatz, *Man and Society: A Critical Examination of Some Important Social and Political Theories from Machiavelli to Marx* (New York: McGraw-Hill, 1963), vol. 1, pp. 49–50 and 415–16.

5. M. I. Finley, *Politics in the Ancient World* (Cambridge: Cambridge University Press, 1983).

6. For instance, Norberto Bobbio, "Kant e le due libertà," in his *Da Hobbes a Marx* (1964; Naples: Morano, 1971), 147.

7. Charles Taylor, "What's Wrong with Negative Liberty," in Alan Ryan, ed., *The Idea of Freedom—Essays in Honour of Isaiah Berlin* (Oxford and New York: Oxford University Press, 1979), 175–93.

8. Bobbio, "Kant e le due libertà," 149.

9. For a discussion of liberalisms in several "domestic contexts," see Maurice Cranston, *Freedom: A New Analysis* (London: Longmans, 1953).

10. For a scholarly account of civic humanism in the Italian Renais-

sance, see Hans Baron, *The Crisis of the Early Italian Renaissance* (Princeton: Princeton University Press, 1966).

11. For a critique of "totalitarian" misconstructions of Rousseau, see my *Rousseau and Weber: Two Studies in the Theory of Legitimacy* (London and Boston: Routledge & Kegan Paul, 1980), 35–57; for a recent interpretation of Rousseau's democratism, see James Miller, *Rousseau, Dreamer of Democracy* (New Haven: Yale University Press, 1984).

12. Ellen Meiksins Woods, "The State and Popular Sovereignty in French Political Thought: A Genealogy of Rousseau's General Will," *History of Political Thought* 4 (Summer 1983): 287. The general-versus-particular problem in Rousseau and before him has been cogently examined by Patrick Riley in *The General Will Before Rousseau: The Transformation of the Divine into the Civic* (Princeton: Princeton University Press, 1986), especially ch. 5. For a good analysis of French political thought from Bodin to Rousseau, see Nannerl O. Keohane, *Philosophy and the State in France: The Renaissance to the Enlightenment* (Princeton: Princeton University Press, 1980).

13. Wood, "The State and Popular Sovereignty," 305 (parentheses added and tenses changed).

14. Benjamin Constant, *Cours de politique constitutionnelle,* ed. E. Laboulaye (Paris: Guillaumin, 1872), vol. 1, pp. 279–80; quoted in Stephen Holmes, *Benjamin Constant and the Making of Modern Liberalism* (New Haven: Yale University Press, 1984), 98.

15. On *Bildung* theory, see W. H. Bruford, *The German Tradition of Self-Cultivation* (Cambridge: Cambridge University Press, 1975).

16. Cf. Leonard Krieger, *The German Idea of Freedom* (Chicago: The University of Chicago, 1957).

17. Immanuel Kant, *Metaphysical Principles of Virtue* (1797), trans. J. W. Ellington (Indianapolis: Bobbs-Merrill, 1964), 97.

18. Cf. Alan Macfarlane, *The Origins of English Individualism* (Oxford and New York: Oxford University Press, 1978).

19. Cf. Jacques Julliard, *La Faute à Rousseau—essai sur les conséquences historiques de l'idée de souveraineté populaire* (Paris: Seuil, 1985).

CHAPTER 2

1. Ernst Troeltsch, *Die Bedeutung des Protestantismus für die Entstehung der modernen Welt* (Munich: Oldenburg, 1906). For a fine discussion of Troeltsch's views, see Harry Liebersohn, *Fate and Utopia in German Sociology 1870–1923* (Cambridge, Mass.: MIT Press, 1988), ch. 3.

2. Ch. Wirszubski, *"Libertas" as a Political Idea at Rome during the Late Republic and the Early Principate* (Cambridge University Press, 1950).

3. Michel Villey, *La Formation de la pensée juridique moderne* (Paris: Montchrétien, 1975).

4. Richard Tuck, *Natural Rights Theories: Their Origin and Development* (Cambridge University Press, 1979), 24.

5. Otto Gierke, *Natural Law and the Theory of Society, 1500 to 1800* trans. Ernest Barker (1913; reprint, Cambridge University Press, 1934), 36.

6. Quentin Skinner, *The Foundations of Modern Political Thought*, vol. 2, *The Age of Reformation* (Cambridge University Press, 1978), ch. 5, especially p. 143.

7. Paul E. Sigmund, *Natural Law in Political Thought* (Cambridge, Mass.: Winthrop, 1971), 80.

8. Alessandro Passerin d'Entrèves, *Natural Law* (London: Hutchinson, 1951), ch. 3.

9. Gierke, *Natural Law*, 35.

10. Albrecht Dihle, *The Theory of the Will in Classical Antiquity* (Berkeley: University of California Press, 1982).

11. Sigmund, *Natural Law*, 76, 84.

12. John Dunn, *Locke* (Oxford University Press, 1984), ch. 2.

13. Norberto Bobbio, "Il modello giusnaturalistico," in N. Bobbio and M. Bovero, *Società e stato nella filosofía politica moderna* (Milan: Il Saggiatore, 1979), 88.

14. Kenneth Wheare, *Modern Constitutions* (Oxford University Press, 1966).

15. C. H. McIlwain, *Constitutionalism Ancient and Modern* (New York: Cornell University Press, 1940).

16. J. N. Figgis, *Studies of Political Thought from Gerson to Grotius* (Cambridge University Press, 1907); Brian Tierney, *Religion, Law and the Growth of Constitutional Thought 1150–1650* (Cambridge University Press, 1982), 40.

17. Paul Hazard, *European Thought in the Eighteenth Century* (1946; reprint, London: Hollis and Carter, 1954).

18. Peter Gay, *The Enlightenment: An Interpretation* (New York: Knopf, 1966).

19. Immanuel Kant, "What is Enlightenment?" in Hans Reiss, ed., *Kant's Political Writings* (1784; reprint, Cambridge University Press, 1970).

20. For the concept of court civilization, see Norbert Elias, *The Court Society* (1969; reprint, Oxford: Blackwell, 1983); Giulio Carlo Argan, *The Europe of the Capitals 1600–1700* (Geneva: Skira, 1964).

21. Gianfranco Poggi, *The Development of the Modern State: A Sociological Introduction* (London: Hutchinson, 1978), 73.

22. A. Goodwin, introductory survey to *The New Cambridge Modern History,* vol. 8, *1763–93* (Cambridge University Press, 1971).

23. Leonard Krieger, *An Essay on the Theory of Enlightened Despotism* (University of Chicago Press, 1975), 18.

24. Maurice Cranston, *Philosophers and Pamphleteers: Political Theorists of the Enlightenment* (Oxford University Press, 1986), introduction.

25. Cf. Gibbon's appendix, published in 1781, to chapter 38 of his *Decline and Fall of the Roman Empire.* Gibbon added that even if (against all likelihood) the commercial society of Europe fell to new barbarians, there would remain America, which was already full of European institutions.

26. Albert O. Hirschman, *The Passions and the Interests: Political Arguments for Capitalism before Its Triumph* (Princeton University Press, 1977), 100–113.

27. D. D. Raphael, *Adam Smith* (Oxford University Press, 1985), 71. For a fine discussion of Smith's view on commercial society as "unequal and unvirtuous but not unjust," see the introductory chapter in Istvan Hunt and Michael Ignatieff, *Wealth and Virtue: The Shaping of Political Economy in the Scottish Enlightenment* (Cambridge University Press, 1983).

28. Kenneth Minogue, *The Liberal Mind* (London: Methuen, 1963), 61–68.

29. Michael Oakeshott, *Rationalism in Politics and Other Essays* (London: Methuen, 1962).

30. Ghita Ionescu, *Politics and the Pursuit of Happiness: An Inquiry into the Involvement of Human Beings in the Politics of Industrial Society* (London: Longman, 1984), ch. 4.

31. Nancy Rosenblum, *Another Liberalism: Romanticism and the Reconstruction of Liberal Thought* (Harvard University Press, 1988).

32. Colin Campbell, *The Romantic Ethic and the Spirit of Modern Consumerism* (Oxford: Blackwell, 1987), 203–205.

33. Boyd Hilton, *The Age of Atonement: The Influence of Evangelicanism on Social and Economic Thought, 1785–1865* (Oxford: Clarendon, 1988).

CHAPTER 3

1. Pierre Manent, *Histoire intellectuelle du libéralisme* (Paris: Calmann-Lévy, 1987), 55–56.

2. According to J. G. A. Pocock ("Conservative Enlightenment and Democratic Revolutions: The American and French Cases in British Perspective," *Government and Opposition* 24 [Winter 1989]: 83), the nominalist Hobbes opposed Greek philosophy and scholastics because by

encouraging the belief in the reality of essences, they fueled essentialist claims against the authority of the sovereign. Yet in Ockham's day, nominalism had been used to undermine the case for papal absolutism.

3. Bobbio, *Da Hobbes a Marx*, 88–90 (see note 6 to chapter 1).

4. Harold Laski, *Political Thought in England: From Locke to Bentham* (New York: Holt, 1920); Louis Hartz, *The Liberal Tradition in America: An Interpretation of American Political Thought since the Revolution* (New York: Harcourt, Brace, 1955).

5. J. G. A. Pocock, *The Machiavellian Moment: Florentine Political Thought and the Atlantic Republican Tradition* (Princeton University Press, 1975).

6. Keith Thomas on Pocock, *New York Review of Books* (27 February 1986).

7. Isaac Kramnick, "Republican Revisionism Revisited," *American Historical Review* 87 (1982).

8. J. G. A. Pocock, *Virtue, Commerce and History: Essays on Political Thought and History, Chiefly in the Eighteenth Century* (Cambridge University Press, 1985).

9. Pocock, "Conservative Enlightenment." (see note 2 above).

10. David F. Epstein, *The Political Theory of "The Federalist"* (The University of Chicago Press, 1984), 5, 6, 79, and 92.

11. Thomas L. Pangle, *The Spirit of Modern Republicanism* (The University of Chicago Press, 1988).

12. Ross Harrison, *Bentham* (London: Routledge & Kegan Paul, 1983), ch. 8.

13. Shirley Robin Letwin, *The Pursuit of Certainty* (Hume, Bentham, Mill and Beatrice Webb) (Cambridge University Press, 1965).

14. Elie Halévy, *The Growth of Philosophical Radicalism, 1901–04* (New York: Macmillan, 1928).

15. Arthur J. Taylor, *Laissez-faire and State Intervention in Nineteenth-Century Britain* (London: The Economic History Society, 1972), 36.

16. Eric Hobsbawm, *Industry and Empire* (London: Weidenfeld & Nicolson, 1968), ch. 12.

17. On Hegel's political thought, see Joachim Ritter, *Hegel and the French Revolution*, trans. R. Winfield (1957; reprint, Boston: MIT, 1982); Manfred Riedel, *Between Tradition and Revolution: The Hegelian Transformation of Political Philosophy* (1969; reprint, Cambridge University Press, 1984); George Armstrong Kelly, *Idealism, Politics and History: Sources of Hegelian Thought* (Cambridge University Press, 1969); two readers edited by Z. A. Pelczynski, *Hegel's Political Philosophy: Problems and Perspectives* (1971) and *The State and Civil Society: Studies in Hegel's Political Philosophy* (1984), both published by Cambridge University Press; Norberto Bobbio,

Studi hegeliani (Turin: Einaudi, 1981); and Michelangelo Bovero, *Hegel e il problema politico moderno* (Milan: Angeli, 1985).

18. On Sieyès, see Bronislaw Baczko, "Le contrat social des Français: Sieyès et Rousseau," in K. M. Baker, ed., *The French Revolution and the Creation of Modern Political Culture,* vol. 1 (New York: Pergamon, 1987), 493–513.

19. On this point, see Adolfo Omodeo, *Studi sull'età della Restaurazione* (Turin: Einaudi, 1970), 3, 2, and especially p. 230.

20. On Constant, see the introduction by Marcel Gauchet to his edition of selected writings of Benjamin Constant, *De la liberté chez les modernes* (Paris: Livre de Poche, 1980); S. Holmes, *Constant* (see note 14, chapter 1); and Paul Bastid, *Benjamin Constant et sa doctrine* (Paris: A. Colin, 1966).

21. On Guizot, see Pierre Rosanvallon, *Le Moment Guizot* (Paris: Gallimard, 1985).

22. James T. Schleifer, *The Making of Tocqueville's "Democracy in America"* (Chapel Hill: University of North Carolina Press, 1980), ch. 18; but see Koenraad Swart, "Individualism in the Mid-Nineteenth Century," *Journal of the History of Ideas* (January/March 1962): 77–90.

23. Jean-Claude Lamberti, *Tocqueville and the Two Democracies* trans. A. Goldhammer (1983; reprint, Cambridge, Mass.: Harvard University Press, 1989).

24. Montesquieu, *The Spirit of the Laws,* bk. 5, ch. 7.

25. See Constant, "De l'esprit de conquête et de l'usurpation dans leurs rapports avec la civilisation européenne," in Gauchet, *De la liberté chez les modernes* (see note 20 above).

26. John Plamenatz, "Liberalism," in Philip Wiener, ed., *Dictionary of the History of Ideas* (New York: Scribner's, 1973), vol. 3, p. 50.

27. Constant, "De la perfectibilité de l'espèce humaine," in Gauchet, *De la liberté chez les modernes* (see note 20 above), 580–95.

28. Hugh Brogan, *Tocqueville* (London: Fontana, 1973), 75.

29. Schleifer, *Tocqueville's Democracy in America* (see note 22 above), ch. 18.

30. Ettore Cuomo, *Profilo del liberalismo europeo* (Naples: Edizioni Scientifiche Italiane, 1981).

31. R. J. Halliday, *John Stuart Mill* (London: Allen & Unwin, 1976), ch. 1.

32. As explained by Dennis F. Thompson, *John Stuart Mill and Representative Government* (Princeton University Press, 1976), 195.

33. William Thomas, *Mill* (Oxford University Press, 1985), 111.

34. J. W. Burrow, *Whigs and Liberals: Continuity and Change in English Political Thought* (Oxford: Clarendon, 1988), 106.

35. Alan Ryan, *J. S. Mill* (London: Routledge & Kegan Paul, 1974), ch. 5.

36. John Gray, *Mill on Liberty: A Defence* (London: Routledge & Kegan Paul, 1983), 45.

37. Maurice Cowling, *Mill and Liberalism* (Cambridge University Press, 1963); Gertrude Himmelfarb, *On Liberty and Liberalism: The Case of John Stuart Mill* (New York, 1974). See J. B. Schneewind, ed., *Mill—A Collection of Critical Essays* (New York: Macmillan, 1968), for R. J. Halliday's discussion of Cowling's critique, 354–78; see C. L. Ten, *Mill on Liberty* (Oxford: Clarendon, 1980), 145–66, for a discussion of both Cowling and Himmelfarb. *On Liberty* is the object of the reader edited by A. Phillips Griffiths, *Of Liberty* (Cambridge University Press, 1983).

38. C. L. Ten, *Mill on Liberty*, (see note 37 above), 173.

39. Larry Siedentop, "Two Liberal Traditions," in A. Ryan, ed., *The Idea of Freedom* (see note 7, chapter 1), 153–74.

40. Guido de Ruggiero, *History of European Liberalism*, trans. R. G. Collingwood (1925; Oxford University Press, 1927), vol. 1, ch. 4, sec. 2.

41. Martin Malia, *Alexander Herzen and the Birth of Revolutionary Socialism, 1812–15* (Oxford University Press, 1961).

42. W. B. Yeats, "The Seven Sages," in *The Winding Stair and Other Poems* (1933), in *The Collected Poems of W. B. Yeats* (London: Macmillan, 1977).

CHAPTER 4

1. Donald Southgate, *The Passing of the Whigs, 1832–1886* (London, 1962), quoted in Burrow, *Whigs and Liberals* (see note 34, chapter 3), 12.

2. Anthony Quinton, *The Politics of Imperfection: The Religious and Secular Traditions of Conservative Thought in England from Hooker to Oakeshott* (London: Faber, 1978), 56, 60.

3. J. W. Burrow, *A Liberal Descent: Victorian Historians and the English Past* (Cambridge University Press, 1981), 28.

4. Burrow, *Whigs and Liberals* (see note 34, chapter 3), 132.

5. On James Stephen, see James Colaiaco, *James Fitzjames Stephen and the Crisis of Victorian Thought* (London: Macmillan, 1983).

6. Herbert Spencer, "Over-legislation," in *Essays: Scientific, Political and Speculative* (London: 1868), vol. 2, p. 50. For recent revaluations of Spencer, see AA.VV., *History of Political Thought* 3.3 (1982).

7. I owe this model-shift interpretation of Sarmiento's evolution to Professor Tulio Halperin Donghi's yet-unpublished inaugural lecture at the Simón Bolívar Chair, Universidad Nacional Autónoma de Méx-

ico, April 1989. For a good analysis of liberal themes in Sarmiento, see Paul Verdevoye, *Domingo Faustino Sarmiento, educateur et publiciste (1839–1852)* (Paris: 1964).

8. For this comment, see Alberdi, "Del uso de lo cómico en Sud América," *El Iniciador* 7 (Buenos Aires, 15 July 1838), quoted by Gerald Martin in ch. 18 of Leslie Bethell, ed., *The Cambridge History of Latin America*, vol. 3, *From Independence to c.1870* (Cambridge University Press, 1985).

9. Natalio Botana, *La Tradición republicana: Alberdi, Sarmiento y las ideas políticas de su tiempo* (Buenos Aires: Sudamericana, 1984), 486.

10. Mariano Grondona, *Los Pensadores de la libertad: de John Locke and Robert Nozick* (Buenos Aires: Sudamericana, 1986), 102–103.

11. Grondona, *Los Pensadores*, 112.

12. Botana, *La Tradición republicana*, 480–81.

13. For a brief aperçu of Argentina's political evolution at the time, see my essay "Patterns of State-Building in Brazil and Argentina," in John A. Hall, ed., *States in History* (Oxford: Blackwell, 1986), 264–88.

14. Carlos H. Waisman, *Reversal of Development in Argentina: Postwar Counter-revolutionary Policies and Their Structural Consequences* (Princeton University Press, 1987).

15. Louis Girard, *Les Libéraux français* (Paris: Aubier, 1985), 188–89.

16. E. K. Bramsted and K. J. Melhuish, *Western Liberalism: A History in Documents from Locke to Croce* (New York: Longman, 1978), 398–99.

17. For good assessments of the relationship between Renan and positivism, see D. G. Charlton, *Positivist Thought in France during the Second Empire, 1852–1870* (Oxford University Press, 1959), 100–106, and W. M. Simon, *European Positivism in the Nineteenth Century* (Ithaca: Cornell University Press, 1963), 95–99.

18. See the fine remarks of Laudyce Rétat, "Renan entre révolution et république," *Commentaire* 39 (Fall 1987).

19. I borrow the translation of *Rechtsstaat* proposed by Gottfried Dietze in *Two Concepts of the Rule of Law* (Indianapolis: Liberty Fund, 1973), on whom much of what follows on Mohl and Stahl is based.

20. For this characterization, see Kenneth Dyson, *The State Tradition in Western Europe* (Oxford: Martin Robertson, 1980), 123.

21. Benjamin Constant, "De la liberté des anciens comparée à celle des modernes" (1819), in Constant, *De la liberté chez les modernes* (see note 20, chapter 3), 513.

22. Quoted in Dietze, *Two Concepts of the Rule of Law*, 24.

23. Bramsted and Melhuish, *Western Liberalism*, 389–90.

24. De Ruggiero, *History of European Liberalism* (see note 40, chapter 3), vol. 1, ch. 3, sec. 4.

25. Robert Eden, *Political Leadership and Nihilism: A Study of Weber and Nietzsche* (Tampa: University Presses of Florida, 1984).

26. David Beetham, *Max Weber and the Theory of Modern Politics* (London: Allen & Unwin, 1974), ch. 4.

27. On this "hypodemocratic" character of Weber's theory of legitimacy, see my *Rousseau and Weber: Two Studies in the Theory of Legitimacy* (note 11, chapter 1), 130–35 and 197–98; and its review by Wolfgang Mommsen in *Government and Opposition* 17 (Winter 1982).

28. Norberto Bobbio, *Profilo ideologico del novecento,* vol. 9, *Storia della letteratura italiana* (Milan: Garzanti, 1969), 161–62.

29. On the historical context of Croce's political thought and attitudes, see H. Stuart Hughes, *Consciousness and Society: The Reorientation of European Social Thought, 1890–1930* (1958; reprint, London: Paladin, 1974), 213–29.

30. On this point, see Richard Bellamy, *Modern Italian Social Theory* (Cambridge: Polity, 1987), 91–92.

31. For a fine critical discussion, see Norberto Bobbio, *Politica e cultura* (1955; reprint, Turin: Einaudi, 1980), ch. 13.

32. For a brief reference to Gramsci's debt to—and criticism of—Croce, see my *Western Marxism* (London: Paladin, 1986), 96–98.

33. On Mosca, see Norberto Bobbio, *On Mosca and Pareto* (Geneva: Droz, 1972), Hughes, *Consciousness and Society,* ch. 7; and Geraint Parry, *Political Elites* (London: Allen & Unwin, 1969), 30–42.

34. Most of the philosophical literature on Unamuno and Ortega is dull and epigonic. Exceptions include Alejandro Rossi et al., *José Ortega y Gasset* (Mexico City: Fondo de Cultura Económica, 1984); J. Ferrater Mora, *Unamuno* (University of California Press, 1962); Martin Nozick, *Unamuno* (New York: Twayne, 1971); Rockwell Gray, *The Imperative of Modernity: An Intellectual Biography of José Ortega y Gasset* (University of California Press, 1989); and Andrew Dobson, *An Introduction to the Politics and Philosophy of José Ortega y Gasset* (Cambridge University Press, 1989). Excellent intellectual portraits of both can be found in Ernst Robert Curtius, *Kritische Essays zur europäische Literatur* (Bern: Francke, 1954), and Juan Marichal, *Teoria e historia del essayismo hispánico* (Madrid: Alianza, 1984). Ionescu, *Politics and the Pursuit of Happiness* (see note 30, chapter 2) has a fine discussion of Unamuno.

35. For an overview of Ortega's youthful socialism, see Fernando Salmerón, "El socialismo del joven Ortega," in Rossi et al., *José Ortega y Gasset,* 111–93.

36. See Guillermo Morón, *Historia política de José Ortega y Gasset* (Mexico City: Oasis, 1960).

37. Immanuel Kant, "On the Common Saying: 'This May Be True in Theory, But It Does Not Apply in Practice' " (1793), in Hans Reiss, ed., *Kant's Political Writings* (Cambridge University Press, 1970), 78.

CHAPTER 5

1. F. C. Montague, *The Limits of Individual Liberty* (London: 1885), 2.

2. As noticed by Vittorio Frosini, *La Ragione dello stato: studi sul pensiero politico inglese contemporaneo* (1963; reprint, Milan: Giuffrè, 1976), 33.

3. Crane Brinton, *English Political Thought in the Nineteenth Century* (London: 1949).

4. On this point, see Robert Eccleshall, *British Liberalism: Liberal Thought from the 1640s to 1980s* (New York: Longman, 1986), 39.

5. See Melvin Richter, *The Politics of Conscience: T. H. Green and His Age* (London: Weidenfeld & Nicolson, 1964).

6. Claude Nicolet, *L'Idée républicaine en France (1789–1924)*: *essai d'histoire critique* (Paris: Gallimard, 1982), 152–57. See also John A. Scott, *Republican Ideas and the Liberal Tradition in France 1870–1914* (New York: 1952).

7. Theodore Zeldin, *France 1848–1945*, vol. 1, *Ambition, Love and Politics* (Oxford: Clarendon, 1973), 483.

8. Ibid., 629–30.

9. For the concept of polytelism, see C. Bouglé, *Leçons de sociologie sur l'évolution des valeurs* (Paris: A. Colin, 1922). Bouglé forged the concept in 1914. On Bouglé's liberalism, see William Logue, "Sociologie et politique: le libéralisme de Célestin Bouglé," *Revue française de sociologie* 20 (1977): 141–61. On polytelism, see W. Paul Vogt, "Un durkheimien ambivalent: C. Bouglé," in the same issue of *Revue française*, 123–39.

10. For a discussion of his claims, see Steven Lukes, *Émile Durkheim, His Life and Work: A Historical and Critical Study* (1973; reprint, Harmondsworth: Penguin, 1975), 338–44.

11. On Duguit, see Dyson, *The State Tradition* (see note 20, chapter 4), 145–49.

12. Burrow, *Whigs and Liberals* (see note 34, chapter 3), 142–52.

13. On Hobson's liberal organicism, see Michael Freeden, *The New Liberalism: An Ideology of Social Reform* (Oxford: Clarendon, 1978), ch. 3.

14. Cf. Peter Clarke, *Liberals and Social Democrats* (Cambridge University Press, 1978), 230–34.

15. Peter Clarke, "In Honor of Hobson," *Times Literary Supplement* (24 March 1978), a review of Freeden, *The New Liberalism*.

16. Cf. Michael Freeden, *Liberalism Divided: A Study in British Political Thought 1914–1939* (Oxford University Press, 1986).

17. A fine short comment on these Italian left liberal positions can be found in Bobbio's *Profilo ideologico del novecento* (see note 28, chapter 4), 186–98, 209–16.

18. Three good volumes on C. Schmitt—one of the ablest challengers of liberalism in our century—are Joseph Bendersky, *Carl Schmitt, Theorist for the Reich* (Princeton University Press, 1983), the special issue of *Telos* 72 (Summer 1987); and the reader edited by Giuseppe Duso, *La Politica oltre lo stato: Carl Schmitt* (Venice: Arsenale, 1981).

19. For a knowledgeable background to Kelsen's political theory, see Roberto Racinaro's long introduction to the Italian translation of *Sozialismus und Staat* (Bari: De Donato, 1978).

20. On Wilson, see Richard Hofstadter, *The American Political Tradition, and the Men Who Made It* (New York: Knopf, 1948, 1973), ch. 10.

21. For a good account of Dewey's philosophy, see James Gouinlock, *John Dewey's Philosophy of Value* (New York: Humanities Press, 1972).

22. For a good summary of Trotsky's essay and Dewey's reply, see Baruch Knei-Paz's masterful *The Social and Political Thought of Leon Trotsky* (Oxford: Clarendon, 1978), 556–67.

23. Robert Skidelsky draws attention to this wordview background in the first instalment of his biography, *John Maynard Keynes, Hopes Betrayed 1883–1920* (London: Macmillan, 1983).

24. I owe this remark to Marcello de Cecco of Siena. See his contribution to Robert Skidelsky, ed., *The End of the Keynesian Era* (London: Macmillan, 1977), 22.

25. Cf. Samuel Brittan, *The Economic Consequences of Democracy* (London: Temple Smith, 1977).

26. For these criticisms, see Bhikhu Parekh, *Contemporary Political Thinkers* (Oxford: Martin Robertson, 1982), 149–52.

27. See Anthony Quinton's chapter on Popper ("Politics without Essences") in Anthony de Crespigny and Kenneth Minogue, eds., *Contemporary Political Philosophers* (New York: Dodd, Mead & Co., 1975). For a fine critical examination of Popper's antihistoricism, see Burleigh Taylor Wilkins, *Has History Any Meaning? A Critique of Popper's Philosophy of History* (Ithaca, N.Y.: University Press, 1978).

28. Michael Walzer, *The Company of Critics: Social Criticism and Political Commitment in the Twentieth Century* (New York: Basic Books, 1988), ch. 7.

29. See for instance the disgracefully bad essays edited by Christopher Norris as *Inside the Myth—Orwell: Views on Orwell from the Left*

(London: Lawrence & Wishart, 1984). For better analysis, see Bernard Crick, *George Orwell: A Life* (London: Secker & Warburg, 1981); Jeffrey Meyers, ed., *George Orwell: The Critical Heritage* (London: Routledge, 1975); Alex Zwerdling, *Orwell and the Left* (Yale University Press, 1974); George Woodcock, *The Crystal Spirit: A Study of George Orwell* (New York: Schocken, 1984), and Simon Leys, *Orwell ou l'horreur de la politique* (Paris: Hermann, 1984).

30. On Camus, see Philip Thody, *Albert Camus 1930–1960* (London: Hamish Hamilton, 1961). A sensitive, judicious assessment of the Algerian war issue can be found in chapter 8 of Walzer, *Company of Critics.*

31. "Historical Inevitability" was first published in 1954 by Oxford University Press; it was reprinted in Isaiah Berlin, *Four Essays on Liberty* (New York: Oxford University Press, 1969).

32. Also reprinted in *Four Essays on Liberty.*

33. Cf. Merquior, *Rousseau and Weber* (see note 11, chapter 1), 82–83.

34. Joseph Raz, *The Morality of Freedom* (Oxford: Clarendon, 1987).

35. For a fine discussion of Rathenau, see Dagmar Barnouw, *Weimar Intellectuals and the Threat of Modernity* (Indiana University Press, 1988), ch. 1.

36. Cf. Richard Rosecrance, *The Rise of the Trading State: Commerce and Conquest in the Modern World* (New York: Basic Books, 1986).

37. F. A. Hayek, *The Constitution of Liberty* (London: Routledge, 1960), 59.

38. See Michael Oakeshott, *Rationalism in Politics and Other Essays* (London: Methuen, 1962).

39. F. A. Hayek, *Law, Legislation and Liberty,* vol. 3, *The Political Order of a Free People* (Chicago University Press, 1973–79), 174.

40. "The Three Sources of Human Values" (London School of Economics, 1978).

41. Hayek, *Constitution of Liberty,* 398.

42. Samuel Brittan, *The Role and Limits of Government: Essays in Political Economy* (London: Temple Smith, 1983), ch. 3.

43. For a terse criticism on this line, see Dallas L. Clouatre, "Making Sense of Hayek" (a review of Gray's book), *Critical Review* 1 (Winter 1987), 73–89.

44. F. A. Hayek, *Studies in Philosophy, Politics and Economics* (London: Routledge, 1967), 165.

45. For this line of criticism, see Anthony de Crespigny "F. A. Hayek: Freedom for Progress," in Crespigny and Minogue, eds., *Contemporary Political Philosophers* (see note 27 above), 49–66.

46. James Buchanan, *Liberty, Market and State—Political Economy in the 1980s* (New York University Press, 1985), 19 and 123–39.

47. Henri Lepage, *Tomorrow, Capitalism: The Economics of Economic Freedom* (La Salle: Open Court, 1982); Guy Sorman, *La Nouvelle richesse des nations* (Paris: Fayard, 1987); Peter Berger, *The Capitalist Revolution* (New York: Basic Books, 1986); and Murray N. Rothbard, *Man, Economy and State* (Menlo Park, Calif.: Institute for Human Studies, 1970), and *Ethics of Liberty* (Atlantic Highlands, N.J.: Humanities Press, 1982).

48. Robert Nisbet, *The Sociological Tradition* (New York: Basic Books, 1966).

49. Alvin Gouldner, *The Coming Crisis of Western Sociology* (New York: Avon Books, 1970).

50. This point about the autonomy of politics is well emphasized in Ghita Ionescu, "Raymond Aron: A Modern Classicist," in Crespigny and Minogue, *Contemporary Political Philosophers* (see note 27 above), 198.

51. Robert Colquhoun, *Raymond Aron*, vol. 2, *The Sociologist in Society, 1955–83* (London and Beverly Hills: Sage, 1986), 85–86.

52. On Aron, see especially Gaston Fessard, *La Philosophie historique de Raymond Aron* (Paris: Julliard, 1980) and Robert Colquhoun, *Raymond Aron*, vol. 1, *The Philosopher in History, 1905–55*, and vol. 2, *The Sociologist in Society, 1955–83* (London and Beverly Hills: Sage, 1986). Key works by Aron concerning our brief discussion are *The Opium of the Intellectuals* (New York: Doubleday, 1957); *Eighteen Lectures on Industrial Society* (1967) and *Democracy and Totalitarianism* (1968), both London: Weidenfeld and Nicolson; *An Essay on Freedom* (New York: World, 1970); and *Études politiques* (Paris: Gallimard, 1972).

53. Collected into Ralf Dahrendorf, *Essay in the Theory of Society* (Stanford University Press, 1968).

54. For a fine summary of Dahrendorf's views on social conflict, see John A. Hall, *Diagnoses of Our Time: Six Views of Our Social Condition* (London: Heinemann, 1981), ch. 5.

55. Ralf Dahrendorf, "Tertium Non Datur: A Comment on the Andrew Shonfield lectures," in *Government and Opposition* 24 (Spring 1989): 133, 135.

56. Ibid., 172.

57. Ibid., 18.

58. Cf. Brian Barry, *The Liberal Theory of Justice: A Critical Examination of the Principal Doctrines in "A Theory of Justice" by John Rawls* (Oxford University Press, 1973).

59. For the consumerist charge, see C. B. Macpherson, *Democratic Theory: Essays in Retrieval* (Oxford University Press, 1973), ch. 4, 3.

60. Ronald Dworkin, *Taking Rights Seriously* (London: Duckworth), ch. 6.

61. Daniel Bell, *The Cultural Contradiction of Capitalism* (New York: Basic Books), ch. 6 in fine.

62. Cf. John Rawls, "Kantian Constructivism in Moral Theory," *Journal of Philsophy* 77 (1980); and "The Basic Liberties and Their Priority," *The Tanner Lectures on Human Values*, vol. 3, S. M. McMurrin, ed., (University of Utah Press, 1982).

63. Robert Nozick, *Anarchy, State and Utopia* (New York: Basic Books, 1974), 160.

64. For typical liberal strictures, see Brian Barry's review in *Political Theory* 3 (August 1975). For a critical reader, see Jeffrey Paul, ed., *Reading Nozick: Essays on "Anarchy, State and Utopia"* (Oxford: Blackwell, 1982).

65. Norberto Bobbio, *Quale socialismo?* (Turin: Einaudi, 1976), 15, 100.

66. See Perry Anderson, "The Affinities of Norberto Bobbio," *New Left Review* 170 (July–August 1988), and my refutation, "Defensa de Bobbio," in *Nexos* 1 (Mexico City, 1988).

67. Bobbio, *Quale socialismo?* 10.

68. Bobbio's reply to Della Volpe, "Della libertà dei moderni comparata a quella dei posteri" (a witty allusion to Constant's famous lecture) and Della Volpe's own text, "Il problema della libertà equalitaria nello sviluppo della moderna democrazia," are reprinted in Alessandro Passerin d'Entrèves, ed., *La Libertà politica* (Verona: Edizioni di Comunità, 1974).

69. Anderson, "Affinities," 19.

70. Norberto Bobbio, *Stato, governo, società:* per una teoria generale della politica (Turin: Einaudi, 1985), 16, 41–42.

71. Ibid., 109; see also Norberto Bobbio, *Il Futuro della democrazia* (Turin: Einaudi, 1984), 132–38.

72. Cf. Celso Lafer, *Ensaios sobre a liberdade* (São Paulo: Perspectiva, 1980).

73. Norberto Bobbio, *Politica e cultura* (Turin: Einaudi, 1955, 1980), 178.

74. Bobbio, *Il Futuro della democrazia,* 111.

75. Richard Bellamy, *Modern Italian Social Theory: Ideology and Politics from Pareto to the Present* (Cambridge: Polity Press, 1987), 165–66.

Further Reading

The liberalism literature grows by the month. The monographs, readers, and historical surveys cited in the notes to the five chapters will not be mentioned again here, in particular the histories of liberalism by De Ruggiero, Laski, Manning, Clarke, Girard, Manent, Freeden, and Burrow. Modern global historical accounts can be found in R. D. Cumming, *Human Nature and History: A Study of the Development of Liberal Political Thought* (Chicago University Press, 1969), Nicola Matteucci, *Il liberalismo in un mondo in trasformazione* (Bologna: Il Mulino, 1972), Massimo Salvadori, *The Liberal Heresy, Origins and Historical Development* (London: Macmillan, 1977), Georges Burdeau, *Le libéralisme* (Paris: Seuil, 1979), and vol. 3 of Jean-Jacques Chevallier, *Histoire de la pensée politique* (Paris: Payot, 1984). Salvadori's approach, like the earlier short book by J. Salwyn Schapiro, *Liberalism, Its Meaning and History* (New York: Van Nostrand, 1965), focuses on social ideology and the history of liberal institutions as much as on liberal theory. The latter is, by contrast, the subject of Giuseppe Bedeschi, *Storia del pensiero liberale* (Bari: Laterza, 1990), a recent history covering liberalism from Locke to Croce and Kelsen.

Critical reassessments of liberalism written from a radical standpoint include Anthony Arblaster, *The Rise and Decline of Western Liberalism* (Oxford: Blackwell, 1984). Robert Paul Wolff's earlier *The Poverty of Liberalism* (Boston: Beacon Press, 1968) criticizes liberal thought by examining the concepts of liberty, tolerance, loyalty, and power. Kirk F. Koerner's *Liberalism and its Critics* (London: Croom Helm, 1985), defends liberalism against the strictures of Macpherson, Marcuse, Strauss, and Oakeshott. John Gray's *Liberalism* (Milton Keynes: The Open University Press, 1986), adds a fine conceptual analysis of liberty, market, and state to an authoritative historical sketch of liberal thought. John A. Hall's *Liberalism* (London: Paladin, 1987) is a sober, insightful attempt at a qualified defense of liberal ideas and institutions in terms of historical sociology, though it also discusses the intellectual origins of liberal doctrine.

The 1980s saw some remarkable responses to Rawls's revival of contractarianism. While Amy Gutman's *Liberal Equality* (Cambridge University Press, 1980), advocated a liberal egalitarianism close to market socialism, Bruce Ackerman's *Social Justice in the Liberal State* (Yale University Press, 1980) took up conjectural contractarianism with a vengeance by imagining a planet of pioneer settlers with anti-utilitarian feelings, no inherited wealth, and no privileged starts in life. On the other hand, Michael Sandel's *Liberalism and the Limits of Justice* (Cambridge University Press, 1982) questioned a metaphysical tenet allegedly underlying all the liberal tradition, including Rawls: the ontological priority of the self; and he accordingly proposes a communitarian supersession of liberal individualism. The reader *Liberalism Reconsidered*, edited by Douglas Maclean and Claudia Mills (Totowa, N.J.: Rowan & Allanheld, 1983) probes the philosophical assumptions of the liberal creed in several essays by, inter alii, Ronald Dworkin, Theda Skocpol, and Christopher Lasch.

Harvey C. Mansfield's *The Spirit of Liberalism* (Harvard University Press, 1978) is a clever Straussian discussion ending up with a critique of "cucumber liberalism" in Rawls and Nozick. Gottfried Dietze's *Liberalism Proper and Proper Liberalism* (Johns Hopkins University Press, 1985) examines Montesquieu, Smith, Kant, and Jefferson as theorists of responsible, law-abiding liberty. Michael Walzer's *Spheres of Justice: A Defense of Pluralism and Equality* (New York: Basic Books, 1983) ofers a sensible new vindication of distributive justice based on liberal pluralism. The most insistent upholder of *liberism* on libertarian grounds has been Mises's American disciple Murray Rothbard (*Man, Economy and State*, Menlo Park, Cal.: Institute for Humane Studies, 1970).

The French liberist paladins are Henri Lepage (*Demain le libéralisme* [Paris: Livre de Poche, 1980]) and Guy Sorman (*La solution libérale* [Paris: Fayard, 1984]). Serge-Christophe Kolm (*Le contrat social libéral* [Paris: PUF, 1983]) is more egalitarian, whereas Jean-Marie

Benoist (*Les outils de la liberté* [Paris: Laffont, 1985]) rather tends toward a neoconservative neighborhood of thought. French neo-liberals still in their 40s have been preceded by the prolific work of Jean-François Revel, a sharp critic of totalitarianism and statism; but save for Benoist, they discuss liberalism as a social practice rather than in its philosophical premises. Liberal politics were also revisited in England by George Watson in *The Idea of Liberalism: Studies for a New Map of Politics* (London: Macmillan, 1985) and in America by Robert B. Reich in *The Resurgent Liberal and Other Unfashionable Prophecies* (New York: Random House, 1989). Finally, it is worth mentioning that some developments in the so-called postmodern philosophy have addressed the nature of a liberal culture, most conspicuously in the recent work of the American philosopher Richard Rorty (*Contingency, Irony and Solidarity* [Cambridge University Press, 1989]).

Index

The Author

José Guilherme Merquior studied law and philosophy in Rio de Janeiro before receiving a literary doctorate from the University of Paris and a Ph.D. in sociology from the London School of Economics and Political Science. A member of the Brazilian Academy of Arts and Letters, he was professor of political science at the University of Brasilia until 1982 and has been a visiting professor at King's College, London. His diplomatic career has taken him to posts in Paris, Bonn, London, Montevideo, and Mexico City, where he served as Brazilian ambassador from 1987 to 1989.

He is the author of, among other books, *Rousseau and Weber: Two Studies in the Theory of Legitimacy* (1980), *Foucault* (1985) and *Western Marxism* (1986) and has been translated into several languages.

Currently the Brazilian ambassador to UNESCO in Paris, Dr. Merquior is married and has two children.

The Editor

Michael S. Roth is the Hartley Burr Alexander Professor of Humanities at Scripps College and professor of history at the Claremont Graduate School. He is the author of *Psycho-Analysis as History: Negation and Freedom in Freud* (1987) and *Knowing and History: Appropriations of Hegel in 20th-Century France* (1988), both published by Cornell University Press. He is currently writing about contemporary strategies for representing the past in the humanities and about conceptualizations of memory disorders in the nineteenth century.